D0885102

Basic Equations of ENGINEERING SCIENCE

By

WILLIAM F. HUGHES, Ph.D.
Associate Professor of Electrical and Mechanical Engineering
Carnegie Institute of Technology

and

EBER W. GAYLORD, Ph.D.
Associate Professor of Mechanical Engineering
Carnegie Institute of Technology

SCHAUM'S OUTLINE SERIES
McGRAW-HILL BOOK COMPANY
New York, St. Louis, San Francisco, Toronto, Sydney

31109

4 5 6 7 8 9 0 SHSH 7 2 1

Preface

The authors, having been confronted countless times with the need to know a basic equation in some given coordinate system and the ensuing frustration of leafing through texts or tedious derivation, realized that it would be extremely useful to have drawn together in one concise volume a compendium of the more useful forms of the basic equations of continuum mechanics. This book is a result of that idea.

We believe that modern engineering and science (with the exception of modern physics) is based primarily on the classical ideas of continuum mechanics. Nearly every graduate curriculum in engineering or science includes one or more courses in fluid mechanics, elasticity, classical mechanics, or electromagnetic theory. We have included fundamental relationships in each of these disciplines. Of course it would be a hopeless task to present all the equations which an engineer or scientist uses, and it is the intent here to include those forms of especial use to the research engineer or student.

The book is intended as a reference or "think book" for the student or engineer who is already familiar with the basic ideas and laws and who wishes to establish the exact form of an equation in a given coordinate system. The structure of the book also lends itself to use as a supplement to textbooks in the basic engineering sciences. In many instances certain of the more subtle assumptions are recorded in order to make the book as self-contained as possible. For example, the chapter on electromagnetic theory contains observations on the derivation and applicability of some of the equations which are difficult to find in most textbooks.

The student must be cautioned against indiscriminate use of these equations; he should understand their derivation and limitations. Many of the so-called fundamental equations of engineering and science are approximations which can be used at times only under rather stringent but subtle conditions. A list of references is included at the end of each chapter so that the reader may study the derivation, physical implications, and applications of the various mathematical forms.

W. F. Hughes
E. W. Gaylord

Carnegie Institute of Technology
August, 1964

Table of Contents

Chapter 1

Fluid Mechanics

1.1 CONTINUITY FOR A GENERAL COMPRESSIBLE FLUID

$\mathbf{V}$ = Velocity vector
t = Time
ρ = Density

(a) Vector.

$$\frac{\partial \rho}{\partial t} + \nabla \cdot (\rho \mathbf{V}) = 0 \qquad \textbf{1.1}$$

or

$$\frac{D\rho}{Dt} + \rho \nabla \cdot \mathbf{V} = 0 \qquad \textbf{1.2}$$

where the operator $\frac{D}{Dt}$, called the material, substantial, or Stokes derivative, is given in Section 1.5 or the Appendix.

(b) Cartesian Tensor.

w_i is the velocity in the x_i direction.

$$\frac{\partial \rho}{\partial t} + \frac{\partial(\rho w_i)}{\partial x_i} = 0 \qquad \textbf{1.3}$$

(c) Cartesian.

$u, v,$ and w are the velocities in the $x, y,$ and z directions respectively.

$$\frac{\partial \rho}{\partial t} + \frac{\partial}{\partial x}(\rho u) + \frac{\partial}{\partial y}(\rho v) + \frac{\partial}{\partial z}(\rho w) = 0 \qquad \textbf{1.4}$$

(d) Cylindrical.

$v_r, v_\theta,$ and v_z are the velocities in the $r, \theta,$ and z directions respectively.

$$\frac{\partial \rho}{\partial t} + \frac{1}{r}\frac{\partial}{\partial r}(r\rho v_r) + \frac{1}{r}\frac{\partial}{\partial \theta}(\rho v_\theta) + \frac{\partial}{\partial z}(\rho v_z) = 0 \qquad \textbf{1.5}$$

(e) Spherical.

$v_r, v_\theta,$ and v_ϕ are the velocities in the $r, \theta,$ and ϕ directions respectively.

$$\frac{\partial \rho}{\partial t} + \frac{1}{r^2}\frac{\partial}{\partial r}(r^2\rho v_r) + \frac{1}{r \sin\theta}\frac{\partial}{\partial \theta}(\rho v_\theta \sin\theta) + \frac{1}{r \sin\theta}\frac{\partial}{\partial \phi}(\rho v_\phi) = 0 \qquad \textbf{1.6}$$

1.2 CONTINUITY FOR AN INCOMPRESSIBLE FLUID

(a) Vector.

$\mathbf{V}$ = Velocity vector

$$\nabla \cdot \mathbf{V} = 0 \qquad \textbf{1.7}$$

(b) Cartesian Tensor.

w_i is the velocity in the x_i direction.

$$\frac{\partial w_i}{\partial x_i} = 0 \qquad \textbf{1.8}$$

(c) Cartesian.

u, v, and w are the velocities in the x, y, and z directions respectively.

$$\frac{\partial u}{\partial x} + \frac{\partial v}{\partial y} + \frac{\partial w}{\partial z} = 0 \qquad \textbf{1.9}$$

(d) Cylindrical.

v_r, v_θ, and v_z are the velocities in the r, θ, and z directions respectively.

$$\frac{1}{r}\frac{\partial}{\partial r}(rv_r) + \frac{1}{r}\frac{\partial v_\theta}{\partial \theta} + \frac{\partial v_z}{\partial z} = 0 \qquad \textbf{1.10}$$

(e) Spherical.

v_r, v_θ, and v_ϕ are the velocities in the r, θ, and ϕ directions respectively.

$$\frac{1}{r^2}\frac{\partial}{\partial r}(r^2 v_r) + \frac{1}{r \sin\theta}\frac{\partial}{\partial \theta}(v_\theta \sin\theta) + \frac{1}{r \sin\theta}\frac{\partial v_\phi}{\partial \phi} = 0 \qquad \textbf{1.11}$$

1.3 STRAIN RATE RELATIONSHIPS

The deformation rate tensor is written (in Cartesian tensor notation) as $\dfrac{\partial w_i}{\partial x_j}$, where w_i is the velocity. The symmetrical part of the deformation rate tensor is the strain rate tensor, and the antisymmetrical part is the rotation tensor, which is further discussed in Sections 1.22 and 2.1. The strain rate tensor is denoted as e_{ij} and the rotation tensor as ω_{ij}. The deformation rate tensor can then be written in terms of e_{ij} and ω_{ij} as $\dfrac{\partial w_i}{\partial x_j} = e_{ij} + \omega_{ij}$ in Cartesian tensor notation. The components of the strain rate tensor and rotation tensor are given in various coordinate systems so that the deformation rate tensor can be found by adding them together.

The rotation term can be related to the angular velocity ω_j of an infinitesimal fluid element as $\omega_j = \omega_{ik}$ and is indicated below.

The diagonal (normal) components of the strain rate tensor can be identified directly with the true normal strain rate. However, the off-diagonal terms (shear rate components), e_{ij}, $i \neq j$, are equal to one-half the true rate of shear strain components, which are denoted as γ_{ij}. The one-half factor is necessary in order to make e_{ij} a true tensor. We can write then: $e_{ii} = \gamma_{ii}$, and $e_{ij} = \frac{1}{2}\gamma_{ij}$ $(i \neq j)$.

(a) Cartesian Tensor.

$$e_{ji} = e_{ij} = \frac{1}{2}\left(\frac{\partial w_i}{\partial x_j} + \frac{\partial w_j}{\partial x_i}\right) \tag{1.12}$$

$$-\omega_k = \omega_{ij} = -\omega_{ji} = \frac{1}{2}\left(\frac{\partial w_i}{\partial x_j} - \frac{\partial w_j}{\partial x_i}\right) \tag{1.13}$$

(b) Orthogonal Curvilinear.

$w_1, w_2,$ and w_3 are the velocities in the $x_1, x_2,$ and x_3 directions respectively. $h_1, h_2,$ and h_3 are defined by the line element (see Appendix).

$$e_{11} = \frac{1}{h_1}\frac{\partial w_1}{\partial x_1} + \frac{w_2}{h_1 h_2}\frac{\partial h_1}{\partial x_2} + \frac{w_3}{h_3 h_1}\frac{\partial h_1}{\partial x_3} \tag{1.14}$$

$$e_{22} = \frac{1}{h_2}\frac{\partial w_2}{\partial x_2} + \frac{w_3}{h_2 h_3}\frac{\partial h_2}{\partial x_3} + \frac{w_1}{h_1 h_2}\frac{\partial h_2}{\partial x_1}$$

$$e_{33} = \frac{1}{h_3}\frac{\partial w_3}{\partial x_3} + \frac{w_1}{h_3 h_1}\frac{\partial h_3}{\partial x_1} + \frac{w_2}{h_2 h_3}\frac{\partial h_3}{\partial x_2}$$

$$e_{23} = e_{32} = \frac{1}{2}\left\{\frac{h_3}{h_2}\frac{\partial}{\partial x_2}\left(\frac{w_3}{h_3}\right) + \frac{h_2}{h_3}\frac{\partial}{\partial x_3}\left(\frac{w_2}{h_2}\right)\right\}$$

$$e_{13} = e_{31} = \frac{1}{2}\left\{\frac{h_1}{h_3}\frac{\partial}{\partial x_3}\left(\frac{w_1}{h_1}\right) + \frac{h_3}{h_1}\frac{\partial}{\partial x_1}\left(\frac{w_3}{h_3}\right)\right\}$$

$$e_{12} = e_{21} = \frac{1}{2}\left\{\frac{h_2}{h_1}\frac{\partial}{\partial x_1}\left(\frac{w_2}{h_2}\right) + \frac{h_1}{h_2}\frac{\partial}{\partial x_2}\left(\frac{w_1}{h_1}\right)\right\}$$

$$\omega_1 = \omega_{32} = -\omega_{23} = \frac{1}{2h_2h_3}\left\{\frac{\partial}{\partial x_2}(w_3h_3) - \frac{\partial}{\partial x_3}(w_2h_2)\right\} \tag{1.15}$$

$$\omega_2 = \omega_{13} = -\omega_{31} = \frac{1}{2h_3h_1}\left\{\frac{\partial}{\partial x_3}(w_1h_1) - \frac{\partial}{\partial x_1}(w_3h_3)\right\}$$

$$\omega_3 = \omega_{21} = -\omega_{12} = \frac{1}{2h_1h_2}\left\{\frac{\partial}{\partial x_1}(w_2h_2) - \frac{\partial}{\partial x_2}(w_1h_1)\right\}$$

(c) Cartesian.

$u, v,$ and w are the velocities in the $x, y,$ and z directions respectively.

$$e_{xx} = \frac{\partial u}{\partial x}, \qquad e_{xy} = e_{yx} = \frac{1}{2}\left(\frac{\partial u}{\partial y} + \frac{\partial v}{\partial x}\right) \tag{1.16}$$

$$e_{yy} = \frac{\partial v}{\partial y}, \qquad e_{yz} = e_{zy} = \frac{1}{2}\left(\frac{\partial v}{\partial z} + \frac{\partial w}{\partial y}\right)$$

$$e_{zz} = \frac{\partial w}{\partial z}, \qquad e_{xz} = e_{zx} = \frac{1}{2}\left(\frac{\partial w}{\partial x} + \frac{\partial u}{\partial z}\right)$$

$$\omega_x = \omega_{zy} = -\omega_{yz} = \frac{1}{2}\left(\frac{\partial w}{\partial y} - \frac{\partial v}{\partial z}\right) \qquad \textbf{1.17}$$

$$\omega_y = \omega_{xz} = -\omega_{zx} = \frac{1}{2}\left(\frac{\partial u}{\partial z} - \frac{\partial w}{\partial x}\right)$$

$$\omega_z = \omega_{yx} = -\omega_{xy} = \frac{1}{2}\left(\frac{\partial v}{\partial x} - \frac{\partial u}{\partial y}\right)$$

(d) Cylindrical.

v_r, v_θ, and v_z are the velocities in the r, θ, and z directions respectively.

$$e_{rr} = \frac{\partial v_r}{\partial r}, \qquad e_{r\theta} = e_{\theta r} = \frac{1}{2}\left(\frac{1}{r}\frac{\partial v_r}{\partial \theta} + \frac{\partial v_\theta}{\partial r} - \frac{v_\theta}{r}\right) \qquad \textbf{1.18}$$

$$e_{\theta\theta} = \frac{1}{r}\frac{\partial v_\theta}{\partial \theta} + \frac{v_r}{r}, \qquad e_{rz} = e_{zr} = \frac{1}{2}\left(\frac{\partial v_r}{\partial z} + \frac{\partial v_z}{\partial r}\right)$$

$$e_{zz} = \frac{\partial v_z}{\partial z}, \qquad e_{\theta z} = e_{z\theta} = \frac{1}{2}\left(\frac{1}{r}\frac{\partial v_z}{\partial \theta} + \frac{\partial v_\theta}{\partial z}\right)$$

$$\omega_r = \omega_{z\theta} = -\omega_{\theta z} = \frac{1}{2}\left(\frac{1}{r}\frac{\partial v_z}{\partial \theta} - \frac{\partial v_\theta}{\partial z}\right) \qquad \textbf{1.19}$$

$$\omega_\theta = \omega_{rz} = -\omega_{zr} = \frac{1}{2}\left(\frac{\partial v_r}{\partial z} - \frac{\partial v_z}{\partial r}\right)$$

$$\omega_z = \omega_{\theta r} = -\omega_{r\theta} = \frac{1}{2}\left\{\frac{1}{r}\frac{\partial}{\partial r}(r v_\theta) - \frac{1}{r}\frac{\partial v_r}{\partial \theta}\right\}$$

(e) Spherical.

v_r, v_θ, and v_ϕ are the velocities in the r, θ, and ϕ directions respectively.

$$e_{rr} = \frac{\partial v_r}{\partial r} \qquad \textbf{1.20}$$

$$e_{\theta\theta} = \frac{1}{r}\frac{\partial v_\theta}{\partial \theta} + \frac{v_r}{r}$$

$$e_{\phi\phi} = \frac{1}{r \sin\theta}\frac{\partial v_\phi}{\partial \phi} + \frac{v_r}{r} + \frac{v_\theta \cot\theta}{r}$$

$$e_{r\theta} = e_{\theta r} = \frac{1}{2}\left\{r\frac{\partial}{\partial r}\left(\frac{v_\theta}{r}\right) + \frac{1}{r}\frac{\partial v_r}{\partial \theta}\right\}$$

$$e_{r\phi} = e_{\phi r} = \frac{1}{2}\left\{\frac{1}{r\sin\theta}\frac{\partial v_r}{\partial \phi} + r\frac{\partial}{\partial r}\left(\frac{v_\phi}{r}\right)\right\}$$

$$e_{\theta\phi} = e_{\phi\theta} = \frac{1}{2}\left\{\frac{\sin\theta}{r}\frac{\partial}{\partial \theta}\left(\frac{v_\phi}{\sin\theta}\right) + \frac{1}{r\sin\theta}\frac{\partial v_\theta}{\partial \phi}\right\}$$

$$\omega_r = \omega_{\phi\theta} = -\omega_{\theta\phi} = \frac{1}{2r^2\sin\theta}\left\{\frac{\partial}{\partial \theta}(r v_\phi \sin\theta) - \frac{\partial}{\partial \phi}(r v_\theta)\right\} \qquad \textbf{1.21}$$

$$\omega_\theta = \omega_{r\phi} = -\omega_{\phi r} = \frac{1}{2r\sin\theta}\left\{\frac{\partial v_r}{\partial \phi} - \frac{\partial}{\partial r}(r v_\phi \sin\theta)\right\}$$

$$\omega_\phi = \omega_{\theta r} = -\omega_{r\theta} = \frac{1}{2r}\left\{\frac{\partial}{\partial r}(r v_\theta) - \frac{\partial v_r}{\partial \theta}\right\}$$

(f) Dilatation.

The fluid dilatation ϕ is defined as $e_{11} + e_{22} + e_{33}$ and is exactly equal to the divergence of the velocity. Hence: $\phi = \nabla \cdot \mathbf{V}$. The components are not written out here but are given by equations 1.7 through 1.11.

1.4 STRESS-STRAIN RATE RELATIONSHIPS

The stress in a fluid may be related to the strain rate by the stress-strain rate relationships. We confine ourselves to linear relationships here, but more general relationships, e.g. viscoelastic and nonlinear, may be useful in some physical situations.

Referring to Fig. 1-1, the components of stress have the following physical significance. The first subscript denotes the normal plane on which the stress acts, and the second subscript denotes the direction in which the stress acts. On the negative normal plane the direction is reversed.

The stress tensor must be symmetrical in order to satisfy equilibrium requirements.

In this book two definitions of the second coefficient of viscosity are used, λ and ζ, both of which are in current usage. For a monatomic gas the second coefficient of viscosity λ is $-\frac{2}{3}\mu$, where μ is the ordinary coefficient of viscosity. ζ is defined as $\zeta = \lambda + \frac{2}{3}\mu$ and is zero for a monatomic gas. The kinematic viscosity ν is μ/ρ, where ρ is the mass density.

In the following, P is pressure, σ_{ij} is the stress tensor, and σ'_{ij} is defined as $\sigma_{ij} + P\delta_{ij}$ and physically is the shear-stress tensor plus any normal component due to the second coefficient of viscosity.

δ_{ij} is the Kronecker delta defined as: $\delta_{ij} = 1,\ i = j;\ \ \delta_{ij} = 0,\ i \neq j.$

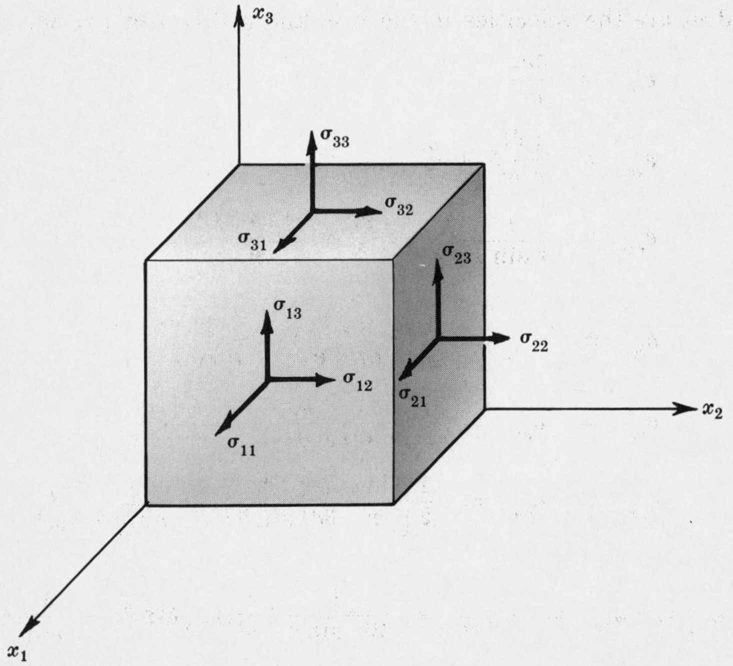

Fig. 1-1. The Stress State on an Elemental Cube.

A surface is denoted by the axis to which it is perpendicular. The stresses shown in the figure are on the positive surfaces. On the opposite or negative surfaces the stresses are in the opposite directions.

The stress-strain rate relationships are as follows:

(a) Cartesian Tensor.

w_i is the velocity in the x_i direction. ϕ is dilatation, $\nabla \cdot \mathbf{V}$.

$$\sigma_{ij} = -P\delta_{ij} + \sigma'_{ij} = -P\delta_{ij} + 2\mu e_{ij} + \delta_{ij}\lambda\phi \qquad \textbf{1.22}$$

$$= -P\delta_{ij} + \mu\left(\frac{\partial w_i}{\partial x_j} + \frac{\partial w_j}{\partial x_i}\right) + \lambda\delta_{ij}\frac{\partial w_k}{\partial x_k}$$

$$= -P\delta_{ij} + \mu\left(\frac{\partial w_i}{\partial x_j} + \frac{\partial w_j}{\partial x_i} - \tfrac{2}{3}\delta_{ij}\frac{\partial w_k}{\partial x_k}\right) + \zeta\delta_{ij}\frac{\partial w_k}{\partial x_k}$$

(b) Orthogonal Curvilinear.

w_1, w_2, and w_3 are the velocities in the x_1, x_2, and x_3 directions respectively. h_1, h_2, and h_3 are defined by the line element (see Appendix).

$$\sigma_{11} = -P + \sigma'_{11} = -P + 2\mu e_{11} + \lambda\nabla\cdot\mathbf{V} \qquad \textbf{1.23}$$

$$= -P + 2\mu\left(\frac{1}{h_1}\frac{\partial w_1}{\partial x_1} + \frac{w_2}{h_1 h_2}\frac{\partial h_1}{\partial x_2} + \frac{w_3}{h_3 h_1}\frac{\partial h_1}{\partial x_3}\right)$$
$$+ \lambda\frac{1}{h_1 h_2 h_3}\left\{\frac{\partial}{\partial x_1}(h_2 h_3 w_1) + \frac{\partial}{\partial x_2}(h_3 h_1 w_2) + \frac{\partial}{\partial x_3}(h_1 h_2 w_3)\right\}$$

$$\sigma_{22} = -P + \sigma'_{22} = -P + 2\mu e_{22} + \lambda\nabla\cdot\mathbf{V}$$

$$= -P + 2\mu\left(\frac{1}{h_2}\frac{\partial w_2}{\partial x_2} + \frac{w_3}{h_2 h_3}\frac{\partial h_2}{\partial x_3} + \frac{w_1}{h_1 h_2}\frac{\partial h_2}{\partial x_1}\right)$$
$$+ \lambda\frac{1}{h_1 h_2 h_3}\left\{\frac{\partial}{\partial x_1}(h_2 h_3 w_1) + \frac{\partial}{\partial x_2}(h_3 h_1 w_2) + \frac{\partial}{\partial x_3}(h_1 h_2 w_3)\right\}$$

$$\sigma_{33} = -P + \sigma'_{33} = -P + 2\mu e_{33} + \lambda\nabla\cdot\mathbf{V}$$

$$= -P + 2\mu\left(\frac{1}{h_3}\frac{\partial w_3}{\partial x_3} + \frac{w_1}{h_3 h_1}\frac{\partial h_3}{\partial x_1} + \frac{w_2}{h_2 h_3}\frac{\partial h_3}{\partial x_2}\right)$$
$$+ \lambda\frac{1}{h_1 h_2 h_3}\left\{\frac{\partial}{\partial x_1}(h_2 h_3 w_1) + \frac{\partial}{\partial x_2}(h_3 h_1 w_2) + \frac{\partial}{\partial x_3}(h_1 h_2 w_3)\right\}$$

$$\sigma_{23} = \sigma_{32} = 2\mu e_{23} = \mu\left\{\frac{h_3}{h_2}\frac{\partial}{\partial x_2}\left(\frac{w_3}{h_3}\right) + \frac{h_2}{h_3}\frac{\partial}{\partial x_3}\left(\frac{w_2}{h_2}\right)\right\}$$

$$\sigma_{13} = \sigma_{31} = 2\mu e_{13} = \mu\left\{\frac{h_1}{h_3}\frac{\partial}{\partial x_3}\left(\frac{w_1}{h_1}\right) + \frac{h_3}{h_1}\frac{\partial}{\partial x_1}\left(\frac{w_3}{h_3}\right)\right\}$$

$$\sigma_{12} = \sigma_{21} = 2\mu e_{12} = \mu\left\{\frac{h_2}{h_1}\frac{\partial}{\partial x_1}\left(\frac{w_2}{h_2}\right) + \frac{h_1}{h_2}\frac{\partial}{\partial x_2}\left(\frac{w_1}{h_1}\right)\right\}$$

(c) Cartesian.

u, v, and w are the velocities in the x, y, and z directions respectively.

$$\sigma_{xx} = -P + \sigma'_{xx} = -P + 2\mu e_{xx} + \lambda \nabla \cdot \mathbf{V} \tag{1.24}$$
$$= -P + 2\mu \frac{\partial u}{\partial x} + \lambda\left(\frac{\partial u}{\partial x} + \frac{\partial v}{\partial y} + \frac{\partial w}{\partial z}\right)$$

$$\sigma_{yy} = -P + \sigma'_{yy} = -P + 2\mu e_{yy} + \lambda \nabla \cdot \mathbf{V}$$
$$= -P + 2\mu \frac{\partial v}{\partial y} + \lambda\left(\frac{\partial u}{\partial x} + \frac{\partial v}{\partial y} + \frac{\partial w}{\partial z}\right)$$

$$\sigma_{zz} = -P + \sigma'_{zz} = -P + 2\mu e_{zz} + \lambda \nabla \cdot \mathbf{V}$$
$$= -P + 2\mu \frac{\partial w}{\partial z} + \lambda\left(\frac{\partial u}{\partial x} + \frac{\partial v}{\partial y} + \frac{\partial w}{\partial z}\right)$$

$$\sigma_{xy} = \sigma_{yx} = 2\mu e_{xy} = \mu\left(\frac{\partial u}{\partial y} + \frac{\partial v}{\partial x}\right)$$

$$\sigma_{xz} = \sigma_{zx} = 2\mu e_{xz} = \mu\left(\frac{\partial w}{\partial x} + \frac{\partial u}{\partial z}\right)$$

$$\sigma_{yz} = \sigma_{zy} = 2\mu e_{yz} = \mu\left(\frac{\partial v}{\partial z} + \frac{\partial w}{\partial y}\right)$$

(d) Cylindrical.

v_r, v_θ, and v_z are the velocities in the r, θ, and z directions respectively.

$$\sigma_{rr} = -P + \sigma'_{rr} = -P + 2\mu e_{rr} + \lambda \nabla \cdot \mathbf{V} \tag{1.25}$$
$$= -P + 2\mu \frac{\partial v_r}{\partial r} + \lambda\left\{\frac{1}{r}\frac{\partial}{\partial r}(rv_r) + \frac{1}{r}\frac{\partial v_\theta}{\partial \theta} + \frac{\partial v_z}{\partial z}\right\}$$

$$\sigma_{\theta\theta} = -P + \sigma'_{\theta\theta} = -P + 2\mu e_{\theta\theta} + \lambda \nabla \cdot \mathbf{V}$$
$$= -P + 2\mu\left(\frac{1}{r}\frac{\partial v_\theta}{\partial \theta} + \frac{v_r}{r}\right) + \lambda\left\{\frac{1}{r}\frac{\partial}{\partial r}(rv_r) + \frac{1}{r}\frac{\partial v_\theta}{\partial \theta} + \frac{\partial v_z}{\partial z}\right\}$$

$$\sigma_{zz} = -P + \sigma'_{zz} = -P + 2\mu e_{zz} + \lambda \nabla \cdot \mathbf{V}$$
$$= -P + 2\mu \frac{\partial v_z}{\partial z} + \lambda\left\{\frac{1}{r}\frac{\partial}{\partial r}(rv_r) + \frac{1}{r}\frac{\partial v_\theta}{\partial \theta} + \frac{\partial v_z}{\partial z}\right\}$$

$$\sigma_{r\theta} = \sigma_{\theta r} = 2\mu e_{r\theta} = \mu\left(\frac{1}{r}\frac{\partial v_r}{\partial \theta} + \frac{\partial v_\theta}{\partial r} - \frac{v_\theta}{r}\right)$$

$$\sigma_{rz} = \sigma_{zr} = 2\mu e_{rz} = \mu\left(\frac{\partial v_r}{\partial z} + \frac{\partial v_z}{\partial r}\right)$$

$$\sigma_{\theta z} = \sigma_{z\theta} = 2\mu e_{\theta z} = \mu\left(\frac{1}{r}\frac{\partial v_z}{\partial \theta} + \frac{\partial v_\theta}{\partial z}\right)$$

(e) Spherical.

v_r, v_θ, and v_ϕ are the velocities in the r, θ, and ϕ directions respectively.

$$\sigma_{rr} = -P + \sigma'_{rr} = -P + 2\mu e_{rr} + \lambda \nabla \cdot \mathbf{V} \qquad \mathbf{1.26}$$

$$= -P + 2\mu\frac{\partial v_r}{\partial r} + \lambda\left\{\frac{1}{r^2}\frac{\partial}{\partial r}(r^2 v_r) + \frac{1}{r\sin\theta}\frac{\partial}{\partial\theta}(v_\theta \sin\theta) + \frac{1}{r\sin\theta}\frac{\partial v_\phi}{\partial\phi}\right\}$$

$$\sigma_{\theta\theta} = -P + \sigma'_{\theta\theta} = -P + 2\mu e_{\theta\theta} + \lambda \nabla \cdot \mathbf{V}$$

$$= -P + 2\mu\left(\frac{1}{r}\frac{\partial v_\theta}{\partial\theta} + \frac{v_r}{r}\right) + \lambda\left\{\frac{1}{r^2}\frac{\partial}{\partial r}(r^2 v_r)\right.$$

$$\left. + \frac{1}{r\sin\theta}\frac{\partial}{\partial\theta}(v_\theta \sin\theta) + \frac{1}{r\sin\theta}\frac{\partial v_\phi}{\partial\phi}\right\}$$

$$\sigma_{\phi\phi} = -P + \sigma'_{\phi\phi} = -P + 2\mu e_{\phi\phi} + \lambda \nabla \cdot \mathbf{V}$$

$$= -P + 2\mu\left(\frac{1}{r\sin\theta}\frac{\partial v_\phi}{\partial\phi} + \frac{v_r}{r} + \frac{v_\theta \cot\theta}{r}\right)$$

$$+ \lambda\left\{\frac{1}{r^2}\frac{\partial}{\partial r}(r^2 v_r) + \frac{1}{r\sin\theta}\frac{\partial}{\partial\theta}(v_\theta \sin\theta) + \frac{1}{r\sin\theta}\frac{\partial v_\phi}{\partial\phi}\right\}$$

$$\sigma_{r\theta} = \sigma_{\theta r} = 2\mu e_{r\theta} = \mu\left\{r\frac{\partial}{\partial r}\left(\frac{v_\theta}{r}\right) + \frac{1}{r}\frac{\partial v_r}{\partial\theta}\right\}$$

$$\sigma_{r\phi} = \sigma_{\phi r} = 2\mu e_{r\phi} = \mu\left\{\frac{1}{r\sin\theta}\frac{\partial v_r}{\partial\phi} + r\frac{\partial}{\partial r}\left(\frac{v_\theta}{r}\right)\right\}$$

$$\sigma_{\theta\phi} = \sigma_{\phi\theta} = 2\mu e_{\theta\phi} = \mu\left\{\frac{\sin\theta}{r}\frac{\partial}{\partial\theta}\left(\frac{v_\phi}{\sin\theta}\right) + \frac{1}{r\sin\theta}\frac{\partial v_\theta}{\partial\phi}\right\}$$

1.5 EQUATIONS OF MOTION IN TERMS OF STRESS

In this section the following symbols are used:

P = Pressure

ρ = Mass density

$\mathbf{F}$ = Body force density

σ_{ij} = Stress tensor

(a) Cartesian Tensor.

w_i is the velocity in the x_i direction.

$$\rho\left(\frac{\partial w_i}{\partial t} + w_j\frac{\partial w_i}{\partial x_j}\right) = F_i + \frac{\partial \sigma_{ij}}{\partial x_j} \qquad \mathbf{1.27}$$

(b) Vector.

The term $\nabla \cdot \boldsymbol{\sigma}$ represents the tensor divergence of the stress tensor $\boldsymbol{\sigma}$.

$$\rho \frac{D\mathbf{V}}{Dt} = \rho\left[\frac{\partial \mathbf{V}}{\partial t} + (\mathbf{V}\cdot\nabla)\mathbf{V}\right] \qquad \textbf{1.28}$$

$$= \rho\left[\frac{\partial \mathbf{V}}{\partial t} + \nabla\left(\frac{V^2}{2}\right) - \mathbf{V}\times(\nabla\times\mathbf{V})\right] = \mathbf{F} + \nabla\cdot\boldsymbol{\sigma}$$

(c) Orthogonal Curvilinear.

w_1, w_2, and w_3 are the velocities in the x_1, x_2, and x_3 directions respectively. h_1, h_2, and h_3 are defined by the line element (see Appendix).

$$\rho\left\{\frac{\partial w_1}{\partial t} + \frac{w_1}{h_1}\frac{\partial w_1}{\partial x_1} + \frac{w_2}{h_2}\frac{\partial w_1}{\partial x_2} + \frac{w_3}{h_3}\frac{\partial w_1}{\partial x_3}\right. \qquad \textbf{1.29}$$

$$\left. - w_2\left[\frac{w_2}{h_2h_1}\frac{\partial h_2}{\partial x_1} - \frac{w_1}{h_1h_2}\frac{\partial h_1}{\partial x_2}\right] + w_3\left[\frac{w_1}{h_1h_3}\frac{\partial h_1}{\partial x_3} - \frac{w_3}{h_3h_1}\frac{\partial h_3}{\partial x_1}\right]\right\}$$

$$= \frac{1}{h_1h_2h_3}\left[\frac{\partial}{\partial x_1}(h_2h_3\sigma_{11}) + \frac{\partial}{\partial x_2}(h_3h_1\sigma_{21}) + \frac{\partial}{\partial x_3}(h_1h_2\sigma_{31})\right]$$

$$+ \frac{\sigma_{12}}{h_1h_2}\frac{\partial h_1}{\partial x_2} + \frac{\sigma_{31}}{h_1h_3}\frac{\partial h_1}{\partial x_3} - \frac{\sigma_{22}}{h_1h_2}\frac{\partial h_2}{\partial x_1} - \frac{\sigma_{33}}{h_1h_3}\frac{\partial h_3}{\partial x_1} + F_1$$

$$\rho\left\{\frac{\partial w_2}{\partial t} + \frac{w_1}{h_1}\frac{\partial w_2}{\partial x_1} + \frac{w_2}{h_2}\frac{\partial w_2}{\partial x_2} + \frac{w_3}{h_3}\frac{\partial w_2}{\partial x_3}\right.$$

$$\left. - w_3\left[\frac{w_3}{h_3h_2}\frac{\partial h_3}{\partial x_2} - \frac{w_2}{h_2h_3}\frac{\partial h_2}{\partial x_3}\right] + w_1\left[\frac{w_2}{h_2h_1}\frac{\partial h_2}{\partial x_1} - \frac{w_1}{h_1h_2}\frac{\partial h_1}{\partial x_2}\right]\right\}$$

$$= \frac{1}{h_1h_2h_3}\left[\frac{\partial}{\partial x_1}(h_2h_3\sigma_{12}) + \frac{\partial}{\partial x_2}(h_3h_1\sigma_{22}) + \frac{\partial}{\partial x_3}(h_1h_2\sigma_{32})\right]$$

$$+ \frac{\sigma_{23}}{h_2h_3}\frac{\partial h_2}{\partial x_3} + \frac{\sigma_{12}}{h_2h_1}\frac{\partial h_2}{\partial x_1} - \frac{\sigma_{33}}{h_2h_3}\frac{\partial h_3}{\partial x_2} - \frac{\sigma_{11}}{h_2h_1}\frac{\partial h_1}{\partial x_2} + F_2$$

$$\rho\left\{\frac{\partial w_3}{\partial t} + \frac{w_1}{h_1}\frac{\partial w_3}{\partial x_1} + \frac{w_2}{h_2}\frac{\partial w_3}{\partial x_2} + \frac{w_3}{h_3}\frac{\partial w_3}{\partial x_3}\right.$$

$$\left. - w_1\left[\frac{w_1}{h_1h_3}\frac{\partial h_1}{\partial x_3} - \frac{w_3}{h_3h_1}\frac{\partial h_3}{\partial x_1}\right] + w_2\left[\frac{w_3}{h_3h_2}\frac{\partial h_3}{\partial x_2} - \frac{w_2}{h_2h_3}\frac{\partial h_2}{\partial x_3}\right]\right\}$$

$$= \frac{1}{h_1h_2h_3}\left[\frac{\partial}{\partial x_1}(h_2h_3\sigma_{13}) + \frac{\partial}{\partial x_2}(h_3h_1\sigma_{23}) + \frac{\partial}{\partial x_3}(h_1h_2\sigma_{33})\right]$$

$$+ \frac{\sigma_{31}}{h_1h_3}\frac{\partial h_3}{\partial x_1} + \frac{\sigma_{23}}{h_3h_2}\frac{\partial h_3}{\partial x_2} - \frac{\sigma_{11}}{h_3h_1}\frac{\partial h_1}{\partial x_3} - \frac{\sigma_{22}}{h_3h_2}\frac{\partial h_2}{\partial x_3} + F_3$$

(d) Cartesian.

u, v, and w are the velocities in the x, y, and z directions respectively. $\frac{D}{Dt}$ is the material derivative defined in Cartesian coordinates as: $\frac{D}{Dt} = \frac{\partial}{\partial t} + u\frac{\partial}{\partial x} + v\frac{\partial}{\partial y} + w\frac{\partial}{\partial z}$.

$$\rho\frac{Du}{Dt} = \rho\left(\frac{\partial u}{\partial t} + u\frac{\partial u}{\partial x} + v\frac{\partial u}{\partial y} + w\frac{\partial u}{\partial z}\right) = F_x + \frac{\partial\sigma_{xx}}{\partial x} + \frac{\partial\sigma_{yx}}{\partial y} + \frac{\partial\sigma_{zx}}{\partial z} \qquad \mathbf{1.30}$$

$$\rho\frac{Dv}{Dt} = \rho\left(\frac{\partial v}{\partial t} + u\frac{\partial v}{\partial x} + v\frac{\partial v}{\partial y} + w\frac{\partial v}{\partial z}\right) = F_y + \frac{\partial\sigma_{xy}}{\partial x} + \frac{\partial\sigma_{yy}}{\partial y} + \frac{\partial\sigma_{zy}}{\partial z}$$

$$\rho\frac{Dw}{Dt} = \rho\left(\frac{\partial w}{\partial t} + u\frac{\partial w}{\partial x} + v\frac{\partial w}{\partial y} + w\frac{\partial w}{\partial z}\right) = F_z + \frac{\partial\sigma_{xz}}{\partial x} + \frac{\partial\sigma_{yz}}{\partial y} + \frac{\partial\sigma_{zz}}{\partial z}$$

(e) Cylindrical.

v_r, v_θ, and v_z are the velocities in the r, θ, and z directions respectively.

$$\frac{D}{Dt} = \frac{\partial}{\partial t} + v_r\frac{\partial}{\partial r} + \frac{v_\theta}{r}\frac{\partial}{\partial\theta} + v_z\frac{\partial}{\partial z}$$

$$\rho\left(\frac{Dv_r}{Dt} - \frac{v_\theta^2}{r}\right) = \rho\left(\frac{\partial v_r}{\partial t} + v_r\frac{\partial v_r}{\partial r} + \frac{v_\theta}{r}\frac{\partial v_r}{\partial\theta} + v_z\frac{\partial v_r}{\partial z} - \frac{v_\theta^2}{r}\right) \qquad \mathbf{1.31}$$

$$= F_r + \frac{1}{r}\left[\frac{\partial}{\partial r}(r\sigma_{rr}) + \frac{\partial}{\partial\theta}(\sigma_{\theta r}) + \frac{\partial}{\partial z}(r\sigma_{zr})\right] - \frac{\sigma_{\theta\theta}}{r}$$

$$\rho\left(\frac{Dv_\theta}{Dt} + \frac{v_r v_\theta}{r}\right) = \rho\left(\frac{\partial v_\theta}{\partial t} + v_r\frac{\partial v_\theta}{\partial r} + \frac{v_\theta}{r}\frac{\partial v_\theta}{\partial\theta} + v_z\frac{\partial v_\theta}{\partial z} + \frac{v_r v_\theta}{r}\right)$$

$$= F_\theta + \frac{1}{r}\left[\frac{\partial}{\partial r}(r\sigma_{r\theta}) + \frac{\partial\sigma_{\theta\theta}}{\partial\theta} + \frac{\partial}{\partial z}(r\sigma_{z\theta})\right] + \frac{\sigma_{r\theta}}{r}$$

$$\rho\left(\frac{Dv_z}{Dt}\right) = \rho\left(\frac{\partial v_z}{\partial t} + v_r\frac{\partial v_z}{\partial r} + \frac{v_\theta}{r}\frac{\partial v_z}{\partial\theta} + v_z\frac{\partial v_z}{\partial z}\right)$$

$$= F_z + \frac{1}{r}\left[\frac{\partial}{\partial r}(r\sigma_{rz}) + \frac{\partial\sigma_{\theta z}}{\partial\theta} + \frac{\partial}{\partial z}(r\sigma_{zz})\right]$$

(f) Spherical.

v_r, v_θ, and v_ϕ are the velocities in the r, θ, and ϕ directions respectively.

$$\frac{D}{Dt} = \frac{\partial}{\partial t} + v_r\frac{\partial}{\partial r} + \frac{v_\theta}{r}\frac{\partial}{\partial\theta} + \frac{v_\phi}{r\sin\theta}\frac{\partial}{\partial\phi}$$

$$\rho\left(\frac{Dv_r}{Dt} - \frac{v_\theta^2 + v_\phi^2}{r}\right) \qquad \mathbf{1.32}$$

$$= \left(\frac{\partial v_r}{\partial t} + v_r\frac{\partial v_r}{\partial r} + \frac{v_\theta}{r}\frac{\partial v_r}{\partial\theta} + \frac{v_\phi}{r\sin\theta}\frac{\partial v_r}{\partial\phi} - \frac{v_\theta^2 + v_\phi^2}{r}\right)$$

$$= F_r + \frac{1}{r^2\sin\theta}\left[\frac{\partial}{\partial r}(r^2\sin\theta\,\sigma_{rr}) + \frac{\partial}{\partial\theta}(r\sin\theta\,\sigma_{\theta r}) + \frac{\partial}{\partial\phi}(r\sigma_{\phi r})\right] - \frac{\sigma_{\theta\theta} + \sigma_{\phi\phi}}{r}$$

$$\rho\left(\frac{Dv_\theta}{Dt} + \frac{v_r v_\theta}{r} - \frac{v_\phi^2 \cot\theta}{r}\right)$$

$$= \rho\left(\frac{\partial v_\theta}{\partial t} + v_r\frac{\partial v_\theta}{\partial r} + \frac{v_\theta}{r}\frac{\partial v_\theta}{\partial \theta} + \frac{v_\phi}{r\sin\theta}\frac{\partial v_\theta}{\partial \phi} + \frac{v_r v_\theta}{r} - \frac{v_\phi^2\cot\theta}{r}\right)$$

$$= F_\theta + \frac{1}{r^2\sin\theta}\left[\frac{\partial}{\partial r}(r^2\sin\theta\,\sigma_{r\theta}) + \frac{\partial}{\partial\theta}(r\sin\theta\,\sigma_{\theta\theta}) + \frac{\partial}{\partial\phi}(r\sigma_{\phi\theta})\right] - \frac{\sigma_{\phi\phi}\cot\theta}{r} + \frac{\sigma_{r\theta}}{r}$$

$$\rho\left(\frac{Dv_\phi}{Dt} + \frac{v_\phi v_r}{r} + \frac{v_\theta v_\phi\cot\theta}{r}\right)$$

$$= \rho\left(\frac{\partial v_\phi}{\partial t} + v_r\frac{\partial v_\phi}{\partial r} + \frac{v_\theta}{r}\frac{\partial v_\phi}{\partial \theta} + \frac{v_\phi}{r\sin\theta}\frac{\partial v_\phi}{\partial \phi} + \frac{v_\phi v_r}{r} + \frac{v_\theta v_\phi\cot\theta}{r}\right)$$

$$= F_\phi + \frac{1}{r^2\sin\theta}\left[\frac{\partial}{\partial r}(r^2\sin\theta\,\sigma_{r\phi}) + \frac{\partial}{\partial\theta}(r\sin\theta\,\sigma_{\theta\phi}) + \frac{\partial}{\partial\phi}(r\sigma_{\phi\phi})\right] + \frac{\sigma_{r\phi}}{r} + \frac{\sigma_{\theta\phi}\cot\theta}{r}$$

1.6 NAVIER-STOKES EQUATIONS OF MOTION FOR A COMPRESSIBLE FLUID (EULERIAN COORDINATES)

P = Pressure

$\mathbf{F}$ = Body force density

μ = Viscosity

λ = Second coefficient of viscosity ($\lambda = -\frac{2}{3}\mu$ for a monatomic gas).

ζ = Another second coefficient of viscosity defined in terms of λ as $\zeta = \lambda + \frac{2}{3}\mu$, and hence ζ is zero for a monatomic gas. Both definitions of the second coefficient of viscosity are in current usage.

(a) Vector.

$\mathbf{V}$ is the velocity vector.

$$\rho\frac{D\mathbf{V}}{Dt} = \rho\left[\frac{\partial\mathbf{V}}{\partial t} + (\mathbf{V}\cdot\nabla)\mathbf{V}\right] = \rho\left[\frac{\partial\mathbf{V}}{\partial t} + \nabla\left(\frac{V^2}{2}\right) - \mathbf{V}\times(\nabla\times\mathbf{V})\right] \quad \textbf{1.33}$$

$$= -\nabla P + \mathbf{F} - \nabla\times[\mu(\nabla\times\mathbf{V})] + \nabla[(\zeta + \tfrac{4}{3}\mu)\nabla\cdot\mathbf{V}]$$

or in terms of λ:

$$\rho\left[\frac{\partial\mathbf{V}}{\partial t} + (\mathbf{V}\cdot\nabla)\mathbf{V}\right] = \rho\left[\frac{\partial\mathbf{V}}{\partial t} + \nabla\left(\frac{V^2}{2}\right) - \mathbf{V}\times(\nabla\times\mathbf{V})\right] \quad \textbf{1.34}$$

$$= -\nabla P + \mathbf{F} - \nabla\times[\mu(\nabla\times\mathbf{V})] + \nabla[(\lambda + 2\mu)\nabla\cdot\mathbf{V}]$$

(b) Cartesian Tensor.

w_i is the velocity in the x_i direction.

$$\rho\left[\frac{\partial w_i}{\partial t} + w_j\frac{\partial w_i}{\partial x_j}\right] = -\frac{\partial P}{\partial x_i} + F_i + \frac{\partial}{\partial x_j}\left[\mu\left(\frac{\partial w_i}{\partial x_j} + \frac{\partial w_j}{\partial x_i} - \tfrac{2}{3}\delta_{ij}\frac{\partial w_k}{\partial x_k}\right)\right] + \frac{\partial}{\partial x_i}\left(\zeta\frac{\partial w_k}{\partial x_k}\right) \quad \textbf{1.35}$$

or in terms of λ:

$$\rho\left[\frac{\partial w_i}{\partial t} + w_j\frac{\partial w_i}{\partial x_j}\right] = -\frac{\partial P}{\partial x_i} + F_i + \frac{\partial}{\partial x_j}\left[\mu\left(\frac{\partial w_i}{\partial x_j} + \frac{\partial w_j}{\partial x_i}\right)\right] + \frac{\partial}{\partial x_i}\left(\lambda\frac{\partial w_k}{\partial x_k}\right) \quad \textbf{1.36}$$

(c) *Orthogonal Curvilinear.*

These equations may be obtained directly from equation 1.29 by substituting for the stress in terms of the strain rate from equation 1.23.

w_1, w_2, and w_3 are the velocities in the x_1, x_2, and x_3 directions respectively. h_1, h_2, and h_3 are defined in terms of the line element (see Appendix).

x_1 COMPONENT:

$$\rho\left[\frac{\partial w_1}{\partial t} + \frac{w_1}{h_1}\frac{\partial w_1}{\partial x_1} + \frac{w_2}{h_2}\frac{\partial w_1}{\partial x_2} + \frac{w_3}{h_3}\frac{\partial w_1}{\partial x_3} - w_2\left(\frac{w_2}{h_2h_1}\frac{\partial h_2}{\partial x_1} - \frac{w_1}{h_1h_2}\frac{\partial h_1}{\partial x_2}\right) + w_3\left(\frac{w_1}{h_1h_3}\frac{\partial h_1}{\partial x_3} - \frac{w_3}{h_3h_1}\frac{\partial h_3}{\partial x_1}\right)\right] \tag{1.37}$$

$$= F_1 - \frac{1}{h_1}\frac{\partial P}{\partial x_1} + \frac{1}{h_1}\frac{\partial}{\partial x_1}(\lambda\nabla\cdot\mathbf{V})$$

$$+ \frac{1}{h_1h_2h_3}\left[\frac{\partial}{\partial x_1}\left\{2\mu h_2h_3\left(\frac{1}{h_1}\frac{\partial w_1}{\partial x_1} + \frac{w_2}{h_1h_2}\frac{\partial h_1}{\partial x_2} + \frac{w_3}{h_3h_1}\frac{\partial h_1}{\partial x_3}\right)\right\}\right.$$

$$+ \frac{\partial}{\partial x_2}\left\{h_3h_1\mu\left[\frac{h_2}{h_1}\frac{\partial}{\partial x_1}\left(\frac{w_2}{h_2}\right) + \frac{h_1}{h_2}\frac{\partial}{\partial x_2}\left(\frac{w_1}{h_1}\right)\right]\right\}$$

$$\left. + \frac{\partial}{\partial x_3}\left\{h_1h_2\mu\left[\frac{h_1}{h_3}\frac{\partial}{\partial x_3}\left(\frac{w_1}{h_1}\right) + \frac{h_3}{h_1}\frac{\partial}{\partial x_1}\left(\frac{w_3}{h_3}\right)\right]\right\}\right]$$

$$+ \frac{\mu}{h_1h_2}\left\{\frac{h_2}{h_1}\frac{\partial}{\partial x_1}\left(\frac{w_2}{h_2}\right) + \frac{h_1}{h_2}\frac{\partial}{\partial x_2}\left(\frac{w_1}{h_1}\right)\right\}\cdot\frac{\partial h_1}{\partial x_2}$$

$$+ \frac{\mu}{h_1h_3}\left\{\frac{h_1}{h_3}\frac{\partial}{\partial x_3}\left(\frac{w_1}{h_1}\right) + \frac{h_3}{h_1}\frac{\partial}{\partial x_1}\left(\frac{w_3}{h_3}\right)\right\}\cdot\frac{\partial h_1}{\partial x_3}$$

$$- \frac{2\mu}{h_1h_2}\left\{\frac{1}{h_2}\frac{\partial w_2}{\partial x_2} + \frac{w_3}{h_2h_3}\frac{\partial h_2}{\partial x_3} - \frac{w_1}{h_1h_2}\frac{\partial h_2}{\partial x_1}\right\}\cdot\frac{\partial h_2}{\partial x_1}$$

$$- \frac{2\mu}{h_1h_3}\left\{\frac{1}{h_3}\frac{\partial w_3}{\partial x_3} + \frac{w_1}{h_3h_1}\frac{\partial h_3}{\partial x_1} + \frac{w_3}{h_2h_3}\frac{\partial h_3}{\partial x_2}\right\}\cdot\frac{\partial h_3}{\partial x_1}$$

x_2 COMPONENT:

$$\rho\left[\frac{\partial w_2}{\partial t} + \frac{w_1}{h_1}\frac{\partial w_2}{\partial x_1} + \frac{w_2}{h_2}\frac{\partial w_2}{\partial x_2} + \frac{w_3}{h_3}\frac{\partial w_2}{\partial x_3} - w_3\left(\frac{w_3}{h_3h_2}\frac{\partial h_3}{\partial x_2} - \frac{w_2}{h_2h_3}\frac{\partial h_2}{\partial x_3}\right) + w_1\left(\frac{w_2}{h_2h_1}\frac{\partial h_2}{\partial x_1} - \frac{w_1}{h_1h_2}\frac{\partial h_1}{\partial x_2}\right)\right]$$

$$= F_2 - \frac{1}{h_2}\frac{\partial P}{\partial x_2} + \frac{1}{h_2}\frac{\partial}{\partial x_2}(\lambda\nabla\cdot\mathbf{V})$$

$$+ \frac{1}{h_1h_2h_3}\left[\frac{\partial}{\partial x_1}\left\{h_2h_3\mu\left[\frac{h_2}{h_1}\frac{\partial}{\partial x_1}\left(\frac{w_2}{h_2}\right) + \frac{h_1}{h_2}\frac{\partial}{\partial x_2}\left(\frac{w_1}{h_1}\right)\right]\right\}\right.$$

$$+ \frac{\partial}{\partial x_2}\left\{2\mu h_3h_1\left(\frac{1}{h_2}\frac{\partial w_2}{\partial x_2} + \frac{w_3}{h_2h_3}\frac{\partial h_2}{\partial x_3} + \frac{w_1}{h_1h_2}\frac{\partial h_2}{\partial x_1}\right)\right\}$$

$$\left. + \frac{\partial}{\partial x_3}\left\{h_1h_2\mu\left[\frac{h_3}{h_2}\frac{\partial}{\partial x_2}\left(\frac{w_3}{h_3}\right) + \frac{h_2}{h_3}\frac{\partial}{\partial x_3}\left(\frac{w_2}{h_2}\right)\right]\right\}\right]$$

$$+ \frac{\mu}{h_2 h_3}\left\{\frac{h_3}{h_2}\frac{\partial}{\partial x_2}\left(\frac{w_3}{h_3}\right) + \frac{h_2}{h_3}\frac{\partial}{\partial x_3}\left(\frac{w_2}{h_2}\right)\right\}\cdot\frac{\partial h_2}{\partial x_3}$$

$$+ \frac{\mu}{h_2 h_1}\left\{\frac{h_2}{h_1}\frac{\partial}{\partial x_1}\left(\frac{w_2}{h_2}\right) + \frac{h_1}{h_2}\frac{\partial}{\partial x_2}\left(\frac{w_1}{h_1}\right)\right\}\cdot\frac{\partial h_2}{\partial x_1}$$

$$- \frac{2\mu}{h_2 h_3}\left\{\frac{1}{h_3}\frac{\partial w_3}{\partial x_3} + \frac{w_1}{h_3 h_1}\frac{\partial h_3}{\partial x_1} + \frac{w_2}{h_2 h_3}\frac{\partial h_3}{\partial x_2}\right\}\cdot\frac{\partial h_3}{\partial x_2}$$

$$- \frac{2\mu}{h_2 h_1}\left\{\frac{1}{h_1}\frac{\partial w_1}{\partial x_1} + \frac{w_2}{h_1 h_2}\frac{\partial h_1}{\partial x_2} + \frac{w_3}{h_3 h_1}\frac{\partial h_1}{\partial x_3}\right\}\cdot\frac{\partial h_1}{\partial x_2}$$

x_3 COMPONENT:

$$\rho\left[\frac{\partial w_3}{\partial t} + \frac{w_1}{h_1}\frac{\partial w_3}{\partial x_1} + \frac{w_2}{h_2}\frac{\partial w_3}{\partial x_2} + \frac{w_3}{h_3}\frac{\partial w_3}{\partial x_3} - w_1\left(\frac{w_1}{h_1 h_3}\frac{\partial h_1}{\partial x_3} - \frac{w_3}{h_3 h_1}\frac{\partial h_3}{\partial x_1}\right)\right.$$
$$\left. + w_2\left(\frac{w_3}{h_3 h_2}\frac{\partial h_3}{\partial x_2} - \frac{w_2}{h_2 h_3}\frac{\partial h_2}{\partial x_3}\right)\right]$$

$$= F_3 - \frac{1}{h_3}\frac{\partial P}{\partial x_3} + \frac{1}{h_3}\frac{\partial}{\partial x_3}(\lambda\nabla\cdot\mathbf{V})$$
$$+ \frac{1}{h_1 h_2 h_3}\left[\frac{\partial}{\partial x_1}\left\{h_2 h_3 \mu\left[\frac{h_1}{h_3}\frac{\partial}{\partial x_3}\left(\frac{w_1}{h_1}\right) + \frac{h_3}{h_1}\frac{\partial}{\partial x_1}\left(\frac{w_3}{h_3}\right)\right]\right\}\right.$$
$$+ \frac{\partial}{\partial x_2}\left\{h_3 h_1 \mu\left[\frac{h_3}{h_2}\frac{\partial}{\partial x_2}\left(\frac{w_3}{h_3}\right) + \frac{h_2}{h_3}\frac{\partial}{\partial x_3}\left(\frac{w_2}{h_2}\right)\right]\right\}$$
$$\left. + \frac{\partial}{\partial x_3}\left\{2\mu h_1 h_2\left(\frac{1}{h_3}\frac{\partial w_3}{\partial x_3} + \frac{w_1}{h_3 h_1}\frac{\partial h_3}{\partial x_1} + \frac{w_2}{h_2 h_3}\frac{\partial h_3}{\partial x_2}\right)\right\}\right]$$

$$+ \frac{\mu}{h_1 h_3}\left\{\frac{h_1}{h_3}\frac{\partial}{\partial x_3}\left(\frac{w_1}{h_1}\right) + \frac{h_3}{h_1}\frac{\partial}{\partial x_1}\left(\frac{w_3}{h_3}\right)\right\}\cdot\frac{\partial h_3}{\partial x_1}$$

$$+ \frac{\mu}{h_3 h_2}\left\{\frac{h_3}{h_2}\frac{\partial}{\partial x_2}\left(\frac{w_3}{h_3}\right) + \frac{h_2}{h_3}\frac{\partial}{\partial x_3}\left(\frac{w_2}{h_2}\right)\right\}\cdot\frac{\partial h_3}{\partial x_2}$$

$$- \frac{2\mu}{h_3 h_1}\left\{\frac{1}{h_1}\frac{\partial w_1}{\partial x_1} + \frac{w_2}{h_1 h_2}\frac{\partial h_1}{\partial x_2} + \frac{w_3}{h_3 h_1}\frac{\partial h_1}{\partial x_3}\right\}\cdot\frac{\partial h_1}{\partial x_3}$$

$$- \frac{2\mu}{h_3 h_2}\left\{\frac{1}{h_2}\frac{\partial w_2}{\partial x_2} + \frac{w_3}{h_2 h_3}\frac{\partial h_2}{\partial x_3} + \frac{w_1}{h_1 h_2}\frac{\partial h_2}{\partial x_1}\right\}\cdot\frac{\partial h_2}{\partial x_3}$$

(d) Cartesian.

u, v, and w are the velocities in the x, y, and z directions respectively. In the following section:

$$\frac{D}{Dt} = \frac{\partial}{\partial t} + u\frac{\partial}{\partial x} + v\frac{\partial}{\partial y} + w\frac{\partial}{\partial z}$$

and
$$\nabla\cdot\mathbf{V} = \frac{\partial u}{\partial x} + \frac{\partial v}{\partial y} + \frac{\partial w}{\partial z}$$

$$\rho\frac{Du}{Dt} = \rho\left(\frac{\partial u}{\partial t} + u\frac{\partial u}{\partial x} + v\frac{\partial u}{\partial y} + w\frac{\partial u}{\partial z}\right) \tag{1.38}$$

$$= F_x - \frac{\partial P}{\partial x} + \frac{\partial}{\partial x}\left[2\mu\frac{\partial u}{\partial x} + (\zeta - \tfrac{2}{3}\mu)\nabla\cdot\mathbf{V}\right] + \frac{\partial}{\partial y}\left[\mu\left(\frac{\partial u}{\partial y} + \frac{\partial v}{\partial x}\right)\right] + \frac{\partial}{\partial z}\left[\mu\left(\frac{\partial w}{\partial x} + \frac{\partial u}{\partial z}\right)\right]$$

$$\rho\frac{Dv}{Dt} = \rho\left(\frac{\partial v}{\partial t} + u\frac{\partial v}{\partial x} + v\frac{\partial v}{\partial y} + w\frac{\partial v}{\partial z}\right)$$

$$= F_y - \frac{\partial P}{\partial y} + \frac{\partial}{\partial y}\left[2\mu\frac{\partial v}{\partial y} + (\zeta - \tfrac{2}{3}\mu)\nabla\cdot\mathbf{V}\right] + \frac{\partial}{\partial z}\left[\mu\left(\frac{\partial v}{\partial z} + \frac{\partial w}{\partial y}\right)\right] + \frac{\partial}{\partial x}\left[\mu\left(\frac{\partial u}{\partial y} + \frac{\partial v}{\partial x}\right)\right]$$

$$\rho\frac{Dw}{Dt} = \rho\left(\frac{\partial w}{\partial t} + u\frac{\partial w}{\partial x} + v\frac{\partial w}{\partial y} + w\frac{\partial w}{\partial z}\right)$$

$$= F_z - \frac{\partial P}{\partial z} + \frac{\partial}{\partial z}\left[2\mu\frac{\partial w}{\partial z} + (\zeta - \tfrac{2}{3}\mu)\nabla\cdot\mathbf{V}\right] + \frac{\partial}{\partial x}\left[\mu\left(\frac{\partial w}{\partial x} + \frac{\partial u}{\partial z}\right)\right] + \frac{\partial}{\partial y}\left[\mu\left(\frac{\partial v}{\partial z} + \frac{\partial w}{\partial y}\right)\right]$$

or in terms of λ:

$$\rho\frac{Du}{Dt} = F_x - \frac{\partial P}{\partial x} + \frac{\partial}{\partial x}\left[2\mu\frac{\partial u}{\partial x} + \lambda\nabla\cdot\mathbf{V}\right] + \frac{\partial}{\partial y}\left[\mu\left(\frac{\partial u}{\partial y} + \frac{\partial v}{\partial x}\right)\right] + \frac{\partial}{\partial z}\left[\mu\left(\frac{\partial w}{\partial x} + \frac{\partial u}{\partial z}\right)\right] \tag{1.39}$$

$$\rho\frac{Dv}{Dt} = F_y - \frac{\partial P}{\partial y} + \frac{\partial}{\partial y}\left[2\mu\frac{\partial v}{\partial y} + \lambda\nabla\cdot\mathbf{V}\right] + \frac{\partial}{\partial z}\left[\mu\left(\frac{\partial v}{\partial z} + \frac{\partial w}{\partial y}\right)\right] + \frac{\partial}{\partial x}\left[\mu\left(\frac{\partial u}{\partial y} + \frac{\partial v}{\partial x}\right)\right]$$

$$\rho\frac{Dw}{Dt} = F_z - \frac{\partial P}{\partial z} + \frac{\partial}{\partial z}\left[2\mu\frac{\partial w}{\partial z} + \lambda\nabla\cdot\mathbf{V}\right] + \frac{\partial}{\partial x}\left[\mu\left(\frac{\partial w}{\partial x} + \frac{\partial u}{\partial z}\right)\right] + \frac{\partial}{\partial y}\left[\mu\left(\frac{\partial v}{\partial z} + \frac{\partial w}{\partial y}\right)\right]$$

(e) Cylindrical.

v_r, v_θ, and v_z are the velocities in the r, θ, and z directions respectively. In the following section:

$$\frac{D}{Dt} = \frac{\partial}{\partial t} + v_r\frac{\partial}{\partial r} + \frac{v_\theta}{r}\frac{\partial}{\partial \theta} + v_z\frac{\partial}{\partial z}$$

and $$\nabla\cdot\mathbf{V} = \frac{1}{r}\frac{\partial}{\partial r}(rv_r) + \frac{1}{r}\frac{\partial v_\theta}{\partial \theta} + \frac{\partial v_z}{\partial z} = \frac{\partial v_r}{\partial r} + \frac{v_r}{r} + \frac{1}{r}\frac{\partial v_\theta}{\partial \theta} + \frac{\partial v_z}{\partial z}$$

$$\rho\left[\frac{Dv_r}{Dt} - \frac{v_\theta^2}{r}\right] \tag{1.40}$$

$$= F_r - \frac{\partial P}{\partial r} + \frac{\partial}{\partial r}\left[2\mu\frac{\partial v_r}{\partial r} + (\zeta - \tfrac{2}{3}\mu)\nabla\cdot\mathbf{V}\right] + \frac{1}{r}\frac{\partial}{\partial\theta}\left[\mu\left(\frac{1}{r}\frac{\partial v_r}{\partial\theta} + \frac{\partial v_\theta}{\partial r} - \frac{v_\theta}{r}\right)\right]$$

$$+ \frac{\partial}{\partial z}\left[\mu\left(\frac{\partial v_r}{\partial z} + \frac{\partial v_z}{\partial r}\right)\right] + \frac{2\mu}{r}\left(\frac{\partial v_r}{\partial r} - \frac{1}{r}\frac{\partial v_\theta}{\partial\theta} - \frac{v_r}{r}\right)$$

$$\rho\left[\frac{Dv_\theta}{Dt} + \frac{v_r v_\theta}{r}\right]$$

$$= F_\theta - \frac{1}{r}\frac{\partial P}{\partial\theta} + \frac{1}{r}\frac{\partial}{\partial\theta}\left[\frac{2\mu}{r}\frac{\partial v_\theta}{\partial\theta} + (\zeta - \tfrac{2}{3}\mu)\nabla\cdot\mathbf{V}\right] + \frac{\partial}{\partial z}\left[\mu\left(\frac{1}{r}\frac{\partial v_z}{\partial\theta} + \frac{\partial v_\theta}{\partial z}\right)\right]$$

$$+ \frac{\partial}{\partial r}\left[\mu\left(\frac{1}{r}\frac{\partial v_r}{\partial\theta} + \frac{\partial v_\theta}{\partial r} - \frac{v_\theta}{r}\right)\right] + \frac{2\mu}{r}\left[\frac{1}{r}\frac{\partial v_r}{\partial\theta} + \frac{\partial v_\theta}{\partial r} - \frac{v_\theta}{r}\right]$$

$$\rho\frac{Dv_z}{Dt}$$

$$= F_z - \frac{\partial P}{\partial z} + \frac{\partial}{\partial z}\left[2\mu\frac{\partial v_z}{\partial z} + (\zeta - \tfrac{2}{3}\mu)\nabla\cdot\mathbf{V}\right]$$

$$+ \frac{1}{r}\frac{\partial}{\partial r}\left[\mu r\left(\frac{\partial v_r}{\partial z} + \frac{\partial v_z}{\partial r}\right)\right] + \frac{1}{r}\frac{\partial}{\partial\theta}\left[\mu\left(\frac{1}{r}\frac{\partial v_z}{\partial\theta} + \frac{\partial v_\theta}{\partial z}\right)\right]$$

or in terms of λ:

$$\rho\left[\frac{Dv_r}{Dt} - \frac{v_\theta^2}{r}\right] \tag{1.41}$$

$$= F_r - \frac{\partial P}{\partial r} + \frac{\partial}{\partial r}\left[2\mu\frac{\partial v_r}{\partial r} + \lambda\nabla\cdot\mathbf{V}\right] + \frac{1}{r}\frac{\partial}{\partial\theta}\left[\mu\left(\frac{1}{r}\frac{\partial v_r}{\partial\theta} + \frac{\partial v_\theta}{\partial r} - \frac{v_\theta}{r}\right)\right]$$

$$+ \frac{\partial}{\partial z}\left[\mu\left(\frac{\partial v_r}{\partial z} + \frac{\partial v_z}{\partial r}\right)\right] + \frac{2\mu}{r}\left(\frac{\partial v_r}{\partial r} - \frac{1}{r}\frac{\partial v_\theta}{\partial\theta} - \frac{v_r}{r}\right)$$

$$\rho\left[\frac{Dv_\theta}{Dt} + \frac{v_r v_\theta}{r}\right]$$

$$= F_\theta - \frac{1}{r}\frac{\partial P}{\partial r} + \frac{1}{r}\frac{\partial}{\partial\theta}\left[\frac{2\mu}{r}\frac{\partial v_\theta}{\partial\theta} + \lambda\nabla\cdot\mathbf{V}\right] + \frac{\partial}{\partial z}\left[\mu\left(\frac{1}{r}\frac{\partial v_z}{\partial\theta} + \frac{\partial v_\theta}{\partial z}\right)\right]$$

$$+ \frac{\partial}{\partial r}\left[\mu\left(\frac{1}{r}\frac{\partial v_r}{\partial\theta} + \frac{\partial v_\theta}{\partial r} - \frac{v_\theta}{r}\right)\right] + \frac{2\mu}{r}\left[\frac{1}{r}\frac{\partial v_r}{\partial\theta} + \frac{\partial v_\theta}{\partial r} - \frac{v_\theta}{r}\right]$$

$$\rho\frac{Dv_z}{Dt}$$

$$= F_z - \frac{\partial P}{\partial z} + \frac{\partial}{\partial z}\left[2\mu\frac{\partial v_z}{\partial z} + \lambda\nabla\cdot\mathbf{V}\right] + \frac{1}{r}\frac{\partial}{\partial r}\left[\mu r\left(\frac{\partial v_r}{\partial z} + \frac{\partial v_z}{\partial r}\right)\right]$$

$$+ \frac{1}{r}\frac{\partial}{\partial\theta}\left[\mu\left(\frac{1}{r}\frac{\partial v_z}{\partial\theta} + \frac{\partial v_\theta}{\partial z}\right)\right]$$

(f) Spherical.

v_r, v_θ, and v_ϕ are the velocities in the r, θ, and ϕ directions respectively. In the following section:

$$\frac{D}{Dt} = \frac{\partial}{\partial t} + v_r\frac{\partial}{\partial r} + \frac{v_\theta}{r}\frac{\partial}{\partial \theta} + \frac{v_\phi}{r\sin\theta}\frac{\partial}{\partial\phi}$$

and

$$\nabla\cdot\mathbf{V} = \frac{1}{r^2}\frac{\partial}{\partial r}(r^2 v_r) + \frac{1}{r\sin\theta}\frac{\partial}{\partial\theta}(v_\theta\sin\theta) + \frac{1}{r\sin\theta}\frac{\partial v_\phi}{\partial\phi}$$

1.42

$$\begin{aligned}\rho\left[\frac{Dv_r}{Dt} - \frac{v_\theta^2+v_\phi^2}{r}\right] &= F_r - \frac{\partial P}{\partial r} + \frac{\partial}{\partial r}\left[2\mu\frac{\partial v_r}{\partial r} + (\zeta-\tfrac{2}{3}\mu)\nabla\cdot\mathbf{V}\right] + \frac{1}{r}\frac{\partial}{\partial\theta}\left[\mu\left\{r\frac{\partial}{\partial r}\left(\frac{v_\theta}{r}\right) + \frac{1}{r}\frac{\partial v_r}{\partial\theta}\right\}\right]\\ &\quad + \frac{1}{r\sin\theta}\frac{\partial}{\partial\phi}\left[\mu\left\{\frac{1}{r\sin\theta}\frac{\partial v_r}{\partial\phi} + r\frac{\partial}{\partial r}\left(\frac{v_\phi}{r}\right)\right\}\right]\\ &\quad + \frac{\mu}{r}\left[4\frac{\partial v_r}{\partial r} - \frac{2}{r}\frac{\partial v_\theta}{\partial\theta} - \frac{4v_r}{r} - \frac{2}{r\sin\theta}\frac{\partial v_\phi}{\partial\phi}\right.\\ &\qquad\left. - \frac{2v_\theta\cot\theta}{r} + r\cot\theta\frac{\partial}{\partial r}\left(\frac{v_\theta}{r}\right) + \frac{\cot\theta}{r}\frac{\partial v_r}{\partial\theta}\right]\end{aligned}$$

$$\begin{aligned}\rho\left[\frac{Dv_\theta}{Dt} + \frac{v_r v_\theta}{r} - \frac{v_\phi^2\cot\theta}{r}\right] &= F_\theta - \frac{1}{r}\frac{\partial P}{\partial\theta} + \frac{1}{r}\frac{\partial}{\partial\theta}\left[\frac{2\mu}{r}\left(\frac{\partial v_\theta}{\partial\theta} + v_r\right) + (\zeta-\tfrac{2}{3}\mu)\nabla\cdot\mathbf{V}\right]\\ &\quad + \frac{1}{r\sin\theta}\frac{\partial}{\partial\phi}\left[\mu\left\{\frac{\sin\theta}{r}\frac{\partial}{\partial\theta}\left(\frac{v_\phi}{\sin\theta}\right) + \frac{1}{r\sin\theta}\frac{\partial v_\theta}{\partial\phi}\right\}\right]\\ &\quad + \frac{\partial}{\partial r}\left[\mu\left\{r\frac{\partial}{\partial r}\left(\frac{v_\theta}{r}\right) + \frac{1}{r}\frac{\partial v_r}{\partial\theta}\right\}\right]\\ &\quad + \frac{\mu}{r}\left[2\left(\frac{1}{r}\frac{\partial v_\theta}{\partial\theta} - \frac{1}{r\sin\theta}\frac{\partial v_\phi}{\partial\phi} - \frac{v_\theta\cot\theta}{r}\right)\cdot\cot\theta\right.\\ &\qquad\left. + 3\left\{r\frac{\partial}{\partial r}\left(\frac{v_\theta}{r}\right) + \frac{1}{r}\frac{\partial v_r}{\partial\theta}\right\}\right]\end{aligned}$$

$$\begin{aligned}\rho\left[\frac{Dv_\phi}{Dt} + \frac{v_\phi v_r}{r} + \frac{v_\theta v_\phi\cot\theta}{r}\right] &= F_\phi - \frac{1}{r\sin\theta}\frac{\partial P}{\partial\phi} + \frac{1}{r\sin\theta}\frac{\partial}{\partial\phi}\left[\frac{2\mu}{r}\left(\frac{1}{\sin\theta}\frac{\partial v_\phi}{\partial\phi} + v_r + v_\theta\cot\theta\right) + (\zeta-\tfrac{2}{3}\mu)\nabla\cdot\mathbf{V}\right]\\ &\quad + \frac{\partial}{\partial r}\left[\mu\left\{\frac{1}{r\sin\theta}\frac{\partial v_r}{\partial\phi} + r\frac{\partial}{\partial r}\left(\frac{v_\phi}{r}\right)\right\}\right]\\ &\quad + \frac{1}{r}\frac{\partial}{\partial\theta}\left[\mu\left\{\frac{\sin\theta}{r}\frac{\partial}{\partial\theta}\left(\frac{v_\phi}{\sin\theta}\right) + \frac{1}{r\sin\theta}\frac{\partial v_\theta}{\partial\phi}\right\}\right]\\ &\quad + \frac{\mu}{r}\left[3\left\{\frac{1}{r\sin\theta}\frac{\partial v_r}{\partial\phi} + r\frac{\partial}{\partial r}\left(\frac{v_\phi}{r}\right)\right\}\right.\\ &\qquad\left. + 2\cot\theta\left\{\frac{\sin\theta}{r}\frac{\partial}{\partial\theta}\left(\frac{v_\phi}{\sin\theta}\right) + \frac{1}{r\sin\theta}\frac{\partial v_\theta}{\partial\phi}\right\}\right]\end{aligned}$$

or in terms of λ:

$$\rho\left[\frac{Dv_r}{Dt} - \frac{v_\theta^2 + v_\phi^2}{r}\right] \qquad \textbf{1.43}$$

$$= F_r - \frac{\partial P}{\partial r} + \frac{\partial}{\partial r}\left[2\mu\frac{\partial v_r}{\partial r} + \lambda\nabla\cdot\mathbf{V}\right] + \frac{1}{r}\frac{\partial}{\partial\theta}\left[\mu\left\{r\frac{\partial}{\partial r}\left(\frac{v_\theta}{r}\right) + \frac{1}{r}\frac{\partial v_r}{\partial\theta}\right\}\right]$$

$$+ \frac{1}{r\sin\theta}\frac{\partial}{\partial\phi}\left[\mu\left\{\frac{1}{r\sin\theta}\frac{\partial v_r}{\partial\phi} + r\frac{\partial}{\partial r}\left(\frac{v_\phi}{r}\right)\right\}\right]$$

$$+ \frac{\mu}{r}\left[4\frac{\partial v_r}{\partial r} - \frac{2}{r}\frac{\partial v_\theta}{\partial\theta} - \frac{4v_r}{r} - \frac{2}{r\sin\theta}\frac{\partial v_\phi}{\partial\phi}\right.$$

$$\left. - \frac{2v_\theta\cot\theta}{r} + r\cot\theta\frac{\partial}{\partial r}\left(\frac{v_\theta}{r}\right) + \frac{\cot\theta}{r}\frac{\partial v_r}{\partial\theta}\right]$$

$$\rho\left[\frac{Dv_\theta}{Dt} + \frac{v_r v_\theta}{r} - \frac{v_\phi^2\cot\theta}{r}\right]$$

$$= F_\theta - \frac{1}{r}\frac{\partial P}{\partial\theta} + \frac{1}{r}\frac{\partial}{\partial\theta}\left[\frac{2\mu}{r}\left(\frac{\partial v_\theta}{\partial\theta} + v_r\right) + \lambda\nabla\cdot\mathbf{V}\right]$$

$$+ \frac{1}{r\sin\theta}\frac{\partial}{\partial\phi}\left[\mu\left\{\frac{\sin\theta}{r}\frac{\partial}{\partial\theta}\left(\frac{v_\phi}{\sin\theta}\right) + \frac{1}{r\sin\theta}\frac{\partial v_\theta}{\partial\phi}\right\}\right]$$

$$+ \frac{\partial}{\partial r}\left[\mu\left\{r\frac{\partial}{\partial r}\left(\frac{v_\theta}{r}\right) + \frac{1}{r}\frac{\partial v_r}{\partial\theta}\right\}\right]$$

$$+ \frac{\mu}{r}\left[2\left(\frac{1}{r}\frac{\partial v_\theta}{\partial\theta} - \frac{1}{r\sin\theta}\frac{\partial v_\phi}{\partial\phi} - \frac{v_\theta\cot\theta}{r}\right)\cdot\cot\theta\right.$$

$$\left. + 3\left\{r\frac{\partial}{\partial r}\left(\frac{v_\theta}{r}\right) + \frac{1}{r}\frac{\partial v_r}{\partial\theta}\right\}\right]$$

$$\rho\left[\frac{Dv_\phi}{Dt} + \frac{v_\phi v_r}{r} + \frac{v_\theta v_\phi\cot\theta}{r}\right]$$

$$= F_\phi - \frac{1}{r\sin\theta}\frac{\partial P}{\partial\phi} + \frac{1}{r\sin\theta}\frac{\partial}{\partial\phi}\left[\frac{2\mu}{r}\left(\frac{1}{\sin\theta}\frac{\partial v_\phi}{\partial\phi} + v_r + v_\theta\cot\theta\right) + \lambda\nabla\cdot\mathbf{V}\right]$$

$$+ \frac{\partial}{\partial r}\left[\mu\left\{\frac{1}{r\sin\theta}\frac{\partial v_r}{\partial\phi} + r\frac{\partial}{\partial r}\left(\frac{v_\phi}{r}\right)\right\}\right]$$

$$+ \frac{1}{r}\frac{\partial}{\partial\theta}\left[\mu\left\{\frac{\sin\theta}{r}\frac{\partial}{\partial\theta}\left(\frac{v_\phi}{\sin\theta}\right) + \frac{1}{r\sin\theta}\frac{\partial v_\theta}{\partial\phi}\right\}\right]$$

$$+ \frac{\mu}{r}\left[3\left\{\frac{1}{r\sin\theta}\frac{\partial v_r}{\partial\phi} + r\frac{\partial}{\partial r}\left(\frac{v_\phi}{r}\right)\right\}\right.$$

$$\left. + 2\cot\theta\left\{\frac{\sin\theta}{r}\frac{\partial}{\partial\theta}\left(\frac{v_\phi}{\sin\theta}\right) + \frac{1}{r\sin\theta}\frac{\partial v_\theta}{\partial\phi}\right\}\right]$$

1.7 NAVIER-STOKES EQUATIONS OF MOTION FOR A COMPRESSIBLE FLUID WITH VISCOSITY CONSTANT

In most physical problems the forms of the equations below are sufficiently accurate. Slight variations in viscosity can still be permitted with a high degree of accuracy.

P = Pressure

$\mathbf{F}$ = Body force density

μ = Viscosity

λ = Second coefficient of viscosity ($\lambda = -\frac{2}{3}\mu$ for a monatomic gas).

ζ = Another second coefficient of viscosity defined in terms of λ as $\zeta = \lambda + \frac{2}{3}\mu$, and hence ζ is zero for a monatomic gas. Both definitions of the second coefficient of viscosity are in current usage.

(a) *Vector.*

$\mathbf{V}$ is the velocity vector.

$$\rho\frac{D\mathbf{V}}{Dt} = \rho\left[\frac{\partial \mathbf{V}}{\partial t} + (\mathbf{V}\cdot\nabla)\mathbf{V}\right] = \rho\left[\frac{\partial \mathbf{V}}{\partial t} + \nabla\left(\frac{V^2}{2}\right) - \mathbf{V}\times(\nabla\times\mathbf{V})\right] \qquad \textbf{1.44}$$

$$= -\nabla P + \mu\nabla^2\mathbf{V} + (\zeta + \tfrac{1}{3}\mu)\nabla(\nabla\cdot\mathbf{V}) + \mathbf{F}$$

$$= -\nabla P - \mu\nabla\times(\nabla\times\mathbf{V}) + (\zeta + \tfrac{4}{3}\mu)\nabla(\nabla\cdot\mathbf{V}) + \mathbf{F}$$

or in terms of λ:

$$\rho\left[\frac{\partial \mathbf{V}}{\partial t} + (\mathbf{V}\cdot\nabla)\mathbf{V}\right] = \rho\left[\frac{\partial \mathbf{V}}{\partial t} + \nabla\left(\frac{V^2}{2}\right) - \mathbf{V}\times(\nabla\times\mathbf{V})\right] \qquad \textbf{1.45}$$

$$= -\nabla P + \mu\nabla^2\mathbf{V} + (\lambda + \mu)\nabla(\nabla\cdot\mathbf{V}) + \mathbf{F}$$

$$= -\nabla P - \mu\nabla\times(\nabla\times\mathbf{V}) + (\lambda + 2\mu)\nabla(\nabla\cdot\mathbf{V}) + \mathbf{F}$$

(b) *Cartesian Tensor.*

w_i is the velocity in the x_i direction.

$$\rho\left[\frac{\partial w_i}{\partial t} + w_j\frac{\partial w_i}{\partial x_j}\right] = -\frac{\partial P}{\partial x_i} + \mu\frac{\partial^2 w_i}{\partial x_j \partial x_j} + (\zeta + \tfrac{1}{3}\mu)\frac{\partial}{\partial x_i}\left(\frac{\partial w_j}{\partial x_j}\right) + F_i \qquad \textbf{1.46}$$

or in terms of λ:

$$\rho\left[\frac{\partial w_i}{\partial t} + w_j\frac{\partial w_i}{\partial x_j}\right] = -\frac{\partial P}{\partial x_i} + \mu\frac{\partial^2 w_i}{\partial x_j \partial x_j} + (\lambda + \mu)\frac{\partial}{\partial x_i}\left(\frac{\partial w_j}{\partial x_j}\right) + F_i \qquad \textbf{1.47}$$

(c) *Orthogonal Curvilinear.* **1.48**

These equations are not written out here because of their bulky nature. They can be obtained immediately from equation 1.37 by removing the coefficients of viscosity from inside the derivatives. Such an equation will be referred to as equation 1.48.

(d) *Cartesian.*

u, v, and w are the velocities in the x, y, and z directions respectively. In the following section:

$$\frac{D}{Dt} = \frac{\partial}{\partial t} + u\frac{\partial}{\partial x} + v\frac{\partial}{\partial y} + w\frac{\partial}{\partial z}$$

$$\nabla \cdot \mathbf{V} = \frac{\partial u}{\partial x} + \frac{\partial v}{\partial y} + \frac{\partial w}{\partial z}$$

$$\nabla^2 = \frac{\partial^2}{\partial x^2} + \frac{\partial^2}{\partial y^2} + \frac{\partial^2}{\partial z^2}$$

$$\rho\frac{Du}{Dt} = -\frac{\partial P}{\partial x} + F_x + \mu\left(\frac{\partial^2 u}{\partial x^2} + \frac{\partial^2 u}{\partial y^2} + \frac{\partial^2 u}{\partial z^2}\right) + (\zeta + \tfrac{1}{3}\mu)\frac{\partial}{\partial x}\left(\frac{\partial u}{\partial x} + \frac{\partial v}{\partial y} + \frac{\partial w}{\partial z}\right) \quad \mathbf{1.49}$$

$$= -\frac{\partial P}{\partial x} + F_x + \mu\nabla^2 u + (\zeta + \tfrac{1}{3}\mu)\frac{\partial}{\partial x}(\nabla \cdot \mathbf{V})$$

$$\rho\frac{Dv}{Dt} = -\frac{\partial P}{\partial y} + F_y + \mu\left(\frac{\partial^2 v}{\partial x^2} + \frac{\partial^2 v}{\partial y^2} + \frac{\partial^2 v}{\partial z^2}\right) + (\zeta + \tfrac{1}{3}\mu)\frac{\partial}{\partial y}\left(\frac{\partial u}{\partial x} + \frac{\partial v}{\partial y} + \frac{\partial w}{\partial z}\right)$$

$$= -\frac{\partial P}{\partial y} + F_y + \mu\nabla^2 v + (\zeta + \tfrac{1}{3}\mu)\frac{\partial}{\partial y}(\nabla \cdot \mathbf{V})$$

$$\rho\frac{Dw}{Dt} = -\frac{\partial P}{\partial z} + F_z + \mu\left(\frac{\partial^2 w}{\partial x^2} + \frac{\partial^2 w}{\partial y^2} + \frac{\partial^2 w}{\partial z^2}\right) + (\zeta + \tfrac{1}{3}\mu)\frac{\partial}{\partial z}\left(\frac{\partial u}{\partial x} + \frac{\partial v}{\partial y} + \frac{\partial w}{\partial z}\right)$$

$$= -\frac{\partial P}{\partial z} + F_z + \mu\nabla^2 w + (\zeta + \tfrac{1}{3}\mu)\frac{\partial}{\partial z}(\nabla \cdot \mathbf{V})$$

or in terms of λ:

$$\rho\frac{Du}{Dt} = -\frac{\partial P}{\partial x} + F_x + \mu\nabla^2 u + (\lambda + \mu)\frac{\partial}{\partial x}(\nabla \cdot \mathbf{V}) \quad \mathbf{1.50}$$

$$\rho\frac{Dv}{Dt} = -\frac{\partial P}{\partial y} + F_y + \mu\nabla^2 v + (\lambda + \mu)\frac{\partial}{\partial y}(\nabla \cdot \mathbf{V})$$

$$\rho\frac{Dw}{Dt} = -\frac{\partial P}{\partial z} + F_z + \mu\nabla^2 w + (\lambda + \mu)\frac{\partial}{\partial z}(\nabla \cdot \mathbf{V})$$

(e) *Cylindrical.*

v_r, v_θ, and v_z are the velocities in the r, θ, and z directions respectively. In the following section:

$$\frac{D}{Dt} = \frac{\partial}{\partial t} + v_r\frac{\partial}{\partial r} + \frac{v_\theta}{r}\frac{\partial}{\partial \theta} + v_z\frac{\partial}{\partial z}$$

$$\nabla \cdot \mathbf{V} = \frac{1}{r}\frac{\partial}{\partial r}(rv_r) + \frac{1}{r}\frac{\partial v_\theta}{\partial \theta} + \frac{\partial v_z}{\partial z}$$

$$\nabla^2 = \frac{\partial^2}{\partial r^2} + \frac{1}{r}\frac{\partial}{\partial r} + \frac{1}{r^2}\frac{\partial^2}{\partial \theta^2} + \frac{\partial^2}{\partial z^2}$$

(The above Laplacian operator is for operation on a scalar component only and is used in that manner in the following equations.)

$$\rho\left[\frac{Dv_r}{Dt} - \frac{v_\theta^2}{r}\right] \quad \mathbf{1.51}$$

$$= -\frac{\partial P}{\partial r} + F_r + \mu\left[\nabla^2 v_r - \frac{v_r}{r^2} - \frac{2}{r^2}\frac{\partial v_\theta}{\partial \theta}\right] + (\zeta + \tfrac{1}{3}\mu)\frac{\partial}{\partial r}(\nabla \cdot \mathbf{V})$$

$$\rho\left[\frac{Dv_\theta}{Dt} + \frac{v_r v_\theta}{r}\right]$$

$$= -\frac{1}{r}\frac{\partial P}{\partial \theta} + F_\theta + \mu\left[\nabla^2 v_\theta + \frac{2}{r^2}\frac{\partial v_r}{\partial \theta} - \frac{v_\theta}{r^2}\right] + (\zeta + \tfrac{1}{3}\mu)\frac{1}{r}\frac{\partial}{\partial \theta}(\nabla \cdot \mathbf{V})$$

$$\rho\frac{Dv_z}{Dt} = -\frac{\partial P}{\partial z} + F_z + \mu\nabla^2 v_z + (\zeta + \tfrac{1}{3}\mu)\frac{\partial}{\partial z}(\nabla \cdot \mathbf{V})$$

or in terms of λ:

$$\rho\left[\frac{Dv_r}{Dt} - \frac{v_\theta^2}{r}\right] \qquad \mathbf{1.52}$$

$$= -\frac{\partial P}{\partial r} + F_r + \mu\left[\nabla^2 v_r - \frac{v_r}{r^2} - \frac{2}{r^2}\frac{\partial v_\theta}{\partial \theta}\right] + (\lambda + \mu)\frac{\partial}{\partial r}(\nabla \cdot \mathbf{V})$$

$$\rho\left[\frac{Dv_\theta}{Dt} + \frac{v_r v_\theta}{r}\right]$$

$$= -\frac{1}{r}\frac{\partial P}{\partial \theta} + F_\theta + \mu\left[\nabla^2 v_\theta + \frac{2}{r^2}\frac{\partial v_r}{\partial \theta} - \frac{v_\theta}{r^2}\right] + (\lambda + \mu)\frac{1}{r}\frac{\partial}{\partial \theta}(\nabla \cdot \mathbf{V})$$

$$\rho\frac{Dv_z}{Dt} = -\frac{\partial P}{\partial z} + F_z + \mu\nabla^2 v_z + (\lambda + \mu)\frac{\partial}{\partial z}(\nabla \cdot \mathbf{V})$$

(f) Spherical.

v_r, v_θ, and v_ϕ are the velocities in the r, θ, and ϕ directions respectively. In the following section:

$$\frac{D}{Dt} = \frac{\partial}{\partial t} + v_r\frac{\partial}{\partial r} + \frac{v_\theta}{r}\frac{\partial}{\partial \theta} + \frac{v_\phi}{r\sin\theta}\frac{\partial}{\partial \phi}$$

$$\nabla \cdot \mathbf{V} = \frac{1}{r^2}\frac{\partial}{\partial r}(r^2 v_r) + \frac{1}{r\sin\theta}\frac{\partial}{\partial \theta}(v_\theta \sin\theta) + \frac{1}{r\sin\theta}\frac{\partial v_\phi}{\partial \phi}$$

$$\nabla^2 = \frac{1}{r^2}\frac{\partial}{\partial r}\left(r^2\frac{\partial}{\partial r}\right) + \frac{1}{r^2\sin\theta}\frac{\partial}{\partial \theta}\left(\sin\theta\frac{\partial}{\partial \theta}\right) + \frac{1}{r^2\sin^2\theta}\frac{\partial^2}{\partial \phi^2}$$

(The above Laplacian is for operation on a scalar component only and is used in that manner in the following equations.)

$$\rho\left[\frac{Dv_r}{Dt} - \frac{v_\theta^2 + v_\phi^2}{r}\right] \qquad \mathbf{1.53}$$

$$= -\frac{\partial P}{\partial r} + F_r + \mu\left[\nabla^2 v_r - \frac{2v_r}{r^2} - \frac{2}{r^2}\frac{\partial v_\theta}{\partial \theta} - \frac{2v_\theta\cot\theta}{r^2} - \frac{2}{r^2\sin\theta}\frac{\partial v_\phi}{\partial \phi}\right]$$

$$+ (\zeta + \tfrac{1}{3}\mu)\frac{\partial}{\partial r}(\nabla \cdot \mathbf{V})$$

$$\rho\left[\frac{Dv_\theta}{Dt} + \frac{v_r v_\theta - v_\phi^2\cot\theta}{r}\right]$$

$$= -\frac{1}{r}\frac{\partial P}{\partial \theta} + F_\theta + \mu\left[\nabla^2 v_\theta + \frac{2}{r^2}\frac{\partial v_r}{\partial \theta} - \frac{v_\theta}{r^2\sin^2\theta} - \frac{2\cos\theta}{r^2\sin^2\theta}\frac{\partial v_\phi}{\partial \phi}\right]$$

$$+ (\zeta + \tfrac{1}{3}\mu)\cdot\frac{1}{r}\frac{\partial}{\partial \theta}(\nabla \cdot \mathbf{V})$$

$$\rho\left[\frac{Dv_\phi}{Dt} + \frac{v_\phi v_r + v_\theta v_\phi \cot\theta}{r}\right]$$
$$= -\frac{1}{r\sin\theta}\frac{\partial P}{\partial\phi} + F_\phi + \mu\left[\nabla^2 v_\phi - \frac{v_\phi}{r^2\sin^2\theta} + \frac{2}{r^2\sin^2\theta}\frac{\partial v_r}{\partial\phi} + \frac{2\cos\theta}{r^2\sin^2\theta}\frac{\partial v_\theta}{\partial\phi}\right]$$
$$+ (\zeta + \tfrac{1}{3}\mu)\frac{1}{r\sin\theta}\frac{\partial}{\partial\phi}(\nabla\cdot\mathbf{V})$$

or in terms of λ:

$$\rho\left[\frac{Dv_r}{Dt} - \frac{v_\theta^2 + v_\phi^2}{r}\right] \qquad \textbf{1.54}$$
$$= -\frac{\partial P}{\partial r} + F_r + \mu\left[\nabla^2 v_r - \frac{2v_r}{r^2} - \frac{2}{r^2}\frac{\partial v_\theta}{\partial\theta} - \frac{2v_\theta\cot\theta}{r^2} - \frac{2}{r^2\sin\theta}\frac{\partial v_\phi}{\partial\phi}\right]$$
$$+ (\lambda + \mu)\frac{\partial}{\partial r}(\nabla\cdot\mathbf{V})$$

$$\rho\left[\frac{Dv_\theta}{Dt} + \frac{v_r v_\theta - v_\phi^2\cot\theta}{r}\right]$$
$$= -\frac{1}{r}\frac{\partial P}{\partial\theta} + F_\theta + \mu\left[\nabla^2 v_\theta + \frac{2}{r^2}\frac{\partial v_r}{\partial\theta} - \frac{v_\theta}{r^2\sin^2\theta} - \frac{2\cos\theta}{r^2\sin^2\theta}\frac{\partial v_\phi}{\partial\phi}\right]$$
$$+ (\lambda + \mu)\frac{1}{r}\frac{\partial}{\partial\theta}(\nabla\cdot\mathbf{V})$$

$$\rho\left[\frac{Dv_\phi}{Dt} + \frac{v_\phi v_r + v_\theta v_\phi\cot\theta}{r}\right]$$
$$= -\frac{1}{r\sin\theta}\frac{\partial P}{\partial\phi} + F_\phi + \mu\left[\nabla^2 v_\phi - \frac{v_\phi}{r^2\sin^2\theta} + \frac{2}{r^2\sin^2\theta}\frac{\partial v_r}{\partial\phi} + \frac{2\cos\theta}{r^2\sin^2\theta}\frac{\partial v_\theta}{\partial\phi}\right]$$
$$+ (\lambda + \mu)\frac{1}{r\sin\theta}\frac{\partial}{\partial\phi}(\nabla\cdot\mathbf{V})$$

1.8 NAVIER-STOKES EQUATIONS OF MOTION FOR AN INCOMPRESSIBLE FLUID

These equations are the same as those in section 1.6 except that the term $\nabla\cdot\mathbf{V}$ is taken as zero. In the following section the following symbols are used.

P = Pressure
$\mathbf{F}$ = Body force density
μ = Viscosity

(a) Vector.

$\mathbf{V}$ is the velocity vector.

$$\rho\frac{D\mathbf{V}}{Dt} = \rho\left[\frac{\partial\mathbf{V}}{\partial t} + (\mathbf{V}\cdot\nabla)\mathbf{V}\right] = \rho\left[\frac{\partial\mathbf{V}}{\partial t} + \nabla\left(\frac{V^2}{2}\right) - \mathbf{V}\times(\nabla\times\mathbf{V})\right] \qquad \textbf{1.55}$$
$$= -\nabla P + \mathbf{F} - \nabla\times[\mu(\nabla\times\mathbf{V})]$$

(b) Cartesian Tensor.

w_i is the velocity in the x_i direction.

$$\rho\left[\frac{\partial w_i}{\partial t} + w_j\frac{\partial w_i}{\partial x_j}\right] = -\frac{\partial P}{\partial x_i} + F_i + \frac{\partial}{\partial x_j}\left[\mu\left(\frac{\partial w_i}{\partial x_j} + \frac{\partial w_j}{\partial x_i}\right)\right] \qquad \textbf{1.56}$$

(c) *Orthogonal Curvilinear.* **1.57**

These equations are not written out explicitly here but can be obtained from equation 1.47 simply by setting the $\nabla \cdot \mathbf{V}$ term equal to zero. We will refer to such an equation as equation 1.57.

(d) *Cartesian.*

u, v, and w are the velocities in the x, y, and z directions respectively. In the following section:

$$\frac{D}{Dt} = \frac{\partial}{\partial t} + u\frac{\partial}{\partial x} + v\frac{\partial}{\partial y} + w\frac{\partial}{\partial z}$$

$$\rho\frac{Du}{Dt} = -\frac{\partial P}{\partial x} + F_x + 2\frac{\partial}{\partial x}\left(\mu\frac{\partial u}{\partial x}\right) + \frac{\partial}{\partial y}\left[\mu\left(\frac{\partial u}{\partial y} + \frac{\partial v}{\partial x}\right)\right] + \frac{\partial}{\partial z}\left[\mu\left(\frac{\partial w}{\partial x} + \frac{\partial u}{\partial z}\right)\right] \qquad \textbf{1.58}$$

$$\rho\frac{Dv}{Dt} = -\frac{\partial P}{\partial y} + F_y + 2\frac{\partial}{\partial y}\left(\mu\frac{\partial v}{\partial y}\right) + \frac{\partial}{\partial z}\left[\mu\left(\frac{\partial v}{\partial z} + \frac{\partial w}{\partial y}\right)\right] + \frac{\partial}{\partial x}\left[\mu\left(\frac{\partial u}{\partial y} + \frac{\partial v}{\partial x}\right)\right]$$

$$\rho\frac{Dw}{Dt} = -\frac{\partial P}{\partial z} + F_z + 2\frac{\partial}{\partial z}\left(\mu\frac{\partial w}{\partial z}\right) + \frac{\partial}{\partial x}\left[\mu\left(\frac{\partial w}{\partial x} + \frac{\partial u}{\partial z}\right)\right] + \frac{\partial}{\partial y}\left[\mu\left(\frac{\partial v}{\partial z} + \frac{\partial w}{\partial y}\right)\right]$$

(e) *Cylindrical.*

v_r, v_θ, and v_z are the velocities in the r, θ, and z directions respectively. In the following section:

$$\frac{D}{Dt} = \frac{\partial}{\partial t} + v_r\frac{\partial}{\partial r} + \frac{v_\theta}{r}\frac{\partial}{\partial \theta} + v_z\frac{\partial}{\partial z}$$

$$\rho\left[\frac{Dv_r}{Dt} - \frac{v_\theta^2}{r}\right] \qquad \textbf{1.59}$$

$$= -\frac{\partial P}{\partial r} + F_r + 2\frac{\partial}{\partial r}\left(\mu\frac{\partial v_r}{\partial r}\right) + \frac{1}{r}\frac{\partial}{\partial \theta}\left[\mu\left(\frac{1}{r}\frac{\partial v_r}{\partial \theta} + \frac{\partial v_\theta}{\partial r} - \frac{v_\theta}{r}\right)\right]$$
$$+ \frac{\partial}{\partial z}\left[\mu\left(\frac{\partial v_r}{\partial z} + \frac{\partial v_z}{\partial r}\right)\right] + \frac{2\mu}{r}\left(\frac{\partial v_r}{\partial r} - \frac{1}{r}\frac{\partial v_\theta}{\partial \theta} - \frac{v_r}{r}\right)$$

$$\rho\left[\frac{Dv_\theta}{Dt} + \frac{v_r v_\theta}{r}\right]$$

$$= -\frac{1}{r}\frac{\partial P}{\partial \theta} + F_\theta + \frac{2}{r}\frac{\partial}{\partial \theta}\left(\frac{\mu}{r}\frac{\partial v_\theta}{\partial \theta}\right) + \frac{\partial}{\partial z}\left[\mu\left(\frac{1}{r}\frac{\partial v_z}{\partial \theta} + \frac{\partial v_\theta}{\partial z}\right)\right]$$
$$+ \frac{\partial}{\partial r}\left[\mu\left(\frac{1}{r}\frac{\partial v_r}{\partial \theta} + \frac{\partial v_\theta}{\partial r} - \frac{v_\theta}{r}\right)\right] + \frac{2\mu}{r}\left[\frac{1}{r}\frac{\partial v_r}{\partial \theta} + \frac{\partial v_\theta}{\partial r} - \frac{v_\theta}{r}\right]$$

$$\rho\frac{Dv_z}{Dt}$$

$$= -\frac{\partial P}{\partial z} + F_z + 2\frac{\partial}{\partial z}\left(\mu\frac{\partial v_z}{\partial z}\right) + \frac{1}{r}\frac{\partial}{\partial r}\left[\mu r\left(\frac{\partial v_r}{\partial z} + \frac{\partial v_z}{\partial r}\right)\right]$$
$$+ \frac{1}{r}\frac{\partial}{\partial \theta}\left[\mu\left(\frac{1}{r}\frac{\partial v_z}{\partial \theta} + \frac{\partial v_\theta}{\partial z}\right)\right]$$

(f) Spherical.

v_r, v_θ, and v_ϕ are the velocities in the r, θ, and ϕ directions respectively. In the following section:

$$\frac{D}{Dt} = \frac{\partial}{\partial t} + v_r \frac{\partial}{\partial r} + \frac{v_\theta}{r}\frac{\partial}{\partial \theta} + \frac{v_\phi}{r \sin\theta}\frac{\partial}{\partial \phi}$$

$$\rho\left[\frac{Dv_r}{Dt} - \frac{v_\theta^2 + v_\phi^2}{r}\right] \qquad \mathbf{1.60}$$

$$= -\frac{\partial P}{\partial r} + F_r + 2\frac{\partial}{\partial r}\left(\mu\frac{\partial v_r}{\partial r}\right)$$

$$+ \frac{1}{r}\frac{\partial}{\partial \theta}\left[\mu\left\{r\frac{\partial}{\partial r}\left(\frac{v_\theta}{r}\right) + \frac{1}{r}\frac{\partial v_r}{\partial \theta}\right\}\right]$$

$$+ \frac{1}{r\sin\theta}\frac{\partial}{\partial\phi}\left[\mu\left\{\frac{1}{r\sin\theta}\frac{\partial v_r}{\partial\phi} + r\frac{\partial}{\partial r}\left(\frac{v_\phi}{r}\right)\right\}\right]$$

$$+ \frac{\mu}{r}\left[4\frac{\partial v_r}{\partial r} - \frac{2}{r}\frac{\partial v_\theta}{\partial\theta} - \frac{4v_r}{r} - \frac{2}{r\sin\theta}\frac{\partial v_\phi}{\partial\phi} - \frac{2v_\theta\cot\theta}{r}\right.$$

$$\left. + r\cot\theta\frac{\partial}{\partial r}\left(\frac{v_\theta}{r}\right) + \frac{\cot\theta}{r}\frac{\partial v_r}{\partial\theta}\right]$$

$$\rho\left[\frac{Dv_\theta}{Dt} + \frac{v_r v_\theta}{r} - \frac{v_\phi^2\cot\theta}{r}\right]$$

$$= -\frac{1}{r}\frac{\partial P}{\partial\theta} + F_\theta + \frac{2}{r}\frac{\partial}{\partial\theta}\left(\frac{\mu}{r}\frac{\partial v_\theta}{\partial\theta} + \frac{\mu}{r}v_r\right)$$

$$+ \frac{1}{r\sin\theta}\frac{\partial}{\partial\phi}\left[\mu\left\{\frac{\sin\theta}{r}\frac{\partial}{\partial\theta}\left(\frac{v_\phi}{\sin\theta}\right) + \frac{1}{r\sin\theta}\frac{\partial v_\theta}{\partial\phi}\right\}\right]$$

$$+ \frac{\partial}{\partial r}\left[\mu\left\{r\frac{\partial}{\partial r}\left(\frac{v_\theta}{r}\right) + \frac{1}{r}\frac{\partial v_r}{\partial\theta}\right\}\right]$$

$$+ \frac{\mu}{r}\left[2\left(\frac{1}{r}\frac{\partial v_\theta}{\partial\theta} - \frac{1}{r\sin\theta}\frac{\partial v_\phi}{\partial\phi} - \frac{v_\theta\cot\theta}{r}\right)\cot\theta + 3\left\{r\frac{\partial}{\partial r}\left(\frac{v_\theta}{r}\right) + \frac{1}{r}\frac{\partial v_r}{\partial\theta}\right\}\right]$$

$$\rho\left[\frac{Dv_\phi}{Dt} + \frac{v_\phi v_r}{r} + \frac{v_\theta v_\phi\cot\theta}{r}\right]$$

$$= -\frac{1}{r\sin\theta}\frac{\partial P}{\partial\phi} + F_\phi + \frac{2}{r\sin\theta}\frac{\partial}{\partial\phi}\left(\frac{\mu}{r\sin\theta}\frac{\partial v_\phi}{\partial\phi} + \frac{\mu v_r}{r} + \mu\frac{v_\theta}{r}\cot\theta\right)$$

$$+ \frac{\partial}{\partial r}\left[\mu\left\{\frac{1}{r\sin\theta}\frac{\partial v_r}{\partial\phi} + r\frac{\partial}{\partial r}\left(\frac{v_\phi}{r}\right)\right\}\right]$$

$$+ \frac{1}{r}\frac{\partial}{\partial\theta}\left[\mu\left\{\frac{\sin\theta}{r}\frac{\partial}{\partial\theta}\left(\frac{v_\phi}{\sin\theta}\right) + \frac{1}{r\sin\theta}\frac{\partial v_\theta}{\partial\phi}\right\}\right]$$

$$+ \frac{\mu}{r}\left[3\left\{\frac{1}{r\sin\theta}\frac{\partial v_r}{\partial\phi} + r\frac{\partial}{\partial r}\left(\frac{v_\phi}{r}\right)\right\}\right.$$

$$\left. + 2\cot\theta\left\{\frac{\sin\theta}{r}\frac{\partial}{\partial\theta}\left(\frac{v_\phi}{\sin\theta}\right) + \frac{1}{r\sin\theta}\frac{\partial v_\theta}{\partial\phi}\right\}\right]$$

1.9 NAVIER-STOKES EQUATIONS OF MOTION FOR AN INCOMPRESSIBLE FLUID WITH VISCOSITY CONSTANT

These equations may be used with a high degree of accuracy for problems involving viscosity variations if the viscosity gradient is not too large. In most physical problems this assumption is adequate and the Navier-Stokes equations may be used in most incompressible flow problems. The following symbols are used:

P = Pressure

$\mathbf{F}$ = Body force density

μ = Viscosity

$\frac{D}{Dt}$ = Material derivative (not the same on a component as on a vector).

(a) *Vector.*

$\mathbf{V}$ is the velocity vector.

$$\rho\frac{D\mathbf{V}}{Dt} = \rho\left[\frac{\partial\mathbf{V}}{\partial t} + (\mathbf{V}\cdot\nabla)\mathbf{V}\right] = -\nabla P + \mathbf{F} + \mu\nabla^2\mathbf{V} \qquad \textbf{1.61}$$

The term $(\mathbf{V}\cdot\nabla)\mathbf{V}$ is actually a pseudo-vector expression and care must be used in its expansion in other than Cartesian coordinates. It is convenient to express this acceleration term in true vector form, and the equation of motion may be written in the alternative form:

$$\rho\left[\frac{\partial\mathbf{V}}{\partial t} + \nabla\left(\frac{V^2}{2}\right) - \mathbf{V}\times(\nabla\times\mathbf{V})\right] = -\nabla P + \mathbf{F} + \mu\nabla^2\mathbf{V} \qquad \textbf{1.62}$$

Care must be taken in expanding $\nabla^2\mathbf{V}$, since the operation on a vector is not the same as the operation on a scalar component. The following vector identity is useful:

$$\nabla^2\mathbf{V} = \nabla(\nabla\cdot\mathbf{V}) - \nabla\times(\nabla\times\mathbf{V})$$

(b) *Cartesian Tensor.*

w_i is the velocity in the x_i direction.

$$\rho\left[\frac{\partial w_i}{\partial t} + w_j\frac{\partial w_i}{\partial x_j}\right] = -\frac{\partial P}{\partial x_i} + F_i + \mu\frac{\partial^2 w_i}{\partial x_j\,\partial x_j} \qquad \textbf{1.63}$$

(c) *Orthogonal Curvilinear.* **1.64**

These equations are not written out explicitly here but can be obtained from equation 1.47 by setting the $\frac{\partial w_j}{\partial x_j}$ term equal to zero and removing the viscosity from the derivatives. We will refer to such an equation as 1.64.

(d) *Cartesian.*

u, v, and w are the velocities in the x, y, and z directions respectively. In the following section:

$$\frac{D}{Dt} = \frac{\partial}{\partial t} + u\frac{\partial}{\partial x} + v\frac{\partial}{\partial y} + w\frac{\partial}{\partial z}, \qquad \nabla^2 = \frac{\partial^2}{\partial x^2} + \frac{\partial^2}{\partial y^2} + \frac{\partial^2}{\partial z^2}$$

$$\rho\frac{Du}{Dt} = F_x - \frac{\partial P}{\partial x} + \mu\nabla^2 u \qquad \textbf{1.65}$$

$$\rho\frac{Dv}{Dt} = F_y - \frac{\partial P}{\partial y} + \mu\nabla^2 v$$

$$\rho\frac{Dw}{Dt} = F_z - \frac{\partial P}{\partial z} + \mu\nabla^2 w$$

Written out in full, these become:

$$\rho\left(\frac{\partial u}{\partial t} + u\frac{\partial u}{\partial x} + v\frac{\partial u}{\partial y} + w\frac{\partial u}{\partial z}\right) = -\frac{\partial P}{\partial x} + F_x + \mu\left(\frac{\partial^2 u}{\partial x^2} + \frac{\partial^2 u}{\partial y^2} + \frac{\partial^2 u}{\partial z^2}\right) \qquad \textbf{1.66}$$

$$\rho\left(\frac{\partial v}{\partial t} + u\frac{\partial v}{\partial x} + v\frac{\partial v}{\partial y} + w\frac{\partial v}{\partial z}\right) = -\frac{\partial P}{\partial y} + F_y + \mu\left(\frac{\partial^2 v}{\partial x^2} + \frac{\partial^2 v}{\partial y^2} + \frac{\partial^2 v}{\partial z^2}\right)$$

$$\rho\left(\frac{\partial w}{\partial t} + u\frac{\partial w}{\partial x} + v\frac{\partial w}{\partial y} + w\frac{\partial w}{\partial z}\right) = -\frac{\partial P}{\partial z} + F_z + \mu\left(\frac{\partial^2 w}{\partial x^2} + \frac{\partial^2 w}{\partial y^2} + \frac{\partial^2 w}{\partial z^2}\right)$$

(e) Cylindrical.

v_r, v_θ, and v_z are the velocities in the r, θ, and z directions respectively. In the following section:

$$\frac{D}{Dt} = \frac{\partial}{\partial t} + v_r\frac{\partial}{\partial r} + \frac{v_\theta}{r}\frac{\partial}{\partial \theta} + v_z\frac{\partial}{\partial z}$$

$$\nabla^2 = \frac{\partial^2}{\partial r^2} + \frac{1}{r}\frac{\partial}{\partial r} + \frac{1}{r^2}\frac{\partial^2}{\partial \theta^2} + \frac{\partial^2}{\partial z^2}$$

$$\rho\left[\frac{Dv_r}{Dt} - \frac{v_\theta^2}{r}\right] = F_r - \frac{\partial P}{\partial r} + \mu\left[\nabla^2 v_r - \frac{v_r}{r^2} - \frac{2}{r^2}\frac{\partial v_\theta}{\partial \theta}\right] \qquad \textbf{1.67}$$

$$\rho\left[\frac{Dv_\theta}{Dt} + \frac{v_r v_\theta}{r}\right] = F_\theta - \frac{1}{r}\frac{\partial P}{\partial \theta} + \mu\left[\nabla^2 v_\theta + \frac{2}{r^2}\frac{\partial v_r}{\partial \theta} - \frac{v_\theta}{r^2}\right]$$

$$\rho\frac{Dv_z}{Dt} = F_z - \frac{\partial P}{\partial z} + \mu\nabla^2 v_z$$

Written out in full, these become:

$$\rho\left[\frac{\partial v_r}{\partial t} + v_r\frac{\partial v_r}{\partial r} + \frac{v_\theta}{r}\frac{\partial v_r}{\partial \theta} + v_z\frac{\partial v_r}{\partial z} - \frac{v_\theta^2}{r}\right] \qquad \textbf{1.68}$$

$$= F_r - \frac{\partial P}{\partial r} + \mu\left[\frac{\partial^2 v_r}{\partial r^2} + \frac{1}{r}\frac{\partial v_r}{\partial r} + \frac{1}{r^2}\frac{\partial^2 v_r}{\partial \theta^2} + \frac{\partial^2 v_r}{\partial z^2} - \frac{v_r}{r^2} - \frac{2}{r^2}\frac{\partial v_\theta}{\partial \theta}\right]$$

$$\rho\left[\frac{\partial v_\theta}{\partial t} + v_r\frac{\partial v_\theta}{\partial r} + \frac{v_\theta}{r}\frac{\partial v_\theta}{\partial \theta} + v_z\frac{\partial v_\theta}{\partial z} + \frac{v_r v_\theta}{r}\right]$$

$$= F_\theta - \frac{1}{r}\frac{\partial P}{\partial \theta} + \mu\left[\frac{\partial^2 v_\theta}{\partial r^2} + \frac{1}{r}\frac{\partial v_\theta}{\partial r} + \frac{1}{r^2}\frac{\partial^2 v_\theta}{\partial \theta^2} + \frac{\partial^2 v_\theta}{\partial z^2} + \frac{2}{r^2}\frac{\partial v_r}{\partial \theta} - \frac{v_\theta}{r^2}\right]$$

$$\rho\left[\frac{\partial v_z}{\partial t} + v_r\frac{\partial v_z}{\partial r} + \frac{v_\theta}{r}\frac{\partial v_z}{\partial \theta} + v_z\frac{\partial v_z}{\partial z}\right]$$

$$= F_z - \frac{\partial P}{\partial z} + \mu\left[\frac{\partial^2 v_z}{\partial r^2} + \frac{1}{r}\frac{\partial v_z}{\partial r} + \frac{1}{r^2}\frac{\partial^2 v_z}{\partial \theta^2} + \frac{\partial^2 v_z}{\partial z^2}\right]$$

(f) Spherical.

v_r, v_θ, and v_ϕ are the velocities in the r, θ, and ϕ directions respectively. In the following section:

$$\frac{D}{Dt} = \frac{\partial}{\partial t} + v_r \frac{\partial}{\partial r} + \frac{v_\theta}{r} \frac{\partial}{\partial \theta} + \frac{v_\phi}{r \sin \theta} \frac{\partial}{\partial \phi}$$

$$\nabla^2 = \frac{1}{r^2} \frac{\partial}{\partial r}\left(r^2 \frac{\partial}{\partial r}\right) + \frac{1}{r^2 \sin \theta} \frac{\partial}{\partial \theta}\left(\sin \theta \frac{\partial}{\partial \theta}\right) + \frac{1}{r^2 \sin^2 \theta} \frac{\partial^2}{\partial \phi^2}$$

$$\rho\left[\frac{Dv_r}{Dt} - \frac{v_\theta^2 + v_r^2}{r}\right] \qquad \text{1.69}$$

$$= F_r - \frac{\partial P}{\partial r} + \mu\left[\nabla^2 v_r - \frac{2v_r}{r^2} - \frac{2}{r^2}\frac{\partial v_\theta}{\partial \theta} - \frac{2v_\theta \cot \theta}{r^2} - \frac{2}{r^2 \sin \theta}\frac{\partial v_\phi}{\partial \phi}\right]$$

$$\rho\left[\frac{Dv_\theta}{Dt} + \frac{v_r v_\theta - v_\phi^2 \cot \theta}{r}\right]$$

$$= F_\theta - \frac{1}{r}\frac{\partial P}{\partial \theta} + \mu\left[\nabla^2 v_\theta + \frac{2}{r^2}\frac{\partial v_r}{\partial \theta} - \frac{v_\theta}{r^2 \sin^2 \theta} - \frac{2 \cos \theta}{r^2 \sin^2 \theta}\frac{\partial v_\phi}{\partial \phi}\right]$$

$$\rho\left[\frac{Dv_\phi}{Dt} + \frac{v_\phi v_r}{r} + \frac{v_\theta v_\phi \cot \theta}{r}\right]$$

$$= F_\phi - \frac{1}{r \sin \theta}\frac{\partial P}{\partial \phi} + \mu\left[\nabla^2 v_\phi - \frac{v_\phi}{r^2 \sin^2 \theta} + \frac{2}{r^2 \sin^2 \theta}\frac{\partial v_r}{\partial \phi} + \frac{2 \cos \theta}{r^2 \sin^2 \theta}\frac{\partial v_\theta}{\partial \phi}\right]$$

Written out in full, these become:

$$\rho\left[\frac{\partial v_r}{\partial t} + v_r \frac{\partial v_r}{\partial r} + \frac{v_\theta}{r}\frac{\partial v_r}{\partial \theta} + \frac{v_\phi}{r \sin \theta}\frac{\partial v_r}{\partial \phi} - \frac{v_\theta^2 + v_\phi^2}{r}\right] \qquad \text{1.70}$$

$$= F_r - \frac{\partial P}{\partial r} + \mu\left[\frac{1}{r^2}\frac{\partial}{\partial r}\left(r^2 \frac{\partial v_r}{\partial r}\right) + \frac{1}{r^2 \sin \theta}\frac{\partial}{\partial \theta}\left(\sin \theta \frac{\partial v_r}{\partial \theta}\right)\right.$$

$$\left. + \frac{1}{r^2 \sin^2 \theta}\frac{\partial^2 v_r}{\partial \phi^2} - \frac{2v_r}{r^2} - \frac{2}{r^2}\frac{\partial v_\theta}{\partial \theta} - \frac{2v_\theta \cot \theta}{r^2} - \frac{2}{r^2 \sin \theta}\frac{\partial v_\phi}{\partial \phi}\right]$$

$$\rho\left[\frac{\partial v_\theta}{\partial t} + v_r \frac{\partial v_\theta}{\partial r} + \frac{v_\theta}{r}\frac{\partial v_\theta}{\partial \theta} + \frac{v_\phi}{r \sin \theta}\frac{\partial v_\theta}{\partial \phi} + \frac{v_r v_\theta}{r} - \frac{v_\phi^2 \cot \theta}{r}\right]$$

$$= F_\theta - \frac{1}{r}\frac{\partial P}{\partial \theta} + \mu\left[\frac{1}{r^2}\frac{\partial}{\partial r}\left(r^2 \frac{\partial v_\theta}{\partial r}\right) + \frac{1}{r^2 \sin \theta}\frac{\partial}{\partial \theta}\left(\sin \theta \frac{\partial v_\theta}{\partial \theta}\right)\right.$$

$$\left. + \frac{1}{r^2 \sin^2 \theta}\frac{\partial^2 v_\theta}{\partial \phi^2} + \frac{2}{r^2}\frac{\partial v_r}{\partial \theta} - \frac{v_\theta}{r^2 \sin^2 \theta} - \frac{2 \cos \theta}{r^2 \sin^2 \theta}\frac{\partial v_\phi}{\partial \phi}\right]$$

$$\rho\left[\frac{\partial v_\phi}{\partial t} + v_r\frac{\partial v_\phi}{\partial r} + \frac{v_\theta}{r}\frac{\partial v_\phi}{\partial \theta} + \frac{v_\phi}{r\sin\theta}\frac{\partial v_\phi}{\partial \phi} + \frac{v_\phi v_r}{r} + \frac{v_\theta v_\phi \cot\theta}{r}\right]$$

$$= F_\phi - \frac{1}{r\sin\theta}\frac{\partial P}{\partial \phi} + \mu\left[\frac{1}{r^2}\frac{\partial}{\partial r}\left(r^2\frac{\partial v_\phi}{\partial r}\right) + \frac{1}{r^2\sin\theta}\frac{\partial}{\partial\theta}\left(\sin\theta\frac{\partial v_\phi}{\partial\theta}\right)\right.$$

$$\left. + \frac{1}{r^2\sin^2\theta}\frac{\partial^2 v_\phi}{\partial\phi^2} - \frac{v_\phi}{r^2\sin^2\theta} + \frac{2}{r^2\sin^2\theta}\frac{\partial v_r}{\partial\phi} + \frac{2\cos\theta}{r^2\sin^2\theta}\frac{\partial v_\theta}{\partial\phi}\right]$$

1.10 LAGRANGIAN EQUATIONS OF MOTION

The equations in Lagrangian coordinates differ from those in Eulerian coordinates only in the acceleration term. These equations are not completely written out here because the acceleration terms are identical to those of a particle in Newtonian mechanics, and may be found in detail in the chapter on dynamics in this book. In Cartesian tensor notation the equations in Lagrangian coordinates may be written:

$$\rho\frac{\partial^2 x_i}{\partial t^2} = F_i + \frac{\partial \sigma_{ij}}{\partial x_j} \qquad \textbf{1.71}$$

1.11 ROTATING FRAMES OF REFERENCE (EULERIAN COORDINATES)

We wish to write the equations of motion in terms of a rotating coordinate system. Consider a coordinate system with a fixed origin at O. Let the coordinate system rotate with angular velocity $\mathbf{\Omega}$. (See Fig. 1-2.) The rotating coordinate system is denoted as xyz. The absolute velocity $\mathbf{V}$ has components u, v, and w, and the velocity relative to the rotating frame $\mathbf{V}'$ has components u', v', and w'. The angular velocity $\mathbf{\Omega}$ has components Ω_x, Ω_y, and Ω_z, and is assumed constant in this discussion.

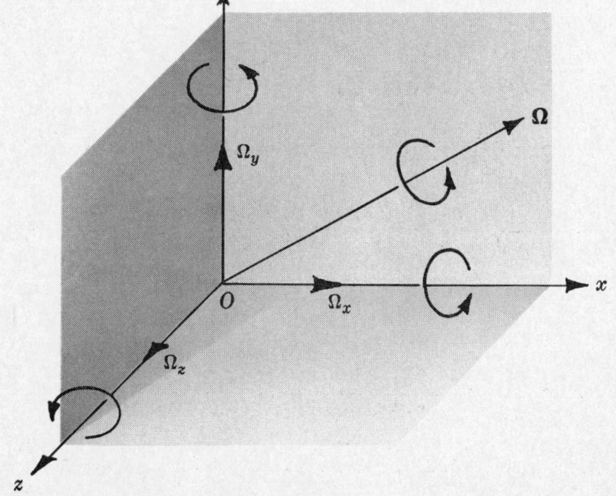

The triad xyz rotates about the fixed point O with angular velocity $\mathbf{\Omega}$.

Fig. 1-2. The rotating Coordinate System.

The absolute velocity in terms of the relative velocity is:

$$\mathbf{V} = \mathbf{V}' + \boldsymbol{\Omega} \times \mathbf{r}$$

where $\mathbf{r}$ is the position vector in the rotating frame. The absolute acceleration $\mathbf{A}$ can be written in terms of the relative acceleration $\mathbf{A}'$ as:

$$\mathbf{A} = \mathbf{A}' + 2\boldsymbol{\Omega} \times \mathbf{V}' + \boldsymbol{\Omega} \times (\boldsymbol{\Omega} \times \mathbf{r})$$

In Eulerian coordinates, that is, including the convective terms, this expression becomes:

$$\mathbf{A} = \frac{\partial \mathbf{V}'}{\partial t} + (\mathbf{V}' \cdot \nabla)\mathbf{V}' + 2\boldsymbol{\Omega} \times \mathbf{V}' + \boldsymbol{\Omega} \times (\boldsymbol{\Omega} \times \mathbf{r})$$

which may also be written:

$$\mathbf{A} = \frac{\partial \mathbf{V}}{\partial t} + (\mathbf{V}' \cdot \nabla)\mathbf{V} + \boldsymbol{\Omega} \times \mathbf{V}$$

By using the vector identities, remembering we are working now with Eulerian coordinates:

$$(\mathbf{V}' \cdot \nabla)\mathbf{V} = (\mathbf{V}' \cdot \nabla)\mathbf{V}' + \boldsymbol{\Omega} \times \mathbf{V}', \qquad \frac{\partial \mathbf{V}}{\partial t} = \frac{\partial \mathbf{V}'}{\partial t}, \qquad \frac{\partial}{\partial t}(\boldsymbol{\Omega} \times \mathbf{r}) = 0$$

$$\begin{aligned} u &= u' - y\Omega_z + z\Omega_y \\ v &= v' - z\Omega_x + x\Omega_z \\ w &= w' - x\Omega_y + y\Omega_x \end{aligned} \qquad \textbf{1.72}$$

The acceleration terms are in Cartesian coordinates:

$$\begin{aligned} &\frac{\partial u}{\partial t} + u'\frac{\partial u}{\partial x} + v'\frac{\partial u}{\partial y} + w'\frac{\partial u}{\partial z} - v\Omega_z + w\Omega_y \\ &\frac{\partial v}{\partial t} + u'\frac{\partial v}{\partial x} + v'\frac{\partial v}{\partial y} + w'\frac{\partial v}{\partial z} - w\Omega_x + u\Omega_z \\ &\frac{\partial w}{\partial t} + u'\frac{\partial w}{\partial x} + v'\frac{\partial w}{\partial y} + w'\frac{\partial w}{\partial z} - u\Omega_y + v\Omega_x \end{aligned} \qquad \textbf{1.73}$$

For the special case of rotation about the z axis only, the equations take the simplified form:

$$\begin{aligned} &\frac{\partial u'}{\partial t} + u'\frac{\partial u'}{\partial x} + v'\frac{\partial u'}{\partial y} + w'\frac{\partial u'}{\partial z} - 2v'\Omega_z - x\Omega_z^2 \\ &\frac{\partial v'}{\partial t} + u'\frac{\partial v'}{\partial x} + v'\frac{\partial v'}{\partial y} + w'\frac{\partial v'}{\partial z} + 2u'\Omega_z - y\Omega_z^2 \\ &\frac{\partial w'}{\partial t} + u'\frac{\partial w'}{\partial x} + v'\frac{\partial w'}{\partial y} + w'\frac{\partial w'}{\partial z} \end{aligned} \qquad \textbf{1.74}$$

The forces, including the viscous stresses, take the same form as in the stationary frame analysis. (That is, the viscous stresses and pressure gradients are written in terms of x, y, z and the velocities u', v', w'.)

The continuity equation in the rotating frame is the same as for a stationary frame, i.e.,

$$\frac{\partial \rho}{\partial t} + \frac{\partial}{\partial x}(\rho u') + \frac{\partial}{\partial y}(\rho v') + \frac{\partial}{\partial z}(\rho w') = 0 \qquad \textbf{1.75}$$

1.12 BOUNDARY LAYER THEORY, THE PRANDTL EQUATIONS

The boundary layer equations are written below in various coordinate systems and for various types of flow. In the following section:

P = Pressure

μ = Viscosity

ρ = Mass density

(a) Cartesian Coordinates.

In Cartesian coordinates for a general compressible fluid the boundary layer equations can be written as follows. The free stream flow is in the x direction and the plane of the plate is the xz plane. u and v are the velocities in the x and y directions respectively. The equations referring to Fig. 1-3 below are:

$$\frac{\partial u}{\partial t} + u\frac{\partial u}{\partial x} + v\frac{\partial u}{\partial y} = -\frac{1}{\rho}\frac{\partial P}{\partial x} + \frac{1}{\rho}\frac{\partial}{\partial y}\left(\mu\frac{\partial u}{\partial y}\right) \qquad \mathbf{1.76}$$

$$\frac{\partial P}{\partial y} = 0$$

$$\frac{\partial \rho}{\partial t} + \frac{\partial}{\partial x}(\rho u) + \frac{\partial}{\partial y}(\rho v) = 0$$

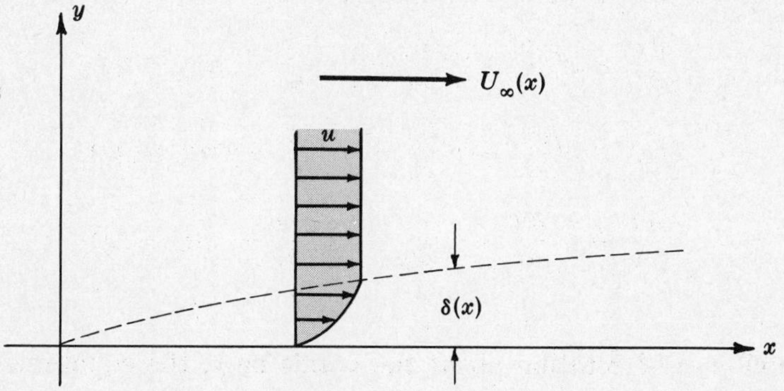

Fig. 1-3. The Boundary Layer over a Flat Plate.

For an incompressible fluid with constant viscosity, the equations become (ν is the kinematic viscosity μ/ρ)

$$\frac{\partial u}{\partial t} + u\frac{\partial u}{\partial x} + v\frac{\partial u}{\partial y} = -\frac{1}{\rho}\frac{\partial P}{\partial x} + \nu\frac{\partial^2 u}{\partial y^2} \qquad \mathbf{1.77}$$

$$\frac{\partial P}{\partial y} = 0$$

$$\frac{\partial u}{\partial x} + \frac{\partial v}{\partial y} = 0$$

(b) Rotating Frames of Reference.

The general case can be deduced from section 1.11. We write here the explicit equations for rotation about the z axis. The free stream flow is along a flat surface in the xy plane. The Cartesian triad xyz rotates with constant angular velocity Ω_z about the z axis. Velocities are measured with respect to the rotating frame of reference and are denoted as u', v', and w' in the x, y, and z directions respectively. ν is the kinematic viscosity,

$$\frac{\partial u'}{\partial t} + u'\frac{\partial u'}{\partial x} + v'\frac{\partial u'}{\partial y} + w'\frac{\partial u'}{\partial z} - 2v'\Omega_z - x\Omega_z^2 = -\frac{1}{\rho}\frac{\partial P}{\partial x} + \nu\frac{\partial^2 u'}{\partial z^2} \qquad \textbf{1.78}$$

$$\frac{\partial v'}{\partial t} + u'\frac{\partial v'}{\partial x} + v'\frac{\partial v'}{\partial y} + w'\frac{\partial v'}{\partial z} - 2u'\Omega_z - y\Omega_z^2 = -\frac{1}{\rho}\frac{\partial P}{\partial y} + \nu\frac{\partial^2 v'}{\partial z^2}$$

$$\frac{\partial P}{\partial z} = 0$$

$$\frac{\partial \rho}{\partial t} + \frac{\partial(\rho u')}{\partial x} + \frac{\partial(\rho v')}{\partial y} + \frac{\partial(\rho w')}{\partial z} = 0$$

(c) Boundary Layer Equations in Orthogonal Curvilinear Coordinates.

In the following section, the surface over which flow occurs is given by the equation $S(x,y,z) = 0$. This surface defines the surface $x_3(x,y,z) =$ constant. There exist two other sets of surfaces, $x_1(x,y,z) =$ constant and $x_2(x,y,z) =$ constant. All three of these surfaces are mutually orthogonal. x, y, and z are the cartesian coordinates, and x_1, x_2, and x_3 are the orthogonal curvilinear coordinates with x_3 a constant on the surface over which the flow takes place. We let h_1, h_2, and h_3 be defined by the line element as

$$ds^2 = h_1^2\,dx_1^2 + h_2^2\,dx_2^2 + h_3^2\,dx_3^2 \qquad \textbf{1.79}$$

The velocity components along x_1, x_2, and x_3 are taken as u, v, and w respectively. K_1 is the principal curvature of the surface $x_1 =$ constant, in the direction of the parameter x_2; and K_2 is the curvature of the surface $x_2 =$ constant, in the direction of the parameter x_1. Written out, then

$$K_1 = -\frac{1}{h_1 h_2}\frac{\partial h_2}{\partial x_1}, \qquad K_2 = -\frac{1}{h_1 h_2}\frac{\partial h_1}{\partial x_2}$$

The boundary layer equations are:

$$\frac{\partial u}{\partial t} + \frac{u}{h_1}\frac{\partial u}{\partial x_1} + \frac{v}{h_2}\frac{\partial u}{\partial x_2} + w\frac{\partial u}{\partial x_3} - K_2 uv + K_1 v^2 = -\frac{1}{\rho h_1}\frac{\partial P}{\partial x_1} + \nu\frac{\partial^2 u}{\partial x_3^2} \qquad \textbf{1.80}$$

$$\frac{\partial v}{\partial t} + \frac{v}{h_1}\frac{\partial v}{\partial x_1} + \frac{v}{h_2}\frac{\partial v}{\partial x_2} + w\frac{\partial v}{\partial x_3} + K_2 u^2 - K_1 uv = -\frac{1}{\rho h_2}\frac{\partial P}{\partial x_2} + \nu\frac{\partial^2 v}{\partial x_3^2}$$

$$\frac{\partial P}{\partial x_3} = 0$$

$$\frac{\partial \rho}{\partial t} + \frac{1}{h_1}\frac{\partial(\rho u)}{\partial x_1} + \frac{1}{h_2}\frac{\partial(\rho v)}{\partial x_2} + \frac{\partial(\rho w)}{\partial x_3} - K_1\rho u - K_2\rho v = 0$$

(d) Boundary Layer Over a Curved Wall.

Consider two dimensional flow over a curved wall. A curvilinear coordinate system is used. The x axis is taken positive in the direction along the wall, and the y axis is taken perpendicular to it. The radius of curvature $R(x)$ of the wall is measured positive when the wall is convex outwards. (See Fig. 1-4.) It may be noted that if there are no sharp changes in curvature such as occur at sharp edges, the following equations are actually unnecessary and the equations of section a may be applied. This is the situation of flow over a cylinder or airfoil where the flat plate equations are used with the appropriate pressure gradient. u and v are the velocities in the x and y directions, and ν is the kinematic viscosity.

$$\frac{\partial u}{\partial t} + \frac{R}{R+y}u\frac{\partial u}{\partial x} + v\frac{\partial u}{\partial y} + \frac{vu}{R+y} \tag{1.81}$$

$$= -\frac{R}{R+y}\frac{1}{\rho}\frac{\partial P}{\partial x} + \nu\left[\frac{R^2}{(R+y)^2}\frac{\partial^2 u}{\partial x^2} + \frac{\partial^2 u}{\partial y^2} + \frac{1}{R+y}\frac{\partial u}{\partial y} - \frac{u}{(R+y)^2} + \frac{2R}{(R+y)^2}\frac{\partial v}{\partial x} - \frac{R}{(R+y)^3}\frac{dR}{dx}v + \frac{Ry}{(R+y)^3}\frac{dR}{dx}\frac{\partial u}{\partial x}\right]$$

$$\frac{\partial v}{\partial t} + \frac{R}{R+y}u\frac{\partial v}{\partial x} + v\frac{\partial v}{\partial y} - \frac{u^2}{R+y}$$

$$= -\frac{1}{\rho}\frac{\partial P}{\partial y} + \nu\left[\frac{\partial^2 v}{\partial y^2} - \frac{2R}{(R+y)^2}\frac{\partial u}{\partial x} + \frac{1}{R+y}\frac{\partial v}{\partial y} + \frac{R^2}{(R+y)^2}\frac{\partial^2 v}{\partial x^2} - \frac{v}{(R+y)^2} + \frac{R}{(R+y)^3}\frac{dR}{dx}u + \frac{Ry}{(R+y)^3}\frac{dR}{dx}\frac{\partial v}{\partial x}\right]$$

$$\frac{\partial \rho}{\partial t} + \frac{R}{R+y}\frac{\partial(u\rho)}{\partial x} + \frac{\partial(v\rho)}{\partial y} + \frac{v\rho}{R+y} = 0$$

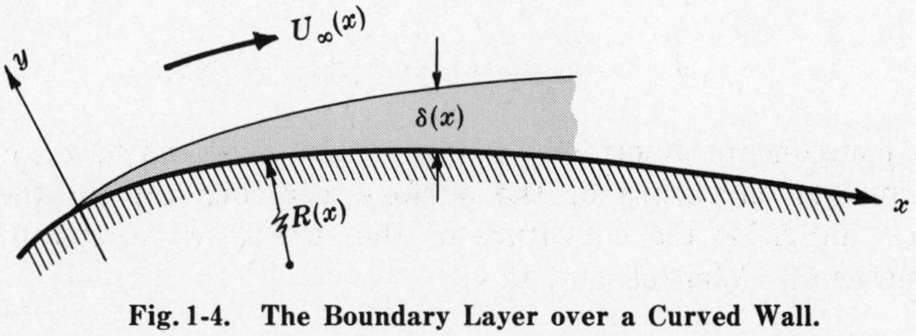

Fig. 1-4. The Boundary Layer over a Curved Wall.

(e) Integral Forms of the Boundary Layer Equations.

The boundary layer equations can be integrated over the boundary layer thickness to give integral equations. For flow over a flat plate with a pressure gradient and free stream velocity U_∞, the equation becomes:

$$\frac{\tau_w}{\rho U_\infty^2} = \frac{\partial \theta}{\partial x} + \frac{1}{U_\infty}\frac{\partial U_\infty}{\partial x}(2\theta + \delta^*) + \frac{1}{U_\infty^2}\frac{\partial}{\partial t}(U_\infty \delta^*) \tag{1.82}$$

where δ^*, the displacement thickness, is defined as:

$$\delta^* = \int_0^\delta \left(1 - \frac{u}{U_\infty}\right) dy \tag{1.83}$$

and θ, the momentum thickness, is defined as:

$$\theta = \int_0^\delta \frac{u}{U_\infty}\left(1 - \frac{u}{U_\infty}\right) dy \tag{1.84}$$

Here δ is the boundary layer thickness which is usually defined as the thickness of the layer between the wall and the position in the free stream where the x component of velocity reaches $0.99\,U_\infty$. U_∞ is the free stream velocity, and τ_w is the wall shear.

The free stream is in the x direction along the wall, and u and v are the velocities in the x and y directions respectively.

1.13 ENERGY EQUATION

In the following section Q is used to represent internal heat generation density such as that due to Joule heating, chemical or nuclear reactions, etc., but not by viscous dissipation which is work accounted for by the mechanical dissipation term Φ. The following symbols are used in this section:

e = Specific internal energy (per unit mass).

P = Pressure.

Q = Internal heat generation.

$\mathbf{q}_r$ = Radiation heat flux vector.

T = Temperature.

κ = Thermal conductivity.

ρ = Mass density.

Φ = Mechanical or viscous dissipation function. See Section 1.15 for a complete description of Φ.

(a) Vector.

$\mathbf{V}$ is the velocity vector. $\dfrac{D}{Dt}$ is the material derivative.

$$\frac{\partial Q}{\partial t} + \Phi + \nabla\cdot(\kappa\nabla T) - \nabla\cdot\mathbf{q}_r = \rho\frac{De}{Dt} + P\,\nabla\cdot\mathbf{V} = \rho\left[\frac{De}{Dt} + P\frac{D}{Dt}\left(\frac{1}{\rho}\right)\right] \qquad \textbf{1.85}$$

For constant κ equation 1.85 becomes:

$$\frac{\partial Q}{\partial t} + \Phi + \kappa\nabla^2 T - \nabla\cdot\mathbf{q}_r = \rho\frac{De}{Dt} + P\,\nabla\cdot\mathbf{V} = \rho\left[\frac{De}{Dt} + P\frac{D}{Dt}\left(\frac{1}{\rho}\right)\right] \qquad \textbf{1.86}$$

For an incompressible fluid:

$$\frac{\partial Q}{\partial t} + \Phi + \nabla\cdot(\kappa\nabla T) - \nabla\cdot\mathbf{q}_r = \rho\frac{De}{Dt} \qquad \textbf{1.87}$$

For an incompressible fluid with constant κ:

$$\frac{\partial Q}{\partial t} + \Phi + \kappa\nabla^2 T - \nabla\cdot\mathbf{q}_r = \rho\frac{De}{Dt} \qquad \textbf{1.88}$$

(b) Cartesian Tensor.

w_i is the velocity vector in the x_i direction. $\dfrac{D}{Dt}$ is the material derivative which is written out below.

$$\frac{\partial Q}{\partial t} + \Phi + \frac{\partial}{\partial x_i}\left(\kappa\frac{\partial T}{\partial x_i}\right) - \frac{\partial q_{ri}}{\partial x_i} = \rho\left[\frac{De}{Dt} + P\frac{D}{Dt}\left(\frac{1}{\rho}\right)\right] = \rho\frac{De}{Dt} + P\frac{\partial w_i}{\partial x_i} \qquad \textbf{1.89}$$

$$= \rho\left[\frac{\partial e}{\partial t} + w_i\frac{\partial e}{\partial x_i}\right] + P\frac{\partial w_i}{\partial x_i}$$

For constant κ, equation 1.89 becomes:

$$\frac{\partial Q}{\partial t} + \Phi + \kappa \frac{\partial^2 T}{\partial x_i \, \partial x_i} - \frac{\partial q_{ri}}{\partial x_i} = \rho \left[\frac{\partial e}{\partial t} + w_i \frac{\partial e}{\partial x_i} \right] + P \frac{\partial w_i}{\partial x_i} \qquad \textbf{1.90}$$

For an incompressible fluid:

$$\frac{\partial Q}{\partial t} + \Phi + \frac{\partial}{\partial x_i}\left(\kappa \frac{\partial T}{\partial x_i}\right) - \frac{\partial q_{ri}}{\partial x_i} = \rho \left[\frac{\partial e}{\partial t} + w_i \frac{\partial e}{\partial x_i} \right] \qquad \textbf{1.91}$$

For an incompressible fluid with constant κ:

$$\frac{\partial Q}{\partial t} + \Phi + \kappa \frac{\partial^2 T}{\partial x_i \, \partial x_i} - \frac{\partial q_{ri}}{\partial x_i} = \rho \left[\frac{\partial e}{\partial t} + w_i \frac{\partial e}{\partial x_i} \right] \qquad \textbf{1.92}$$

(c) Cartesian.

u, v, and w are the velocities in the x, y, and z directions respectively. In the following section:

$$\frac{D}{Dt} = \frac{\partial}{\partial t} + u \frac{\partial}{\partial x} + v \frac{\partial}{\partial y} + w \frac{\partial}{\partial z}$$

$$\nabla \cdot \mathbf{V} = \frac{\partial u}{\partial x} + \frac{\partial v}{\partial y} + \frac{\partial w}{\partial z}$$

$$\nabla^2 = \frac{\partial^2}{\partial x^2} + \frac{\partial^2}{\partial y^2} + \frac{\partial^2}{\partial z^2}$$

The general equation is:

$$\frac{\partial Q}{\partial t} + \Phi + \frac{\partial}{\partial x}\left(\kappa \frac{\partial T}{\partial x}\right) + \frac{\partial}{\partial y}\left(\kappa \frac{\partial T}{\partial y}\right) + \frac{\partial}{\partial z}\left(\kappa \frac{\partial T}{\partial z}\right) - \nabla \cdot \mathbf{q}_r \qquad \textbf{1.93}$$

$$= \rho \left[\frac{De}{Dt} + P \frac{D}{Dt}\left(\frac{1}{\rho}\right) \right] = \rho \frac{De}{Dt} + P \, \nabla \cdot \mathbf{V}$$

For constant κ, equation 1.93 becomes:

$$\frac{\partial Q}{\partial t} + \Phi + \kappa \nabla^2 T - \nabla \cdot \mathbf{q}_r = \rho \left[\frac{De}{Dt} + P \frac{D}{Dt}\left(\frac{1}{\rho}\right) \right] \qquad \textbf{1.94}$$

$$= \rho \frac{De}{Dt} + P \, \nabla \cdot \mathbf{V}$$

For an incompressible fluid:

$$\frac{\partial Q}{\partial t} + \Phi + \frac{\partial}{\partial x}\left(\kappa \frac{\partial T}{\partial x}\right) + \frac{\partial}{\partial y}\left(\kappa \frac{\partial T}{\partial y}\right) + \frac{\partial}{\partial z}\left(\kappa \frac{\partial T}{\partial z}\right) - \nabla \cdot \mathbf{q}_r = \rho \frac{De}{Dt} \qquad \textbf{1.95}$$

For an incompressible fluid with constant κ:

$$\frac{\partial Q}{\partial t} + \Phi + \kappa \nabla^2 T - \nabla \cdot \mathbf{q}_r = \rho \frac{De}{Dt} \qquad \textbf{1.96}$$

(d) Cylindrical.

v_r, v_θ, and v_z are the velocities in the r, θ, and z directions respectively. In the following section:

$$\frac{D}{Dt} = \frac{\partial}{\partial t} + v_r \frac{\partial}{\partial r} + \frac{v_\theta}{r} \frac{\partial}{\partial \theta} + v_z \frac{\partial}{\partial z}$$

$$\nabla \cdot \mathbf{V} = \frac{1}{r} \frac{\partial}{\partial r}(r v_r) + \frac{1}{r} \frac{\partial v_\theta}{\partial \theta} + \frac{\partial v_z}{\partial z}$$

$$\nabla^2 = \frac{\partial^2}{\partial r^2} + \frac{1}{r} \frac{\partial}{\partial r} + \frac{1}{r^2} \frac{\partial^2}{\partial \theta^2} + \frac{\partial^2}{\partial z^2}$$

The general equation is:

$$\frac{\partial Q}{\partial t} + \Phi + \frac{1}{r}\frac{\partial}{\partial r}\left(r\kappa\frac{\partial T}{\partial r}\right) + \frac{1}{r^2}\frac{\partial}{\partial \theta}\left(\kappa\frac{\partial T}{\partial \theta}\right) + \frac{\partial}{\partial z}\left(\kappa\frac{\partial T}{\partial z}\right) - \nabla\cdot\mathbf{q}_r \qquad \mathbf{1.97}$$

$$= \rho\frac{De}{Dt} + P\,\nabla\cdot\mathbf{V} = \rho\left[\frac{De}{Dt} + P\frac{D}{Dt}\left(\frac{1}{\rho}\right)\right]$$

For constant κ, equation 1.97 becomes:

$$\frac{\partial Q}{\partial t} + \Phi + \kappa\nabla^2 T - \nabla\cdot\mathbf{q}_r = \rho\frac{De}{Dt} + P\,\nabla\cdot\mathbf{V} \qquad \mathbf{1.98}$$

$$= \rho\left[\frac{De}{Dt} + P\frac{D}{Dt}\left(\frac{1}{\rho}\right)\right]$$

For an incompressible fluid:

$$\frac{\partial Q}{\partial t} + \Phi + \frac{1}{r}\frac{\partial}{\partial r}\left(r\kappa\frac{\partial T}{\partial r}\right) + \frac{1}{r^2}\frac{\partial}{\partial \theta}\left(\kappa\frac{\partial T}{\partial \theta}\right) + \frac{\partial}{\partial z}\left(\kappa\frac{\partial T}{\partial z}\right) - \nabla\cdot\mathbf{q}_r = \rho\frac{De}{Dt} \qquad \mathbf{1.99}$$

For an incompressible fluid with constant κ:

$$\frac{\partial Q}{\partial t} + \Phi + \kappa\nabla^2 T - \nabla\cdot\mathbf{q}_r = \rho\frac{De}{Dt} \qquad \mathbf{1.100}$$

(e) Spherical.

v_r, v_θ, and v_ϕ are the velocities in the r, θ, and ϕ directions respectively. In the following section:

$$\frac{D}{Dt} = \frac{\partial}{\partial t} + v_r\frac{\partial}{\partial r} + \frac{v_\theta}{r}\frac{\partial}{\partial \theta} + \frac{v_\phi}{r\sin\theta}\frac{\partial}{\partial \phi}$$

$$\nabla\cdot\mathbf{V} = \frac{1}{r^2}\frac{\partial}{\partial r}(r^2 v_r) + \frac{1}{r\sin\theta}\frac{\partial}{\partial \theta}(v_\theta\sin\theta) + \frac{1}{r\sin\theta}\frac{\partial v_\phi}{\partial \phi}$$

$$\nabla^2 = \frac{1}{r^2}\frac{\partial}{\partial r}\left(r^2\frac{\partial}{\partial r}\right) + \frac{1}{r^2\sin\theta}\frac{\partial}{\partial \theta}\left(\sin\theta\frac{\partial}{\partial \theta}\right) + \frac{1}{r^2\sin^2\theta}\frac{\partial^2}{\partial \phi^2}$$

The general equation is:

$$\frac{\partial Q}{\partial t} + \Phi + \frac{1}{r^2}\frac{\partial}{\partial r}\left(r^2\kappa\frac{\partial T}{\partial r}\right) + \frac{1}{r^2\sin\theta}\frac{\partial}{\partial \theta}\left(\kappa\sin\theta\frac{\partial T}{\partial \theta}\right) \qquad \mathbf{1.101}$$

$$+ \frac{1}{r^2\sin^2\theta}\frac{\partial}{\partial \phi}\left(\kappa\frac{\partial T}{\partial \phi}\right) - \nabla\cdot\mathbf{q}_r = \rho\frac{De}{Dt} + P\,\nabla\cdot\mathbf{V} = \rho\left[\frac{De}{Dt} + P\frac{D}{Dt}\left(\frac{1}{\rho}\right)\right]$$

For constant κ, equation 1.101 becomes:

$$\frac{\partial Q}{\partial t} + \Phi + \kappa\nabla^2 T - \nabla\cdot\mathbf{q}_r = \rho\frac{De}{Dt} + P\,\nabla\cdot\mathbf{V} \qquad \mathbf{1.102}$$

$$= \rho\left[\frac{De}{Dt} + P\frac{D}{Dt}\left(\frac{1}{\rho}\right)\right]$$

For an incompressible fluid:

$$\frac{\partial Q}{\partial t} + \Phi + \frac{1}{r^2}\frac{\partial}{\partial r}\left(r^2\kappa\frac{\partial T}{\partial r}\right) + \frac{1}{r^2\sin\theta}\frac{\partial}{\partial\theta}\left(\kappa\sin\theta\frac{\partial T}{\partial\theta}\right) + \frac{1}{r^2\sin^2\theta}\frac{\partial}{\partial\phi}\left(\kappa\frac{\partial T}{\partial\phi}\right) - \nabla\cdot\mathbf{q}_r = \rho\frac{De}{Dt} \quad \textbf{1.103}$$

For an incompressible fluid with constant κ:

$$\frac{\partial Q}{\partial t} + \Phi + \kappa\nabla^2 T - \nabla\cdot\mathbf{q}_r = \rho\frac{De}{Dt} \quad \textbf{1.104}$$

1.14 ENERGY EQUATION IN TERMS OF ENTHALPY AND FOR A PERFECT GAS

The energy equation can, generally, be expressed in terms of enthalpy instead of internal energy. The specific enthalpy (per unit mass) is denoted by h. The material derivative D/Dt has been written out in the previous section for various coordinate systems and is not repeated here. The symbols are all the same as in the previous section.

(a) Vector.

$$\rho\frac{Dh}{Dt} = \frac{DP}{Dt} + \frac{\partial Q}{\partial t} + \Phi + \nabla\cdot(\kappa\nabla T) - \nabla\cdot\mathbf{q}_r \quad \textbf{1.105}$$

For constant κ:

$$\rho\frac{Dh}{Dt} = \frac{DP}{Dt} + \frac{\partial Q}{\partial t} + \Phi + \kappa\nabla^2 T - \nabla\cdot\mathbf{q}_r \quad \textbf{1.106}$$

(b) Cartesian Tensor.

$$\rho\frac{Dh}{Dt} = \frac{DP}{Dt} + \frac{\partial Q}{\partial t} + \Phi + \frac{\partial}{\partial x_i}\left(\kappa\frac{\partial T}{\partial x_i}\right) - \frac{\partial q_{ri}}{\partial x_i} \quad \textbf{1.107}$$

For constant κ:

$$\rho\frac{Dh}{Dt} = \frac{DP}{Dt} + \frac{\partial Q}{\partial t} + \Phi + \kappa\frac{\partial^2 T}{\partial x_i\,\partial x_i} - \frac{\partial q_{ri}}{\partial x_i} \quad \textbf{1.108}$$

(c) Cartesian.

$$\rho\frac{Dh}{Dt} = \frac{DP}{Dt} + \frac{\partial Q}{\partial t} + \Phi + \frac{\partial}{\partial x}\left(\kappa\frac{\partial T}{\partial x}\right) + \frac{\partial}{\partial y}\left(\kappa\frac{\partial T}{\partial y}\right) + \frac{\partial}{\partial z}\left(\kappa\frac{\partial T}{\partial z}\right) - \nabla\cdot\mathbf{q}_r \quad \textbf{1.109}$$

For constant κ:

$$\rho\frac{Dh}{Dt} = \frac{DP}{Dt} + \frac{\partial Q}{\partial t} + \Phi + \kappa\nabla^2 T - \nabla\cdot\mathbf{q}_r \quad \textbf{1.110}$$

(d) Cylindrical.

$$\rho \frac{Dh}{Dt} = \frac{DP}{Dt} + \frac{\partial Q}{\partial t} + \Phi$$

$$+ \frac{1}{r}\frac{\partial}{\partial r}\left(r\kappa \frac{\partial T}{\partial r}\right) + \frac{1}{r^2}\frac{\partial}{\partial \theta}\left(\kappa \frac{\partial T}{\partial \theta}\right) + \frac{\partial}{\partial z}\left(\kappa \frac{\partial T}{\partial z}\right) - \nabla \cdot \mathbf{q}_r \qquad \mathbf{1.111}$$

For constant κ:

$$\rho \frac{Dh}{Dt} = \frac{DP}{Dt} + \frac{\partial Q}{\partial t} + \Phi + \kappa \nabla^2 T - \nabla \cdot \mathbf{q}_r \qquad \mathbf{1.112}$$

(e) Spherical.

$$\rho \frac{Dh}{Dt} = \frac{DP}{Dt} + \frac{\partial Q}{\partial t} + \Phi + \frac{1}{r^2}\frac{\partial}{\partial r}\left(r^2\kappa \frac{\partial T}{\partial r}\right) + \frac{1}{r^2 \sin\theta}\frac{\partial}{\partial \theta}\left(\kappa \sin\theta \frac{\partial T}{\partial \theta}\right) \qquad \mathbf{1.113}$$

$$+ \frac{1}{r^2 \sin^2\theta}\frac{\partial}{\partial \phi}\left(\kappa \frac{\partial T}{\partial \phi}\right) - \nabla \cdot \mathbf{q}_r$$

For constant κ:

$$\rho \frac{Dh}{Dt} = \frac{DP}{Dt} + \frac{\partial Q}{\partial t} + \Phi + \kappa \nabla^2 T - \nabla \cdot \mathbf{q}_r \qquad \mathbf{1.114}$$

(f) Perfect Gas.

For a perfect gas the material derivative of enthalpy or internal energy that occurs in the previous sections can be written as: $\frac{Dh}{Dt} = c_p \frac{DT}{Dt}$ and $\frac{De}{Dt} = c_v \frac{DT}{Dt}$. It should be emphasized that the specific heats can be removed from the derivative regardless of whether or not they are functions of temperature. The only requirement for removal from the derivative is that the fluid be a perfect gas. c_v and c_p are the specific heats at constant volume and constant pressure respectively.

1.15 THE DISSIPATION FUNCTION

The mechanical or viscous dissipation function Φ is defined in generalized orthogonal coordinates as

$$\Phi = \mu[2(e_{11}^2 + e_{22}^2 + e_{33}^2) + (2e_{23})^2 + (2e_{31})^2 + (2e_{12})^2] + \lambda(e_{11} + e_{22} + e_{33})^2$$

(In some texts, the definition of Φ differs by a factor of μ from the one defined here.)

(a) Cartesian Tensor.

$$\Phi = \sigma'_{ij} \frac{\partial w_i}{\partial x_j} \qquad \mathbf{1.115}$$

σ'_{ij} can be written in terms of velocity from section 1.4.

(b) Cartesian.

$$\Phi = 2\mu\left[\left(\frac{\partial u}{\partial x}\right)^2 + \left(\frac{\partial v}{\partial y}\right)^2 + \left(\frac{\partial w}{\partial z}\right)^2 + \frac{1}{2}\left(\frac{\partial u}{\partial y} + \frac{\partial v}{\partial x}\right)^2 + \frac{1}{2}\left(\frac{\partial v}{\partial z} + \frac{\partial w}{\partial y}\right)^2 + \frac{1}{2}\left(\frac{\partial w}{\partial x} + \frac{\partial u}{\partial z}\right)^2\right] + \lambda\left[\frac{\partial u}{\partial x} + \frac{\partial v}{\partial y} + \frac{\partial w}{\partial z}\right]^2 \qquad \mathbf{1.116}$$

(c) Cylindrical.

$$\Phi = \mu\left[2\left\{\left(\frac{\partial v_r}{\partial r}\right)^2 + \left(\frac{1}{r}\frac{\partial v_\theta}{\partial \theta} + \frac{v_r}{r}\right)^2 + \left(\frac{\partial v_z}{\partial z}\right)^2\right\} + \left(\frac{1}{r}\frac{\partial v_z}{\partial \theta} + \frac{\partial v_\theta}{\partial z}\right)^2 + \left(\frac{\partial v_r}{\partial z} + \frac{\partial v_z}{\partial r}\right)^2 + \left(\frac{1}{r}\frac{\partial v_r}{\partial \theta} + \frac{\partial v_\theta}{\partial r} - \frac{v_\theta}{r}\right)^2\right] + \lambda\left[\frac{\partial v_r}{\partial r} + \frac{1}{r}\frac{\partial v_\theta}{\partial \theta} + \frac{v_r}{r} + \frac{\partial v_z}{\partial z}\right]^2 \qquad \mathbf{1.117}$$

(d) Spherical.

$$\Phi = \mu\left[2\left\{\left(\frac{\partial v_r}{\partial r}\right)^2 + \left(\frac{1}{r}\frac{\partial v_\theta}{\partial \theta} + \frac{v_r}{r}\right)^2 + \left(\frac{1}{r\sin\theta}\frac{\partial v_\phi}{\partial \phi} + \frac{v_r}{r} + \frac{v_\theta \cot\theta}{r}\right)^2\right\} + \left\{\frac{1}{r\sin\theta}\frac{\partial v_\theta}{\partial \phi} + \frac{\sin\theta}{r}\frac{\partial}{\partial \theta}\left(\frac{v_\phi}{\sin\theta}\right)\right\}^2 + \left\{\frac{1}{r\sin\theta}\frac{\partial v_r}{\partial \phi} + r\frac{\partial}{\partial r}\left(\frac{v_\phi}{r}\right)\right\}^2 + \left\{r\frac{\partial}{\partial r}\left(\frac{v_\theta}{r}\right) + \frac{1}{r}\frac{\partial v_r}{\partial \theta}\right\}^2\right] + \lambda\left[\frac{\partial v_r}{\partial r} + \frac{1}{r}\frac{\partial v_\theta}{\partial \theta} + \frac{2v_r}{r} + \frac{1}{r\sin\theta}\frac{\partial v_\phi}{\partial \phi} + \frac{v_\theta \cot\theta}{r}\right]^2 \qquad \mathbf{1.118}$$

1.16 ENERGY EQUATION AND ENTROPY PRODUCTION

In terms of specific entropy s, the energy equation can be written in the following manner. We write the equations only in vector and Cartesian tensor form, but the extension to other coordinate systems is obvious from the work of the previous three sections and is not carried out here.

The general energy equation can be written:

$$\rho\frac{Ds}{Dt} = \frac{\Phi}{T} + \frac{1}{T}\frac{\partial Q}{\partial t} + \frac{1}{T}\frac{\partial}{\partial x_i}\left(\kappa\frac{\partial T}{\partial x_i}\right) - \frac{\partial q_{ri}}{\partial x_i} \qquad \mathbf{1.119}$$

or in vector form:

$$\rho\frac{Ds}{Dt} = \frac{\Phi}{T} + \frac{1}{T}\frac{\partial Q}{\partial t} + \frac{1}{T}\nabla\cdot(\kappa\nabla T) - \nabla\cdot\mathbf{q}_r \qquad \mathbf{1.120}$$

The entropy production rate per unit volume, σ, may be introduced:

$$\sigma = \frac{\Phi}{T} + \frac{\kappa}{T^2}\left(\frac{\partial T}{\partial x_i}\cdot\frac{\partial T}{\partial x_i}\right) + \frac{1}{T}\frac{\partial Q}{\partial t} + q_{ri}\frac{\partial}{\partial x_i}\left(\frac{1}{T}\right) \tag{1.121}$$

or in vector form:

$$\sigma = \frac{\Phi}{T} + \frac{\kappa}{T^2}[(\nabla T)\cdot(\nabla T)] + \frac{1}{T}\frac{\partial Q}{\partial t} + \mathbf{q}_r\cdot\nabla\left(\frac{1}{T}\right) \tag{1.122}$$

In the above equations, Φ is the mechanical dissipation function, $\partial Q/\partial t$ is the rate of internal dissipation such as Joule heat, κ is the thermal conductivity, and $\mathbf{q}_r$ is the radiation heat flux vector. A detailed discussion of these terms has been given in the previous few sections.

1.17 INTEGRAL FORMS OF THE BASIC EQUATIONS (FOR A CONTROL VOLUME)

A control volume is shown in Fig. 1-5 below. The velocity vector $\mathbf{V}$ is positive out of the control volume, as is the vector $d\mathbf{A}$. In the following equations the element of volume is denoted as $d\tau$, and τ indicates integration throughout the volume.

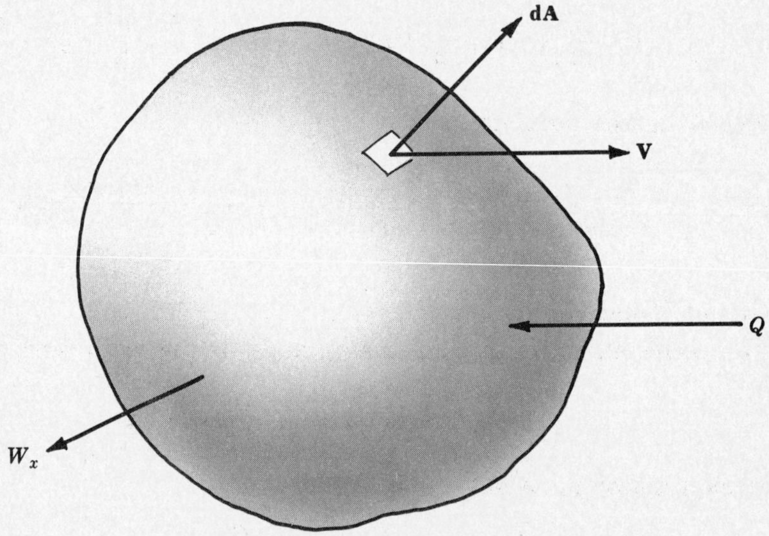

Fig. 1-5. The Control Volume.

(a) Continuity.

ρ is the mass density and $\mathbf{V}$ the velocity vector.

$$\frac{\partial}{\partial t}\int_\tau \rho\, d\tau + \int_A \rho\mathbf{V}\cdot d\mathbf{A} = 0 \tag{1.123}$$

or in Cartesian tensor notation (w_i is the velocity):

$$\frac{\partial}{\partial t}\int_\tau \rho\, d\tau + \int_A \rho w_i\, dA_i = 0 \tag{1.124}$$

(b) *Momentum.*

Here **F** is the sum of the external forces including pressure forces and body forces, and also any shear forces on the surface of the control volume.

$$\mathbf{F} = \frac{\partial}{\partial t}\int_\tau \rho\mathbf{V}\,d\tau + \int_A \rho\mathbf{V}(\mathbf{V}\cdot d\mathbf{A}) \qquad \textbf{1.125}$$

or in Cartesian tensor notation:

$$F_i = \frac{\partial}{\partial t}\int_\tau \rho w_i\,d\tau + \int_A \rho w_i w_j\,dA_j \qquad \textbf{1.126}$$

(c) *Energy Equation.*

Here, Q is the rate of heat transfer into the control volume, including conduction and radiation. W_x is the shaft work which is counted as positive out of the control volume. That is, positive work is done by the material in the control volume on the surroundings. e is the specific internal energy (per unit mass). g is the acceleration due to gravity so that the gz term is the potential energy per unit mass. z is the elevation above an arbitrary datum level. If other forms of internal energy are present they must also be included, such as electromagnetic energy, etc. (The energy equation for electrical conductors in the presence of an electromagnetic field is discussed in the chapter on electromagnetic theory.)

$$Q - W_x = \frac{\partial}{\partial t}\int_\tau \left(e + \frac{V^2}{2} + gz\right)\rho\,d\tau + \int_A \rho\left(e + \frac{V^2}{2} + gz + \frac{P}{\rho}\right)\mathbf{V}\cdot d\mathbf{A} \qquad \textbf{1.127}$$

or in Cartesian tensor notation:

$$Q - W_x = \frac{\partial}{\partial t}\int_\tau \left(e + \frac{w_i w_i}{2} + gz\right)\rho\,d\tau + \int_A \rho\left(e + \frac{w_i w_i}{2} + gz + \frac{P}{\rho}\right)w_i\,dA_i \qquad \textbf{1.128}$$

(d) *Second Law of Thermodynamics.*

s is the specific entropy (per unit mass), and ρ is the mass density.

$$\frac{Q}{T} \leq \frac{\partial}{\partial t}\int_\tau \rho s\,d\tau + \int_A \rho s\mathbf{V}\cdot d\mathbf{A} \qquad \textbf{1.129}$$

or in Cartesian tensor notation:

$$\frac{Q}{T} \leq \frac{\partial}{\partial t}\int_\tau \rho s\,d\tau + \int_A \rho s w_i\,dA_i \qquad \textbf{1.130}$$

(e) *Entropy Production.*

We introduce the entropy production rate per unit volume, σ. κ is the thermal conductivity, T is the temperature, and ρ is the mass density.

$$\int_\tau \sigma\,d\tau + \int_A \frac{\kappa\nabla T}{T}\cdot d\mathbf{A} = \frac{\partial}{\partial t}\int_\tau \rho s\,d\tau + \int_A \rho s\mathbf{V}\cdot d\mathbf{A} \qquad \textbf{1.131}$$

or in Cartesian tensor notation:

$$\int_\tau \sigma\,d\tau + \int_A \frac{\kappa}{T}\frac{\partial T}{\partial x_i}\,dA_i = \frac{\partial}{\partial t}\int_\tau \rho s\,d\tau + \int_A \rho s w_i\,dA_i \qquad \textbf{1.132}$$

1.18 INTEGRAL FORMS OF THE BASIC EQUATIONS FOR CHANNEL FLOW WITH UNIFORM PROPERTIES AND VELOCITY OVER THE CROSS SECTION OF THE CHANNEL

The equations of Section 1.17 can be integrated for channel flow with uniform conditions across the channel or pipe. Such an approximation is valid in a rather wide class of flows. In turbulent flow, the velocity is essentially uniform over the cross section. Fig. 1-6 below shows a channel between the cross sectional planes of integration denoted as 1 and 2. The velocity is assumed from 1 to 2, that is, the flow is in the 1 to 2 direction.

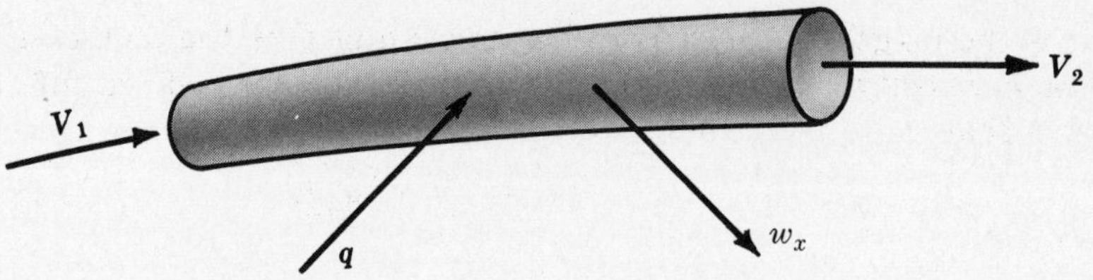

Fig. 1-6. Channel or Pipe Flow.

(a) *Bernoulli Equation, Compressible Unsteady Flow.*

The Bernoulli equation is obtained from the equations of motion as a first integral along a stream line. This equation is valid only for frictionless flow. The Bernoulli equation is sometimes written for steady incompressible flow and the compressible equation is then called the Euler equation. The equation holds along a streamline for frictionless flow, but if the flow is irrotational the equation holds between any two points in the flow. This statement applies to the following special cases of the Bernoulli equation. For the general equation:

$$\int_1^2 \frac{dP}{\rho} + \frac{V_2^2 - V_1^2}{2} + g(z_2 - z_1) = -\int_1^2 \frac{\partial \mathbf{V}}{\partial t} \cdot d\mathbf{s} \qquad \textbf{1.133}$$

(b) *Bernoulli Equation for Steady Compressible Flow, the Euler Equation.*

For steady flow the equation above can be written as follows:

$$\int_1^2 \frac{dP}{\rho} + \frac{V_2^2 - V_1^2}{2} + g(z_2 - z_1) = 0 \qquad \textbf{1.134}$$

which is sometimes referred to as the Euler equation.

(c) *Bernoulli Equation for Steady Incompressible Flow.*

$$\frac{P_2 - P_1}{\rho} + \frac{V_2^2 - V_1^2}{2} + g(z_2 - z_1) = 0 \qquad \textbf{1.135}$$

(d) Head Loss.

For incompressible, steady flow, when friction is present the energy equation can be written with the heat transfer term and the change in internal energy term lumped together in what is known as head loss. w_x is the shaft work done by the fluid per unit mass of fluid flowing. H_{L1-2} is the head loss from point 1 to 2. The equation can be written:

$$-w_x \quad = \quad \frac{P_2 - P_1}{\rho} + \frac{V_2^2 - V_1^2}{2} + g(z_2 - z_1) + H_{L1-2} \qquad \textbf{1.136}$$

The head loss term is often represented in terms of a dimensionless friction factor f as:

$$H_{L1-2} \quad = \quad f\frac{LV^2}{2gD} \qquad \textbf{1.137}$$

where L is the length between points 1 and 2 and D is the diameter of the pipe. V is the average velocity. Sometimes the friction factor is defined differently by a factor of four, so that:

$$H_{L1-2} \quad = \quad f\frac{LV^2}{8gD}$$

(e) Energy.

Here, q is the heat transfer rate into the channel per unit mass of fluid flowing, w_x is the work rate done on the surroundings by the fluid per unit mass of flowing fluid. e is the specific internal energy (per unit mass). See Fig. 1-6.

$$q - w_x \quad = \quad \frac{P_2}{\rho_2} - \frac{P_1}{\rho_1} + \frac{V_2^2 - V_1^2}{2} + g(z_2 - z_1) + e_2 - e_1 \qquad \textbf{1.138}$$

1.19 STREAM FUNCTION

In two dimensional flow a stream function Ψ may be introduced and defined as below. Physically, the stream function is a constant along a streamline. The flow rate between two streamlines is proportional to the numerical difference between the two stream functions. The sign convention used below in the definitions is such that the flow is positive from right to left when passing from streamline Ψ_1 to streamline Ψ_2, and the flow rate is given by $(\Psi_2 - \Psi_1)$. See Fig. 1-7 below.

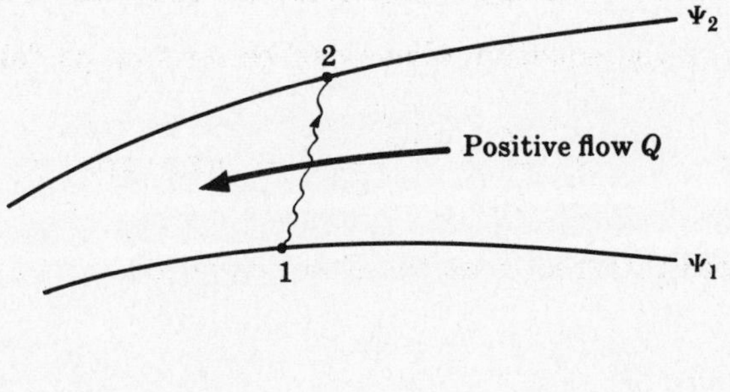

$$\Psi_2 - \Psi_1 \quad = \quad \int_1^2 d\Psi \quad = \quad \int_1^2 \frac{\partial \Psi}{\partial x}dx + \frac{\partial \Psi}{\partial y}dy \quad = \quad \int_1^2 (v\,dx - u\,dy) \quad = \quad Q$$

Fig. 1-7. The Flow Between Two Streamlines.

(a) Streamlines in Two Dimensional Incompressible Flow.

Cartesian coordinates:

u and v are the velocities in the x and y directions respectively.

$$u = -\frac{\partial \Psi}{\partial y}, \qquad v = \frac{\partial \Psi}{\partial x} \tag{1.139}$$

Axial symmetric flow, (about the z axis):

v_z and v_r are the velocities in the z and r directions respectively.

$$v_z = -\frac{1}{r}\frac{\partial \Psi}{\partial r}, \qquad v_r = \frac{1}{r}\frac{\partial \Psi}{\partial z} \tag{1.140}$$

Polar coordinates:

v_r and v_θ are the velocities in the r and θ directions respectively.

$$v_r = -\frac{1}{r}\frac{\partial \Psi}{\partial \theta}, \qquad v_\theta = \frac{\partial \Psi}{\partial r} \tag{1.141}$$

(b) Streamlines in Compressible Flow.

The symbols are as used in the above section a. ρ_0 and ρ are an arbitrary reference density and the ordinary density respectively. In various coordinates then:

Cartesian:

$$u = -\frac{\rho_0}{\rho}\frac{\partial \Psi}{\partial y}, \qquad v = \frac{\rho_0}{\rho}\frac{\partial \Psi}{\partial x} \tag{1.142}$$

Axial symmetric flow (about z axis):

$$v_z = -\frac{\rho_0}{\rho}\frac{1}{r}\frac{\partial \Psi}{\partial r}, \qquad v_r = \frac{\rho_0}{\rho}\frac{1}{r}\frac{\partial \Psi}{\partial z} \tag{1.143}$$

Polar coordinates:

$$v_r = -\frac{\rho_0}{\rho}\frac{1}{r}\frac{\partial \Psi}{\partial \theta}, \qquad v_\theta = \frac{\rho_0}{\rho}\frac{\partial \Psi}{\partial r} \tag{1.144}$$

Various forms of the equations of motion in terms of the stream function are listed in Section 1.22 in the general area of vorticity where the stream function can be related to vorticity. Also, in Section 1.21 the role of the stream function in potential flow theory is discussed.

1.20 VELOCITY POTENTIAL

A velocity potential can be defined if the velocity field is irrotational, i.e. $\nabla \times \mathbf{V} = 0$. The velocity potential Φ is defined in various coordinate systems below.

(a) Cartesian Tensor.

w_i is the velocity in the x_i direction.

$$w_i = -\frac{\partial \Phi}{\partial x_i} \tag{1.145}$$

(b) Vector.

V is the velocity vector.

$$\mathbf{V} = -\nabla\Phi \qquad \textbf{1.146}$$

(c) Cartesian.

u, v, and w are the velocities in the x, y, and z directions respectively.

$$u = -\frac{\partial\Phi}{\partial x}, \qquad v = -\frac{\partial\Phi}{\partial y}, \qquad w = -\frac{\partial\Phi}{\partial z} \qquad \textbf{1.147}$$

(d) Cylindrical.

v_r, v_θ, and v_z are the velocities in the r, θ, and z directions respectively.

$$v_r = -\frac{\partial\Phi}{\partial r}, \qquad v_\theta = -\frac{1}{r}\frac{\partial\Phi}{\partial\theta}, \qquad v_z = -\frac{\partial\Phi}{\partial z} \qquad \textbf{1.148}$$

(e) Spherical.

v_r, v_θ, and v_ϕ are the velocities in the r, θ, and ϕ directions respectively.

$$v_r = -\frac{\partial\Phi}{\partial r}, \qquad v_\theta = -\frac{1}{r}\frac{\partial\Phi}{\partial\theta}, \qquad v_\phi = -\frac{1}{r\sin\theta}\frac{\partial\Phi}{\partial\phi} \qquad \textbf{1.149}$$

(f) Equations for Φ.

Continuity requires that the velocity potential satisfy certain equations. For incompressible flow:

$$\nabla^2\Phi = 0 \qquad \textbf{1.150}$$

and for compressible flow:

$$\frac{\partial^2\Phi}{\partial x^2}\left[1 - \frac{\left(\frac{\partial\Phi}{\partial x}\right)^2}{c^2}\right] + \frac{\partial^2\Phi}{\partial y^2}\left[1 - \frac{\left(\frac{\partial\Phi}{\partial y}\right)^2}{c^2}\right] + \frac{\partial^2\Phi}{\partial z^2}\left[1 - \frac{\left(\frac{\partial\Phi}{\partial z}\right)^2}{c^2}\right] \qquad \textbf{1.151}$$

$$-\frac{2}{c^2}\frac{\partial^2\Phi}{\partial x\,\partial y}\frac{\partial\Phi}{\partial x}\frac{\partial\Phi}{\partial y} - \frac{2}{c^2}\frac{\partial^2\Phi}{\partial y\,\partial z}\frac{\partial\Phi}{\partial y}\frac{\partial\Phi}{\partial z} - \frac{2}{c^2}\frac{\partial^2\Phi}{\partial z\,\partial x}\frac{\partial\Phi}{\partial z}\frac{\partial\Phi}{\partial x} = 0$$

where c denotes the local velocity of sound.

1.21 POTENTIAL FLOW

For two dimensional, incompressible, inviscid (and irrotational) flow, a stream function and a velocity potential can be defined. The condition of zero viscosity implies irrotationality if there are no external rotational body forces. Then, Φ and Ψ are conjugate harmonic functions. Both Φ and Ψ are harmonic:

$$\nabla^2\Phi = \nabla^2\Psi = 0 \qquad \textbf{1.152}$$

The complex potential F is defined:

$$F = \Phi + i\Psi = F(z) = F(x+iy) \qquad \textbf{1.153}$$

The complex velocity can be defined:

$$V = u - iv = -\frac{\partial\Phi}{\partial x} + i\frac{\partial\Phi}{\partial y} = -\frac{\partial\Psi}{\partial y} - i\frac{\partial\Psi}{\partial x} = -\frac{dF}{dz} \qquad 1.154$$

and hence:

$$|\mathbf{V}|^2 = V\bar{V} = u^2 + v^2 = \frac{d\bar{F}}{d\bar{z}}\frac{dF}{dz} \qquad 1.155$$

where the bar indicates the complex conjugate and i is $\sqrt{-1}$.

The Cauchy-Riemann conditions are satisfied:

$$\frac{\partial\Phi}{\partial x} = \frac{\partial\Psi}{\partial y}, \qquad \frac{\partial\Phi}{\partial y} = -\frac{\partial\Psi}{\partial x} \qquad 1.156$$

1.22 VORTICITY AND CIRCULATION

(a) *Vorticity* Ω.

Vorticity is defined as:

$$\mathbf{\Omega} = \nabla\times\mathbf{V} = 2\boldsymbol{\omega}, \qquad \omega_j = \omega_{ik} \qquad 1.157$$

$\boldsymbol{\omega}$ is the angular velocity of an infinitesimal fluid element, and is equal to one half the vorticity vector. The rotation tensor ω_{ij} may be related to the vorticity vector $\mathbf{\Omega}$ as in equation 1.157. The rotation tensor is written in terms of the velocity w_i as:

$$-\omega_k = \omega_{ij} = \frac{1}{2}\left(\frac{\partial w_i}{\partial x_j} - \frac{\partial w_j}{\partial x_i}\right) = -\omega_{ji} \qquad 1.158$$

The rotation tensor is antisymmetric so that $\omega_{ij} = -\omega_{ji}$. In the expression $\omega_j = \omega_{ik}$ care must be taken to use the permutation correctly. A detailed discussion of the components of rotation has been given in Section 1.3.

(b) *Circulation* Γ.

The circulation Γ is defined around a closed path as

$$\Gamma = \oint_C \mathbf{V}\cdot d\mathbf{r} = \int_A (\nabla\times\mathbf{V})\cdot d\mathbf{A} = \int_A \mathbf{\Omega}\cdot d\mathbf{A} \qquad 1.159$$

$\mathbf{r}$ is the position vector of a point on the curve C, and hence $d\mathbf{r}$ is an element of path length. In irrotational flow $\nabla\times\mathbf{V}$ and hence Γ are zero for any closed path unless point singularities exist within the enclosed region.

(c) *Joukowski Lift.*

For an airfoil or object immersed in a flow, the lift in terms of the circulation Γ is given by

$$L = -\rho U\Gamma \qquad 1.160$$

where U is the free stream velocity and ρ is the density. The direction of L is perpendicular to the direction of U, and in the direction of $\mathbf{U}\times\mathbf{\Omega}$ where $\mathbf{\Omega}$ is the net vorticity generating the circulation. The minus sign in the above equation is due to the method of defining Γ positive in a counterclockwise direction. Fig. 1-8 shows the arrangement.

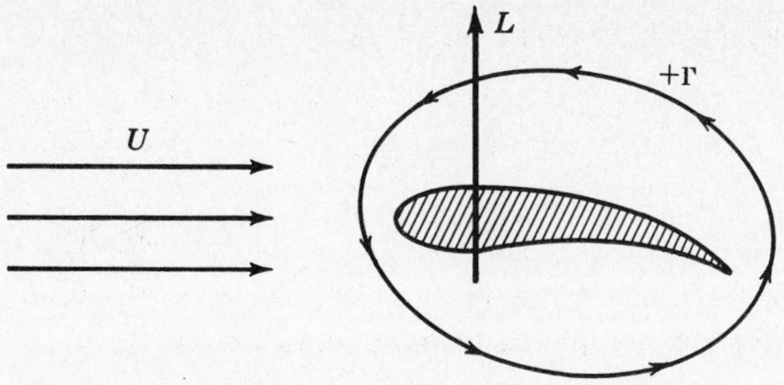

Fig. 1-8. Circulation and Joukowski Lift.

(d) Equations of Motion in Terms of Vorticity.

The vorticity transport equation expresses the equations of motion in terms of the vorticity $\mathbf{\Omega}$. $\mathbf{\Omega}$ has been defined in section *a* above. ν is the kinematic viscosity. In vector form:

$$\frac{\partial \mathbf{\Omega}}{\partial t} - \nabla \times (\mathbf{V} \times \mathbf{\Omega}) = \nu \nabla^2 \mathbf{\Omega} \qquad \mathbf{1.161}$$

where $\mathbf{\Omega} = \nabla \times \mathbf{V}$. The above equation may also be written:

$$\frac{D\mathbf{\Omega}}{Dt} = (\mathbf{\Omega} \cdot \nabla)\mathbf{V} + \nu \nabla^2 \mathbf{\Omega}$$

In Cartesian tensor form:

$$\frac{\partial \Omega_i}{\partial t} + w_j \frac{\partial \Omega_i}{\partial x_j} - \Omega_j \frac{\partial w_i}{\partial x_j} = \nu \frac{\partial^2 \Omega_i}{\partial x_j \, \partial x_j} \qquad \mathbf{1.162}$$

where $\Omega_j = 2\omega_{ik} = \dfrac{\partial w_i}{\partial x_k} - \dfrac{\partial w_k}{\partial x_i}$.

(e) Motion in Terms of Stream Functions.

For two dimensional flow a stream function exists and the above equation becomes:

$$\frac{\partial}{\partial t}(\nabla^2 \Psi) - \frac{\partial \Psi}{\partial x_2} \frac{\partial}{\partial x_1}(\nabla^2 \Psi) + \frac{\partial \Psi}{\partial x_1} \frac{\partial}{\partial x_2}(\nabla^2 \Psi) = \nu \nabla^4 \Psi \qquad \mathbf{1.163}$$

which is written in Cartesian coordinates, x_1, x_2, and x_3. The one component of vorticity Ω_3 is given by $\Omega_3 = \nabla^2 \Psi$ and $w_1 = -\dfrac{\partial \Psi}{\partial x_2}$, $w_2 = \dfrac{\partial \Psi}{\partial x_1}$.

(f) Crocco's Theorem.

The variation of entropy s along a streamline is given by:

$$T \nabla s + \mathbf{V} \times (\nabla \times \mathbf{V}) = \nabla h_0 + \frac{\partial \mathbf{V}}{\partial t} \qquad \mathbf{1.164}$$

where h_0 is the stagnation enthalpy, $h_0 = h + V^2/2$. V is the velocity. T is temperature. $\mathbf{V}$ is the velocity vector, and the entropy is specific entropy (per unit mass).

(g) Kelvin's Vortex Theorem.

In an ideal fluid the circulation around a closed fluid line is constant in time. A fluid line is a line made up of the same fluid particles at all time. Denoting the circulation by Γ, we can write:

$$\frac{D\Gamma}{Dt} = -\oint_c \frac{dP}{\rho} - \oint_c d\Phi + \oint_c \frac{1}{2} d(V^2) = 0 \qquad \mathbf{1.165}$$

where P is pressure, ρ is mass density, V is velocity, and Φ is the gravitational potential (or other conservative body force potential).

For a viscous fluid the flow is not irrotational and the circulation around a fluid line changes, in general, with time. The circulation can also change in time even for an inviscid fluid if rotational body forces are present to generate vorticity. In general the circulation time change around a fluid line is given by:

$$\frac{D\Gamma}{Dt} = \nu \oint_c \nabla^2 \mathbf{V} \cdot d\mathbf{r} + \frac{1}{\rho} \oint_c \mathbf{F} \cdot d\mathbf{r} = -\nu \oint_c (\nabla \times \Omega) \cdot d\mathbf{r} + \frac{1}{\rho} \oint_c \mathbf{F} \cdot d\mathbf{r} \quad \textbf{1.166}$$

where ν is the kinematic viscosity, Ω is the rotation vector, and $\mathbf{F}$ is the body force which may not be irrotational (say if it is generated by electromagnetic means, etc.).

1.23 LINEARIZED PERTURBATION THEORY

Linearized perturbation theory is used to solve flow about thin bodies at high speed where compressibility effects must be considered. Various forms of the general equation which allow simplification of the equation for certain regions of flight velocity will be discussed below.

The main flow of the free stream has velocity U_∞ in the x direction. The small perturbation velocities are then defined as u, v, and w in the x, y, and z directions respectively. u_1, u_2, and u_3 are the total velocities in the x_1, x_2, and x_3 directions respectively. Hence:

$$u_1 = U_\infty + u$$

$$u_2 = v$$

$$u_3 = w$$

and $u, v, w \ll U_\infty$.

In the following M_∞ is the free stream Mach number and $\gamma = c_p/c_v$.

(a) General Equation (for any velocity).

The general equation (for any velocity) is:

$$\begin{aligned}(1-M_\infty)^2 \frac{\partial u}{\partial x_1} + \frac{\partial v}{\partial x_2} + \frac{\partial w}{\partial x_3} &\qquad\qquad \textbf{1.167}\\
= M_\infty^2 \left[(\gamma+1)\frac{u}{U_\infty} + \frac{\gamma+1}{2}\frac{u^2}{U_\infty^2} + \frac{\gamma-1}{2}\frac{v^2+w^2}{U_\infty^2}\right]\frac{\partial u}{\partial x_1} \\
+ M_\infty^2 \left[(\gamma-1)\frac{u}{U_\infty} + \frac{\gamma+1}{2}\frac{v^2}{U_\infty^2} + \frac{\gamma-1}{2}\frac{w^2+u^2}{U_\infty^2}\right]\frac{\partial v}{\partial x_2} \\
+ M_\infty^2 \left[(\gamma-1)\frac{u}{U_\infty} + \frac{\gamma+1}{2}\frac{w^2}{U_\infty^2} + \frac{\gamma-1}{2}\frac{u^2+v^2}{U_\infty^2}\right]\frac{\partial w}{\partial x_3} \\
+ M_\infty^2 \left[\frac{v}{U_\infty}\left(1+\frac{u}{U_\infty}\right)\left(\frac{\partial u}{\partial x_2}+\frac{\partial v}{\partial x_1}\right) + \frac{w}{U_\infty}\left(1+\frac{u}{U_\infty}\right)\left(\frac{\partial u}{\partial x_3}+\frac{\partial w}{\partial x_1}\right)\right. \\
\left. + \frac{vw}{U_\infty^2}\left(\frac{\partial w}{\partial x_2}+\frac{\partial v}{\partial x_3}\right)\right]\end{aligned}$$

(b) For Subsonic or Supersonic Flow.

$$(1-M_\infty^2)\frac{\partial u}{\partial x_1} + \frac{\partial v}{\partial x_2} + \frac{\partial w}{\partial x_3} = 0 \qquad \textbf{1.168}$$

(c) For Subsonic, Transonic, and Supersonic Flow.

$$(1-M_\infty^2)\frac{\partial u}{\partial x_1} + \frac{\partial v}{\partial x_2} + \frac{\partial w}{\partial x_3} = M_\infty^2(\gamma+1)\frac{u}{U_\infty}\frac{\partial u}{\partial x_1} \qquad \textbf{1.169}$$

(d) In Terms of Velocity Potential.

In terms of the velocity potential Φ, the above equations 1.168 and 1.169 can be written respectively, where $\mathbf{V} = -\nabla\Phi$: For subsonic and supersonic flow:

$$(1-M_\infty^2)\frac{\partial^2\Phi}{\partial x_1^2} + \frac{\partial^2\Phi}{\partial x_2^2} + \frac{\partial^2\Phi}{\partial x_3^2} = 0 \qquad \textbf{1.170}$$

and for subsonic, transonic, and supersonic flow:

$$(1-M_\infty^2)\frac{\partial^2\Phi}{\partial x_1^2} + \frac{\partial^2\Phi}{\partial x_2^2} + \frac{\partial^2\Phi}{\partial x_3^2} = -\frac{M_\infty^2(\gamma+1)}{U_\infty}\frac{\partial\Phi}{\partial x_1}\frac{\partial^2\Phi}{\partial x_1^2} \qquad \textbf{1.171}$$

Note. The above equations valid for supersonic flow are not valid for hypersonic flow, i.e. $M_\infty \geqq$ approximately 3.

1.24 ACOUSTIC WAVE EQUATIONS

(a) Sonic Velocity c.

The sonic velocity c is:

For a gas:

$$c = \sqrt{\gamma g R T} = \left(\frac{\partial P}{\partial \rho}\right)_s \qquad \textbf{1.172}$$

For a liquid:

$$c = \sqrt{\beta/\rho} \qquad \textbf{1.173}$$

where β is the bulk compression modulus defined as $\frac{d\rho}{\rho} = \frac{dP}{\beta}$. γ is the ratio of specific heats, c_p/c_v; T is absolute temperature; s is entropy; and R is the gas constant. g is the acceleration due to gravity, necessary if engineering units are used for R.

(b) Wave Equation for an Inviscid Fluid.

The wave equation for an inviscid fluid is:

$$\frac{1}{c^2}\frac{\partial^2 P}{\partial t^2} = \nabla^2 P \qquad \textbf{1.174}$$

$$\frac{1}{c^2}\frac{\partial^2 \rho}{\partial t^2} = \nabla^2 \rho$$

$$\frac{1}{c^2}\frac{\partial^2 \Phi}{\partial t^2} = \nabla^2 \Phi$$

where P is the pressure and ρ is the density. c is the sonic velocity given in section a. Φ is the velocity potential.

(c) Wave Equation for a Viscous Fluid.

The wave equations for a viscous fluid (the Stokes wave equation):

$$\frac{1}{c^2}\frac{\partial^2 P}{\partial t^2} = \nabla^2 P + \frac{(\frac{4}{3}\mu + \zeta)}{\rho_0 c^2}\frac{\partial}{\partial t}(\nabla^2 P) \qquad \textbf{1.175}$$

$$\frac{1}{c^2}\frac{\partial^2 \rho}{\partial t^2} = \nabla^2 \rho + \frac{(\frac{4}{3}\mu + \zeta)}{\rho_0 c^2}\frac{\partial}{\partial t}(\nabla^2 \rho)$$

where ρ_0 is the mean density. ζ is the second coefficient of viscosity defined as zero for a monatomic gas. If the velocity $\mathbf{V}$ is written in terms of a velocity potential Φ and vector potential $\mathbf{A}$ as $\mathbf{V} = -\nabla\Phi + \nabla \times \mathbf{A}$, then the wave equation for Φ is:

$$\frac{1}{c^2}\frac{\partial^2 \Phi}{\partial t^2} = \nabla^2 \Phi + \frac{(\frac{4}{3}\mu + \zeta)}{\rho_0 c^2}\frac{\partial}{\partial t}(\nabla^2 \Phi) \qquad \textbf{1.176}$$

The diffusion equation for $\mathbf{A}$ is:

$$\frac{\rho_0}{\mu}\frac{\partial \mathbf{A}}{\partial t} = -\nabla \times \nabla \times \mathbf{A}$$

which is the same as that for vorticity $\boldsymbol{\Omega}$:

$$\frac{\rho_0}{\mu}\frac{\partial \boldsymbol{\Omega}}{\partial t} = -\nabla \times \nabla \times \boldsymbol{\Omega} = \nabla^2 \boldsymbol{\Omega}$$

Note that $\boldsymbol{\Omega} = \nabla \times \mathbf{V}$ and $\nabla \times \nabla \times \boldsymbol{\Omega} = -\nabla^2\boldsymbol{\Omega} + \nabla(\nabla \cdot \boldsymbol{\Omega})$ but

$$\nabla \cdot \boldsymbol{\Omega} = \nabla \cdot (\nabla \times \mathbf{V}) = 0$$

1.25 SLOW MOTION AND LUBRICATION THEORY

For motion where the inertia terms can be neglected compared to the viscous forces, i.e. low Reynolds number flow, certain simplifications can be made in order to linearize the equations of motion.

1. In two dimensional steady motion the stream function satisfies:

$$\nabla^4 \Psi = 0 \qquad \textbf{1.177}$$

2. Lubrication Theory:

The Reynolds equation for incompressible lubrication flow is

$$\frac{\partial}{\partial x}\left(\frac{h^3}{\mu}\frac{\partial P}{\partial x}\right) + \frac{\partial}{\partial z}\left(\frac{h^3}{\mu}\frac{\partial P}{\partial z}\right) = \frac{\partial}{\partial x}(6Uh) \qquad \textbf{1.178}$$

Here, the coordinates x and z lie in the plane of the lubrication film. h is the thickness which may be a function of x and z. The motion of the slider is in the x direction.

1.26 RANKINE-HUGONIOT RELATIONSHIPS (NORMAL SHOCK FUNCTIONS)

The fluid properties across a normal shock wave may be related by applying the equations of momentum, continuity, and energy. These relationships are known as the Rankine-Hugoniot equations. Here, the subscript 1 refers to conditions upstream before the shock and subscript 2 refers to conditions downstream after the shock. The velocity before a normal shock must be supersonic and the velocity after the shock must be subsonic. The following symbols are used:

P = Pressure
T = Temperature
M = Mach number
c = Sonic velocity
s = Specific entropy
u = Velocity
R = Gas constant
ρ = Mass density
γ = Ratio of specific heats, c_p/c_v.

$$\frac{\rho_2}{\rho_1} = \frac{u_1}{u_2} = \frac{1 + \dfrac{\gamma+1}{\gamma-1}\dfrac{P_2}{P_1}}{\dfrac{\gamma+1}{\gamma-1} + \dfrac{P_2}{P_1}} \quad \textbf{1.179}$$

$$\frac{T_2}{T_1} = \frac{P_2}{P_1}\,\frac{\dfrac{\gamma+1}{\gamma-1} + \dfrac{P_2}{P_1}}{1 + \dfrac{\gamma+1}{\gamma-1}\dfrac{P_2}{P_1}} \quad \textbf{1.180}$$

$$M_2^2 = \frac{1 + \dfrac{\gamma-1}{2}M_1^2}{\gamma M_1^2 - \dfrac{\gamma-1}{2}} \quad \textbf{1.181}$$

$$\frac{P_2}{P_1} = 1 + \frac{2\gamma}{\gamma+1}(M_1^2 - 1) \quad \textbf{1.182}$$

$$\frac{\rho_2}{\rho_1} = \frac{u_1}{u_2} = \frac{(\gamma+1)M_1^2}{(\gamma-1)M_1^2 + 2} \quad \textbf{1.183}$$

$$\frac{P_2 - P_1}{P_1} = \frac{\Delta P}{P_1} = \frac{2\gamma}{\gamma+1}(M_1^2 - 1) \quad \textbf{1.184}$$

$$\frac{T_2}{T_1} = \frac{c_2^2}{c_1^2} = 1 + \frac{2(\gamma-1)}{(\gamma+1)^2}\,\frac{\gamma M_1^2 + 1}{M_1^2}(M_1^2 - 1) \quad \textbf{1.185}$$

$$\frac{s_2 - s_1}{R} = \ln\left\{\left[1 + \frac{2\gamma}{\gamma+1}(M_1^2 - 1)\right]^{1/(\gamma-1)} - \left[\frac{(\gamma+1)M_1^2}{(\gamma-1)M_1^2 + 2}\right]^{-\gamma/(\gamma-1)}\right\} \quad \textbf{1.186}$$

1.27 TURBULENCE (TURBULENT REYNOLDS EQUATIONS)

Average values are denoted by ($\bar{\ }$), and fluctuation values are denoted by ( )′. The stresses $\bar{\sigma}_{ij}$ do not include the pressure and are the same viscous stresses denoted by σ'_{ij} in Section 1.4. In the following P is pressure, ρ is mass density, and w_i is the Cartesian component of velocity.

$$\rho\left(\frac{\partial \bar{w}_i}{\partial t} + \bar{w}_j \frac{\partial \bar{w}_i}{\partial x_j}\right) = -\frac{\partial P}{\partial x_i} + \frac{\partial \bar{\sigma}_{ij}}{\partial x_j} + \frac{\partial \sigma_{ijt}}{\partial x_j} \qquad \textbf{1.187}$$

In Cartesian coordinates:

$$\rho\left(\frac{\partial \bar{u}}{\partial t} + \bar{u}\frac{\partial \bar{u}}{\partial x} + \bar{v}\frac{\partial \bar{u}}{\partial y} + \bar{w}\frac{\partial \bar{u}}{\partial z}\right) \qquad \textbf{1.188}$$

$$= -\frac{\partial \bar{P}}{\partial x} + \frac{\partial \bar{\sigma}_{xx}}{\partial x} + \frac{\partial \bar{\sigma}_{xy}}{\partial y} + \frac{\partial \bar{\sigma}_{xz}}{\partial z} + \frac{\partial \sigma_{xxt}}{\partial x} + \frac{\partial \sigma_{xyt}}{\partial y} + \frac{\partial \sigma_{xzt}}{\partial z}$$

$$\rho\left(\frac{\partial \bar{v}}{\partial t} + \bar{u}\frac{\partial \bar{v}}{\partial x} + \bar{v}\frac{\partial \bar{v}}{\partial y} + \bar{w}\frac{\partial \bar{v}}{\partial z}\right)$$

$$= -\frac{\partial \bar{P}}{\partial y} + \frac{\partial \bar{\sigma}_{yx}}{\partial x} + \frac{\partial \bar{\sigma}_{yy}}{\partial y} + \frac{\partial \bar{\sigma}_{yz}}{\partial z} + \frac{\partial \sigma_{yxt}}{\partial x} + \frac{\partial \sigma_{yyt}}{\partial y} + \frac{\partial \sigma_{yzt}}{\partial z}$$

$$\rho\left(\frac{\partial \bar{w}}{\partial t} + \bar{u}\frac{\partial \bar{w}}{\partial x} + \bar{v}\frac{\partial \bar{w}}{\partial y} + \bar{w}\frac{\partial \bar{w}}{\partial z}\right)$$

$$= -\frac{\partial \bar{P}}{\partial z} + \frac{\partial \bar{\sigma}_{zx}}{\partial x} + \frac{\partial \bar{\sigma}_{zy}}{\partial y} + \frac{\partial \bar{\sigma}_{zz}}{\partial z} + \frac{\partial \sigma_{zxt}}{\partial x} + \frac{\partial \sigma_{zyt}}{\partial y} + \frac{\partial \sigma_{zzt}}{\partial z}$$

In the above equations $\bar{\sigma}_{ij}$ is related to the average strain rate by the formulas of laminar flow. The turbulent Reynolds stresses are given in terms of correlations as:

$$\sigma_{ijt} = -\begin{bmatrix} \rho\overline{u'^2} & \rho\overline{u'v'} & \rho\overline{u'w'} \\ \rho\overline{u'v'} & \rho\overline{v'^2} & \rho\overline{v'w'} \\ \rho\overline{u'w'} & \rho\overline{v'w'} & \rho\overline{w'^2} \end{bmatrix} \qquad \textbf{1.189}$$

where u', v', and w' are the fluctuation velocity components in the x, y, and z directions respectively.

The equations of motion in cylindrical coordinates can be written as follows. The turbulent stresses have been inserted directly into the equations, and the viscous stresses have been neglected. The Reynolds equations for turbulent motion are then:

$$\frac{\partial \bar{v}_r}{\partial t} + \bar{v}_r\frac{\partial \bar{v}_r}{\partial r} + \frac{\bar{v}_\theta}{r}\frac{\partial \bar{v}_r}{\partial \theta} + \bar{v}_z\frac{\partial \bar{v}_r}{\partial z} - \frac{\bar{v}_\theta^2}{r} \qquad \textbf{1.190}$$

$$= -\frac{1}{\rho}\frac{\partial \bar{P}}{\partial r} - \frac{\partial}{\partial r}\overline{v_r'^2} - \frac{1}{r}\frac{\partial}{\partial \theta}(\overline{v_r' v_\theta'}) - \frac{\partial}{\partial z}(\overline{v_r' v_z'}) - \frac{\overline{v_r'^2}}{r} + \frac{\overline{v_\theta'^2}}{r}$$

$$\frac{\partial \bar{v}_\theta}{\partial t} + \bar{v}_r\frac{\partial \bar{v}_\theta}{\partial r} + \frac{\bar{v}_\theta}{r}\frac{\partial \bar{v}_\theta}{\partial \theta} + \bar{v}_z\frac{\partial \bar{v}_\theta}{\partial z} + \frac{\bar{v}_r\bar{v}_\theta}{r}$$

$$= -\frac{1}{\rho}\frac{1}{r}\frac{\partial \bar{P}}{\partial \theta} - \frac{\partial}{\partial r}(\overline{v_r' v_\theta'}) - \frac{1}{r}\frac{\partial}{\partial \theta}(\overline{v_\theta'^2}) - \frac{\partial}{\partial z}(\overline{v_\theta' v_z'}) - \frac{2\overline{v_r' v_\theta'}}{r}$$

$$\frac{\partial \bar{v}_z}{\partial t} + \bar{v}_r \frac{\partial \bar{v}_z}{\partial r} + \frac{\bar{v}_\theta}{r}\frac{\partial \bar{v}_z}{\partial \theta} + \bar{v}_z \frac{\partial \bar{v}_z}{\partial z}$$

$$= -\frac{1}{\rho}\frac{\partial \bar{P}}{\partial z} - \frac{\partial}{\partial r}(\overline{v'_r v'_z}) - \frac{1}{r}\frac{\partial}{\partial \theta}(\overline{v'_\theta v'_z}) - \frac{\partial}{\partial z}(\overline{v'^2_z}) - \frac{\overline{v'_r v'_z}}{r}$$

The continuity equation takes the same form as in laminar flow except that the velocities are now the average values.

$$\frac{\partial \rho}{\partial t} + \frac{\partial(\rho \overline{w}_i)}{\partial x_i} = 0 \qquad \textbf{1.191}$$

1.28 SIMILARITY AND COMMON DIMENSIONLESS PARAMETERS

Some of the more frequently used dimensionless groups in fluid mechanics are listed below. In order to avoid confusion the symbols that are used here are listed below in detail.

Drag Coefficient	C_d	$= D/\frac{1}{2}\rho U^2 A$
Eckert No.	E	$= U^2_\infty / g c_p (\Delta T)_0$
Froude No.	F	$= U^2/gL$
Grashof No.	G	$= g\beta\theta L^3/\nu^2$
Hypersonic Similarity Parameter	K	$= M_\infty \cdot t$
Lift Coefficient	C_L	$= L/\frac{1}{2}\rho U^2 A$
Mach No.	M	$= U/c$
Nusselt No.	Nu	$= hL/\kappa$
Peclet No.	Pe	$= U_\infty L/\alpha = Pr \cdot Re$
Prandtl No.	Pr	$= \nu/\alpha = \mu c_p/\kappa$
Pressure Coefficient	C_p	$= (P - P_0)/\frac{1}{2}\rho U^2$
Reynolds No.	Re	$= \rho LU/\mu = LU/\nu$
Schmidt No.	S	$= \mu/\rho D_f$
Skin Friction Coefficient	C_f	$= \tau_w/\frac{1}{2}\rho U^2$
Sound Wave No.		$= 1/M$
Stanton No.	N_{st}	$= Nu/(Pr \cdot Re) = h/c_p G = h/c_p U \rho$
Strouhal No.	S	$= U\tau/L$
Surface Tension No.		$= T'/g\rho L^2$
Weber No.	We	$= \rho U^2 L/T'$

In the above dimensionless groups the following symbols have been used:

A = Characteristic area.

c = Sonic velocity.

c_p = Specific heat at constant pressure.

D = Drag.

D_f = Material diffusion coefficient.

g = Acceleration due to gravity.

h = Film coefficient.

L = Characteristic length, or Lift.

P = Pressure.

t = Thickness.

T = Temperature.

T' = Surface tension.

$(\Delta T)_0$ = $T_{\text{wall}} - T_\infty$.

U = Characteristic velocity.

$(\ )_\infty$ = Denotes free stream value.

α = Thermal diffusivity. $\alpha = \dfrac{\kappa}{\rho c_p}$.

β = Coefficient of thermal expansion.

θ = $T - T_\infty$.

κ = Thermal conductivity.

μ = Viscosity.

ν = Kinematic viscosity.

ρ = Density.

τ = Characteristic time.

τ_w = Wall shear.

1.29 LIST OF SYMBOLS USED IN CHAPTER 1

Note. Other symbols have been used but were identified explicitly at the time of their use. The following are the most important symbols used throughout the chapter. Occasionally, these symbols were used to represent other quantities but were then explained in the text.

c = Sonic velocity.

c_p = Heat capacity (specific heat) at constant pressure.

c_v = Heat capacity (specific heat) at constant volume.

$\dfrac{D}{Dt}$ = Material or substantial derivative.

e = Internal energy.

e_{ij} = Strain rate tensor.

$\mathbf{F}$ = Body force density.

g = Acceleration due to gravity.

h = Enthalpy; film thickness.

h_i = Defined by space metric or line element if curvilinear coordinates.

L = Lift.

P = Pressure.

q = Heat rate per unit mass.

Q = Heat quantity.

R = Gas constant.

s = Entropy.

u = Velocity in x direction.

v = Velocity in y direction.

$\mathbf{V}$ = Velocity vector.

v_r = Velocity in radial direction.

v_θ = Velocity in θ direction.

v_ϕ = Velocity in ϕ direction.

v_z = Velocity in z direction.

w = Velocity in z direction.

w_i = Velocity in the x_i direction.

W_x = Shaft work or shear work rate.

x_i = Coordinate.

α = Thermal diffusivity.

β = Coefficient of thermal expansion; bulk modulus.

γ_{ij} = Actual shear deformation rate.

Γ = Circulation.

δ_{ij} = Kronecker delta.

ζ = Second coefficient of viscosity. Zero for a monatomic gas. Related to λ by $\zeta = \lambda + \frac{2}{3}\mu$.

κ = Thermal conductivity.

μ = Viscosity.

ν = Kinematic viscosity.

ρ = Density.

σ = Entropy production rate per unit volume.

σ_{ij} = Stress tensor.

σ'_{ij} = Non-pressure part of the stress tensor.

ϕ = Dilatation, $\nabla \cdot \mathbf{V}$.

Φ = Dissipation function. Velocity potential.

Ψ = Stream function.

ω = Angular velocity.

ω_{ij} = Rotation tensor.

$\mathbf{\Omega}$ = Vorticity vector.

1.30 LIST OF REFERENCES

1. Aris, R., *Vectors, Tensors, and the Basic Equations of Fluid Mechanics,* Prentice-Hall, 1962

2. Eringen, A. C., *Nonlinear Theory of Continuous Media,* McGraw-Hill, 1962

3. Goldstein, S., *Modern Developments in Fluid Dynamics,* Vols. I and II, Oxford University Press, 1938

4. Howarth, L., *Modern Developments in Fluid Dynamics, High Speed Flow,* Vols. I and II, Oxford University Press, 1953

5. Lamb, Sir Horace, *Hydrodynamics,* Cambridge University Press, 6th edition, 1932. Also in Dover Publications.

6. Landau, L. D., and Lifshitz, E. M., *Fluid Mechanics,* Addison-Wesley, 1959

7. Liepmann, H. W., and Roshko, A., *Elements of Gasdynamics,* John Wiley, 1957

8. Love, A. E. H., *A Treatise on the Mathematical Theory of Elasticity,* Cambridge University Press, 1927. Also in Dover Publications.

9. Milne-Thompson, L. M., *Theoretical Hydrodynamics,* Macmillan, 1955

10. Pai, S. I., *Viscous Flow Theory,* Vols. I and II, Van Nostrand, 1956

11. Lord Rayleigh, *Theory of Sound,* Vols. I and II, Dover, 1945

12. Robinson, A., and Laurmann, J. A., *Wing Theory,* Cambridge University Press, 1956

13. Schlichting, H., *Boundary Layer Theory,* McGraw-Hill, 1955

14. Shapiro, A., *Dynamics and Thermodynamics of Compressible Flow,* Ronald Press, 1953

15. Sommerfeld, A., *Dynamics of Deformable Media,* Academic Press, 1950

Chapter 2

Elasticity

2.1 STRAIN RELATIONSHIPS

The infinitesimal strain tensor is denoted as e_{ij}. The actual components of strain are related to the strain tensor in the following manner. The normal strains are exactly equal to the normal (or diagonal) terms of the strain tensor, but the shear (off diagonal) terms of the strain tensor are one half the corresponding values of the true strains. Denoting the actual strains as γ_{ij}, we can write: $\gamma_{ij} = 2e_{ij}$, $i \neq j$, and $\gamma_{ij} = e_{ij}$, $i = j$. The strain tensor is defined in this manner so that it will be a true tensor and transform accordingly. The strain tensor is the symmetrical part of the deformation tensor $\dfrac{\partial u_i}{\partial x_j}$, and the rotation tensor ω_{ij} is the antisymmetric part. Here, u_i is the deformation vector. The rotation vector is one half the curl of the deformation vector, $\boldsymbol{\omega} = \frac{1}{2}\nabla \times \mathbf{u}$, and is completely analogous to the rotation vector in fluid mechanics.

The dilatation ϕ is a strain invariant and equal to the divergence of the deformation vector. It is equal to the sum of the normal strains, i.e. $\phi = e_{11} + e_{22} + e_{33}$.

Below are listed the strain tensor and rotation tensor in various coordinate systems. The dilatation is also listed.

(a) Cartesian Tensor.

u_i is the deformation in the x_i direction.

$$e_{ij} = \frac{1}{2}\left(\frac{\partial u_i}{\partial x_j} + \frac{\partial u_j}{\partial x_i}\right) = e_{ji} \qquad \textbf{2.1}$$

The tensor may be written out in matrix form as:

$$e_{ij} = \begin{bmatrix} \dfrac{\partial u_1}{\partial x_1} & \dfrac{1}{2}\left(\dfrac{\partial u_1}{\partial x_2} + \dfrac{\partial u_2}{\partial x_1}\right) & \dfrac{1}{2}\left(\dfrac{\partial u_1}{\partial x_3} + \dfrac{\partial u_3}{\partial x_1}\right) \\ \dfrac{1}{2}\left(\dfrac{\partial u_2}{\partial x_1} + \dfrac{\partial u_1}{\partial x_2}\right) & \dfrac{\partial u_2}{\partial x_2} & \dfrac{1}{2}\left(\dfrac{\partial u_2}{\partial x_3} + \dfrac{\partial u_3}{\partial x_2}\right) \\ \dfrac{1}{2}\left(\dfrac{\partial u_3}{\partial x_1} + \dfrac{\partial u_1}{\partial x_3}\right) & \dfrac{1}{2}\left(\dfrac{\partial u_3}{\partial x_2} + \dfrac{\partial u_2}{\partial x_3}\right) & \dfrac{\partial u_3}{\partial x_3} \end{bmatrix} \qquad \textbf{2.2}$$

The rotation tensor is:

$$-\omega_k = \omega_{ij} = -\omega_{ji} = \frac{1}{2}\left(\frac{\partial u_i}{\partial x_j} - \frac{\partial u_j}{\partial x_i}\right) \qquad \textbf{2.3}$$

The dilatation is:

$$\phi = e_{ii} = \frac{\partial u_i}{\partial x_i} = e_{11} + e_{22} + e_{33} \qquad \textbf{2.4}$$

(b) Orthogonal Curvilinear.

h_1, h_2, and h_3 are defined by the line element (see appendix) and x_1, x_2, and x_3 are the coordinates. In the following the summation convention of tensor notation is not used.

The normal terms are:

$$e_{ii} = \frac{\partial}{\partial x_i}\left(\frac{u_i}{h_i}\right) + \frac{1}{2h_i^2}\sum_{k=1}^{3}\frac{\partial h_i^2}{\partial x_k}\frac{u_k}{h_k} \qquad \mathbf{2.5}$$

and the shear terms are:

$$e_{ij} = \frac{1}{2h_ih_j}\left[h_i^2\frac{\partial}{\partial x_j}\left(\frac{u_i}{h_i}\right) + h_j^2\frac{\partial}{\partial x_i}\left(\frac{u_j}{h_j}\right)\right]; \quad i \neq j \qquad \mathbf{2.6}$$

Written out:

$$e_{11} = \frac{1}{h_1}\frac{\partial u_1}{\partial x_1} + \frac{u_2}{h_1h_2}\frac{\partial h_1}{\partial x_2} + \frac{u_3}{h_3h_1}\frac{\partial h_1}{\partial x_3} \qquad \mathbf{2.7}$$

$$e_{22} = \frac{1}{h_2}\frac{\partial u_2}{\partial x_2} + \frac{u_3}{h_2h_3}\frac{\partial h_2}{\partial x_3} + \frac{u_1}{h_1h_2}\frac{\partial h_2}{\partial x_1}$$

$$e_{33} = \frac{1}{h_3}\frac{\partial u_3}{\partial x_3} + \frac{u_1}{h_3h_1}\frac{\partial h_3}{\partial x_1} + \frac{u_2}{h_2h_3}\frac{\partial h_3}{\partial x_2}$$

$$e_{23} = \frac{1}{2}\left[\frac{h_3}{h_2}\frac{\partial}{\partial x_2}\left(\frac{u_3}{h_3}\right) + \frac{h_2}{h_3}\frac{\partial}{\partial x_3}\left(\frac{u_2}{h_2}\right)\right]$$

$$e_{31} = \frac{1}{2}\left[\frac{h_1}{h_3}\frac{\partial}{\partial x_3}\left(\frac{u_1}{h_1}\right) + \frac{h_3}{h_1}\frac{\partial}{\partial x_1}\left(\frac{u_3}{h_3}\right)\right]$$

$$e_{12} = \frac{1}{2}\left[\frac{h_2}{h_1}\frac{\partial}{\partial x_1}\left(\frac{u_2}{h_2}\right) + \frac{h_1}{h_2}\frac{\partial}{\partial x_2}\left(\frac{u_1}{h_1}\right)\right]$$

The rotation tensor is:

$$\omega_1 = \omega_{32} = \frac{1}{2h_2h_3}\left\{\frac{\partial}{\partial x_2}(u_3h_3) - \frac{\partial}{\partial x_3}(u_2h_2)\right\} \qquad \mathbf{2.8}$$

$$\omega_2 = \omega_{13} = \frac{1}{2h_3h_1}\left\{\frac{\partial}{\partial x_3}(u_1h_1) - \frac{\partial}{\partial x_1}(u_3h_3)\right\}$$

$$\omega_3 = \omega_{21} = \frac{1}{2h_1h_2}\left\{\frac{\partial}{\partial x_1}(u_2h_2) - \frac{\partial}{\partial x_2}(u_1h_1)\right\}$$

The dilatation is:

$$\phi = \frac{1}{h_1h_2h_3}\left\{\frac{\partial}{\partial x_1}(u_1h_2h_3) + \frac{\partial}{\partial x_2}(u_2h_3h_1) + \frac{\partial}{\partial x_3}(u_3h_1h_2)\right\} \qquad \mathbf{2.9}$$

(c) Cartesian.

u, v, and w are the deformations in the x, y, and z directions respectively.

$$e_{xx} = \frac{\partial u}{\partial x} \qquad \mathbf{2.10}$$

$$e_{yy} = \frac{\partial v}{\partial y}$$

$$e_{zz} = \frac{\partial w}{\partial z}$$

$$e_{xz} = \frac{1}{2}\left(\frac{\partial u}{\partial z} + \frac{\partial w}{\partial x}\right)$$

$$e_{xy} = \frac{1}{2}\left(\frac{\partial v}{\partial x} + \frac{\partial u}{\partial y}\right)$$

$$e_{zy} = \frac{1}{2}\left(\frac{\partial w}{\partial y} + \frac{\partial v}{\partial z}\right)$$

The rotation tensor is:

$$\omega_x = \omega_{zy} = \frac{1}{2}\left(\frac{\partial w}{\partial y} - \frac{\partial v}{\partial z}\right) \qquad 2.11$$

$$\omega_y = \omega_{xz} = \frac{1}{2}\left(\frac{\partial u}{\partial z} - \frac{\partial w}{\partial x}\right)$$

$$\omega_z = \omega_{yx} = \frac{1}{2}\left(\frac{\partial v}{\partial x} - \frac{\partial u}{\partial y}\right)$$

The dilatation is:

$$\phi = e_{xx} + e_{yy} + e_{zz} = \frac{\partial u}{\partial x} + \frac{\partial v}{\partial y} + \frac{\partial w}{\partial z} \qquad 2.12$$

(d) Cylindrical.

u_r, u_θ, and u_z are the deformations in the r, θ, and z directions respectively.

$$e_{rr} = \frac{\partial u_r}{\partial r} \qquad 2.13$$

$$e_{\theta\theta} = \frac{1}{r}\frac{\partial u_\theta}{\partial \theta} + \frac{u_r}{r}$$

$$e_{zz} = \frac{\partial u_z}{\partial z}$$

$$e_{r\theta} = \frac{1}{2}\left(\frac{1}{r}\frac{\partial u_r}{\partial \theta} + \frac{\partial u_\theta}{\partial r} - \frac{u_\theta}{r}\right)$$

$$e_{rz} = \frac{1}{2}\left(\frac{\partial u_z}{\partial r} + \frac{\partial u_r}{\partial z}\right)$$

$$e_{\theta z} = \frac{1}{2}\left(\frac{\partial u_\theta}{\partial z} + \frac{1}{r}\frac{\partial u_z}{\partial \theta}\right)$$

The rotation tensor is:

$$\omega_r = \omega_{z\theta} = \frac{1}{2}\left(\frac{1}{r}\frac{\partial u_z}{\partial \theta} - \frac{\partial u_\theta}{\partial z}\right) \qquad 2.14$$

$$\omega_\theta = \omega_{rz} = \frac{1}{2}\left(\frac{\partial u_r}{\partial z} - \frac{\partial u_z}{\partial r}\right)$$

$$\omega_z = \omega_{\theta r} = \frac{1}{2}\left(\frac{1}{r}\frac{\partial (r u_\theta)}{\partial r} - \frac{1}{r}\frac{\partial u_r}{\partial \theta}\right)$$

The dilatation is:

$$\phi = e_{rr} + e_{\theta\theta} + e_{zz} = \frac{\partial u_r}{\partial r} + \frac{1}{r}\frac{\partial u_\theta}{\partial \theta} + \frac{u_r}{r} + \frac{\partial u_z}{\partial z} \qquad 2.15$$

(e) Spherical.

u_r, u_θ, and u_ϕ are the deformations in the r, θ, and ϕ directions respectively.

$$e_{rr} = \frac{\partial u_r}{\partial r} \tag{2.16}$$

$$e_{\theta\theta} = \frac{1}{r}\frac{\partial u_\theta}{\partial \theta} + \frac{u_r}{r}$$

$$e_{\phi\phi} = \frac{1}{r \sin\theta}\frac{\partial u_\phi}{\partial \phi} + \frac{u_r}{r} + u_\theta \frac{\cot\theta}{r}$$

$$e_{r\phi} = \frac{1}{2}\left(\frac{1}{r\sin\theta}\frac{\partial u_r}{\partial \phi} - \frac{u_\phi}{r} + \frac{\partial u_\phi}{\partial r}\right)$$

$$e_{r\theta} = \frac{1}{2}\left(\frac{1}{r}\frac{\partial u_r}{\partial \theta} - \frac{u_\theta}{r} + \frac{\partial u_\theta}{\partial r}\right)$$

$$e_{\phi\theta} = \frac{1}{2}\left(\frac{1}{r}\frac{\partial u_\phi}{\partial \theta} - \frac{u_\phi \cot\theta}{r} + \frac{1}{r\sin\theta}\frac{\partial u_\theta}{\partial \phi}\right)$$

The rotation tensor is:

$$\omega_r = \omega_{\phi\theta} = \frac{1}{2}\frac{1}{r^2 \sin\theta}\left\{\frac{\partial}{\partial\theta}(r u_\phi \sin\theta) - \frac{\partial}{\partial\phi}(r u_\theta)\right\} \tag{2.17}$$

$$\omega_\theta = \omega_{r\phi} = \frac{1}{2}\frac{1}{r\sin\theta}\left\{\frac{\partial u_r}{\partial\phi} - \frac{\partial}{\partial r}(r u_\phi \sin\theta)\right\}$$

$$\omega_\phi = \omega_{\theta r} = \frac{1}{2r}\left\{\frac{\partial}{\partial r}(r u_\theta) - \frac{\partial u_r}{\partial\theta}\right\}$$

The dilatation is:

$$\phi = e_{rr} + e_{\theta\theta} + e_{\phi\phi} = \frac{\partial u_r}{\partial r} + \frac{1}{r}\frac{\partial u_\theta}{\partial\theta} + \frac{2u_r}{r} + \frac{1}{r\sin\theta}\frac{\partial u_\phi}{\partial\phi} + \frac{u_\theta \cot\theta}{r} \tag{2.18}$$

(f) Plane Polar.

$$e_{rr} = \frac{\partial u_r}{\partial r} \tag{2.19}$$

$$e_{\theta\theta} = \frac{1}{r}\frac{\partial u_\theta}{\partial\theta} + \frac{u_r}{r}$$

$$e_{r\theta} = \frac{1}{2r}\left(\frac{\partial u_r}{\partial\theta} - u_\theta + r\frac{\partial u_\theta}{\partial r}\right)$$

(g) Plane Cartesian.

$$e_{xx} = \frac{\partial u}{\partial x} \tag{2.20}$$

$$e_{yy} = \frac{\partial v}{\partial y}$$

$$e_{xy} = \frac{1}{2}\left(\frac{\partial u}{\partial y} + \frac{\partial v}{\partial x}\right)$$

(h) Nonlinear Strain Tensor.

The nonlinear strain tensor to quadratic order may be written in Cartesian coordinates as:

$$e_{ij} = \begin{bmatrix} \frac{\partial u}{\partial x} & \frac{1}{2}\left(\frac{\partial v}{\partial x}+\frac{\partial u}{\partial y}\right) & \frac{1}{2}\left(\frac{\partial w}{\partial x}+\frac{\partial u}{\partial z}\right) \\ \frac{1}{2}\left(\frac{\partial u}{\partial y}+\frac{\partial v}{\partial x}\right) & \frac{\partial v}{\partial y} & \frac{1}{2}\left(\frac{\partial w}{\partial y}+\frac{\partial v}{\partial z}\right) \\ \frac{1}{2}\left(\frac{\partial u}{\partial z}+\frac{\partial w}{\partial x}\right) & \frac{1}{2}\left(\frac{\partial v}{\partial z}+\frac{\partial w}{\partial y}\right) & \frac{\partial w}{\partial z} \end{bmatrix} \tag{2.21}$$

$$+ \frac{1}{2}\begin{bmatrix} \left\{\left(\frac{\partial u}{\partial x}\right)^2+\left(\frac{\partial v}{\partial x}\right)^2+\left(\frac{\partial w}{\partial x}\right)^2\right\} & \left\{\frac{\partial u}{\partial x}\frac{\partial u}{\partial y}+\frac{\partial v}{\partial x}\frac{\partial v}{\partial y}+\frac{\partial w}{\partial x}\frac{\partial w}{\partial y}\right\} & \left\{\frac{\partial u}{\partial x}\frac{\partial u}{\partial z}+\frac{\partial v}{\partial x}\frac{\partial v}{\partial z}+\frac{\partial w}{\partial x}\frac{\partial w}{\partial z}\right\} \\ \left\{\frac{\partial u}{\partial x}\frac{\partial u}{\partial y}+\frac{\partial v}{\partial x}\frac{\partial v}{\partial y}+\frac{\partial w}{\partial x}\frac{\partial w}{\partial y}\right\} & \left\{\left(\frac{\partial u}{\partial y}\right)^2+\left(\frac{\partial v}{\partial y}\right)^2+\left(\frac{\partial w}{\partial y}\right)^2\right\} & \left\{\frac{\partial u}{\partial y}\frac{\partial u}{\partial z}+\frac{\partial v}{\partial y}\frac{\partial v}{\partial z}+\frac{\partial w}{\partial y}\frac{\partial w}{\partial z}\right\} \\ \left\{\frac{\partial u}{\partial x}\frac{\partial u}{\partial z}+\frac{\partial v}{\partial x}\frac{\partial v}{\partial z}+\frac{\partial w}{\partial x}\frac{\partial w}{\partial z}\right\} & \left\{\frac{\partial u}{\partial y}\frac{\partial u}{\partial z}+\frac{\partial v}{\partial y}\frac{\partial v}{\partial z}+\frac{\partial w}{\partial y}\frac{\partial w}{\partial z}\right\} & \left\{\left(\frac{\partial u}{\partial z}\right)^2+\left(\frac{\partial v}{\partial z}\right)^2+\left(\frac{\partial w}{\partial z}\right)^2\right\} \end{bmatrix}$$

(i) Principal Strains.

The principal strains are denoted by e_1, e_2, and e_3 in the directions $\mathbf{A}_1$, $\mathbf{A}_2$, and $\mathbf{A}_3$ respectively. If the coordinate axes are oriented along the vectors **A**, then no shear strains exist. This condition defines the principal axes.

The principal strains are given by the determinantal equation:

$$|e_{ij} - e\delta_{ij}| = 0 \tag{2.22}$$

where δ_{ij} is the Kronecker delta.

The vectors **A** are given by the equation:

$$[e_{ij} - e\delta_{ij}][A_j] = 0 \tag{2.23}$$

Equation 2.22 can be written as:

$$-e^3 + \phi_1 e^2 - \phi_2 e + \phi_3 = 0 \tag{2.24}$$

where the symbols have the following meaning:

$$\phi_1 = \phi = e_1 + e_2 + e_3 = e_{11} + e_{22} + e_{33} \tag{2.25}$$

$$\phi_2 = \begin{vmatrix} e_{22} & e_{23} \\ e_{23} & e_{33} \end{vmatrix} + \begin{vmatrix} e_{11} & e_{31} \\ e_{31} & e_{33} \end{vmatrix} + \begin{vmatrix} e_{11} & e_{12} \\ e_{12} & e_{22} \end{vmatrix}$$

$$= e_2 e_3 + e_3 e_1 + e_1 e_2$$

$$\phi_3 = \begin{vmatrix} e_{11} & e_{12} & e_{31} \\ e_{12} & e_{22} & e_{23} \\ e_{31} & e_{23} & e_{33} \end{vmatrix} = e_1 e_2 e_3$$

The three values ϕ_1, ϕ_2, and ϕ_3 are strain invariants (with respect to orthogonal transformations of coordinates).

2.2 STRESS RELATIONSHIPS

The stress tensor τ_{ij} is a symmetric tensor and can be written:

$$\tau_{ij} = \tau_{ji} = \begin{bmatrix} \tau_{11} & \tau_{12} & \tau_{13} \\ \tau_{21} & \tau_{22} & \tau_{23} \\ \tau_{31} & \tau_{32} & \tau_{33} \end{bmatrix} \qquad \textbf{2.26}$$

The sign convention is illustrated in Fig. 2-1. The first subscript indicates the surface on which the stress acts and indicates the axis to which the surface is perpendicular. The second subscript denotes the direction in which the stress acts on the positive surface (which is the one shown in the figure). On the negative surface the stress acts in the opposite direction.

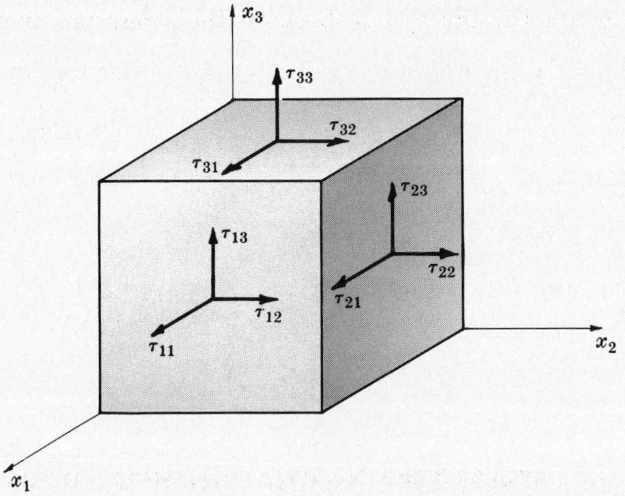

Fig. 2-1. A surface is denoted by the axis to which it is perpendicular. The stresses shown are on the positive surfaces. On the opposite or negative surfaces the stresses are in the opposite directions.

The stress vector **T** is defined as the stress acting on a surface as shown in Fig. 2-2 below.

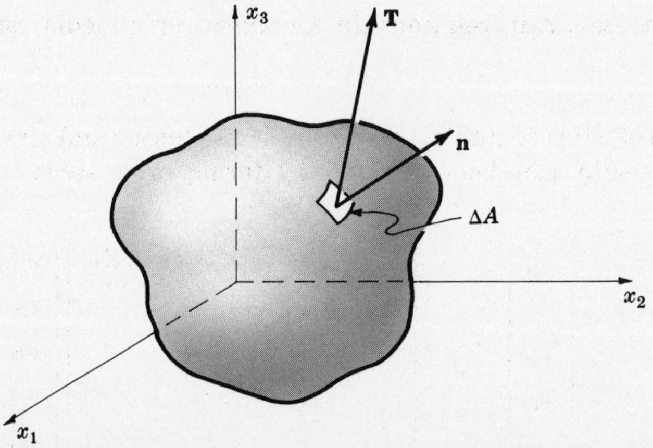

Fig. 2-2. **n** is the normal unit vector on the area ΔA. **T** is not in general in the direction of **n**.

In general, the stress vector at a point in a body is given by:

$$T_i = \tau_{ij} n_j \qquad 2.27$$

where T_i is the component of **T** in the direction x_i.

The principal stresses τ act on the surfaces defined by the vectors **A**. If the coordinate axes are oriented along these vectors there are no shear stresses. The principal stresses are given by:

$$|\tau_{ij} - \tau\delta_{ij}| = 0 \qquad 2.28$$

and the vectors **A** by:

$$[\tau_{ij} - \tau\delta_{ij}][A_j] = 0 \qquad 2.29$$

Equation 2.28 can be written as:

$$|\tau_{ij} - \tau\delta_{ij}| = -\tau^3 + \theta_1\tau^2 - \theta_2\tau + \theta_3 = 0 \qquad 2.30$$

where θ_1, θ_2, and θ_3 are the three invariants of the stress tensor given by:

$$\theta_1 = \tau_1 + \tau_2 + \tau_3 = \tau_{11} + \tau_{22} + \tau_{33} = \theta \qquad 2.31$$

$$\theta_2 = \tau_1\tau_2 + \tau_2\tau_3 + \tau_3\tau_1 = \begin{vmatrix} \tau_{22} & \tau_{23} \\ \tau_{23} & \tau_{33} \end{vmatrix} + \begin{vmatrix} \tau_{11} & \tau_{31} \\ \tau_{31} & \tau_{33} \end{vmatrix} + \begin{vmatrix} \tau_{11} & \tau_{12} \\ \tau_{12} & \tau_{22} \end{vmatrix}$$

$$\theta_3 = \tau_1\tau_2\tau_3 = \begin{vmatrix} \tau_{11} & \tau_{12} & \tau_{13} \\ \tau_{21} & \tau_{22} & \tau_{23} \\ \tau_{31} & \tau_{32} & \tau_{33} \end{vmatrix}$$

2.3 STRESS-STRAIN RELATIONSHIPS, HOOKE'S LAW

The generalized Hooke's law for homogeneous isotropic bodies is listed below in various coordinate systems. The general stress-strain relationship for anisotropic bodies is discussed. Φ is the dilatation ($\Phi = e_{11} + e_{22} + e_{33}$). μ and λ are the Lamé constants and E is the Young's modulus. σ is the Poisson ratio. μ is sometimes denoted as G and is the shear modulus or modulus of rigidity.

The general stress-strain relationship for anisotropic media can be written:

$$\tau_{ij} = C_{ijkl}e_{kl} \qquad 2.32a$$

where C_{ijkl} are the elastic constants. Since the stress tensor and strain tensor are symmetric, the above relationship can be expressed in terms of a second order elastic coefficient matrix as:

$$\begin{bmatrix} \tau_{11} \\ \tau_{22} \\ \tau_{33} \\ \tau_{12} \\ \tau_{23} \\ \tau_{13} \end{bmatrix} = \begin{bmatrix} C_{11} & C_{12} & \cdot & \cdot & \cdot & C_{16} \\ C_{21} & C_{22} & & & & \\ \cdot & & \cdot & & & \\ \cdot & & & \cdot & & \\ \cdot & & & & \cdot & \\ C_{61} & & & & & C_{66} \end{bmatrix} \begin{bmatrix} e_{11} \\ e_{22} \\ e_{33} \\ e_{12} \\ e_{23} \\ e_{13} \end{bmatrix} \qquad 2.32b$$

If the coordinate axes are taken along the principal axes for homogeneous, isotropic material the shear strains and shear stresses are zero, since the principal strain axes and principal stress axes are coincident for homogeneous isotropic material. For homogeneous isotropic media the invariants of stress and strain are related by:

$$\theta = (3\lambda + 2\mu)\phi$$

We now list the generalized Hooke's law for homogeneous isotropic material:

(a) Cartesian Tensor (or Orthogonal Curvilinear).

$$\tau_{ij} = \lambda\delta_{ij}\phi + 2\mu e_{ij} = \frac{E\sigma\phi}{(1+\sigma)(1-2\sigma)}\delta_{ij} + \frac{E}{1+\sigma}e_{ij} \qquad 2.33$$

where δ_{ij} is the Kronecker delta. ϕ is the dilatation.

In terms of strain:

$$e_{ij} = -\frac{\lambda}{2\mu(3\lambda+2\mu)}\delta_{ij}\theta + \frac{1}{2\mu}\tau_{ij} = \frac{1+\sigma}{E}\tau_{ij} - \frac{\sigma}{E}\theta\delta_{ij} \qquad 2.34$$

where θ is the stress invariant, $\theta = \tau_{11} + \tau_{22} + \tau_{33}$.

(b) Cartesian.

$$\tau_{xx} = \frac{E}{(1+\sigma)(1-2\sigma)}[(1-\sigma)e_{xx} + \sigma(e_{yy}+e_{zz})] \qquad 2.35$$

$$\tau_{yy} = \frac{E}{(1+\sigma)(1-2\sigma)}[(1-\sigma)e_{yy} + \sigma(e_{zz}+e_{xx})]$$

$$\tau_{zz} = \frac{E}{(1+\sigma)(1-2\sigma)}[(1-\sigma)e_{zz} + \sigma(e_{xx}+e_{yy})]$$

$$\tau_{yz} = \tau_{zy} = \frac{E}{1+\sigma}e_{yz} = 2\mu e_{yz} = \mu\gamma_{yz}$$

$$\tau_{zx} = \tau_{xz} = \frac{E}{1+\sigma}e_{zx} = 2\mu e_{zx} = \mu\gamma_{zx}$$

$$\tau_{xy} = \tau_{yx} = \frac{E}{1+\sigma}e_{xy} = 2\mu e_{xy} = \mu\gamma_{xy}$$

In terms of strain:

$$e_{xx} = \frac{1}{E}[\tau_{xx} - \sigma(\tau_{yy}+\tau_{zz})] \qquad 2.36$$

$$e_{yy} = \frac{1}{E}[\tau_{yy} - \sigma(\tau_{xx}+\tau_{zz})]$$

$$e_{zz} = \frac{1}{E}[\tau_{zz} - \sigma(\tau_{xx}+\tau_{yy})]$$

$$e_{yz} = \frac{1+\sigma}{E}\tau_{yz} = \frac{1}{2\mu}\tau_{yz} = \frac{1}{2}\gamma_{yz}$$

$$e_{zx} = \frac{1+\sigma}{E}\tau_{zx} = \frac{1}{2\mu}\tau_{zx} = \frac{1}{2}\gamma_{zx}$$

$$e_{xy} = \frac{1+\sigma}{E}\tau_{xy} = \frac{1}{2\mu}\tau_{xy} = \frac{1}{2}\gamma_{xy}$$

(c) Cylindrical.

$$\tau_{rr} = \frac{E}{(1+\sigma)(1-2\sigma)}[(1-\sigma)e_{rr} + \sigma(e_{\theta\theta}+e_{zz})] \quad \mathbf{2.37}$$

$$\tau_{\theta\theta} = \frac{E}{(1+\sigma)(1-2\sigma)}[(1-\sigma)e_{\theta\theta} + \sigma(e_{rr}+e_{zz})]$$

$$\tau_{zz} = \frac{E}{(1+\sigma)(1-2\sigma)}[(1-\sigma)e_{zz} + \sigma(e_{rr}+e_{\theta\theta})]$$

$$\tau_{r\theta} = \frac{E}{(1+\sigma)}e_{r\theta} = 2\mu e_{r\theta} = \mu\gamma_{r\theta}$$

$$\tau_{rz} = \frac{E}{(1+\sigma)}e_{rz} = 2\mu e_{rz} = \mu\gamma_{rz}$$

$$\tau_{\theta z} = \frac{E}{(1+\sigma)}e_{\theta z} = 2\mu e_{\theta z} = \mu\gamma_{\theta z}$$

In terms of strain:

$$e_{rr} = \frac{1}{E}[\tau_{rr} - \sigma(\tau_{\theta\theta}+\tau_{zz})] \quad \mathbf{2.38}$$

$$e_{\theta\theta} = \frac{1}{E}[\tau_{\theta\theta} - \sigma(\tau_{rr}+\tau_{zz})]$$

$$e_{zz} = \frac{1}{E}[\tau_{zz} - \sigma(\tau_{\theta\theta}+\tau_{rr})]$$

$$e_{r\theta} = \frac{1+\sigma}{E}\tau_{r\theta} = \frac{1}{2\mu}\tau_{r\theta} = \frac{1}{2}\gamma_{r\theta}$$

$$e_{rz} = \frac{1+\sigma}{E}\tau_{rz} = \frac{1}{2\mu}\tau_{rz} = \frac{1}{2}\gamma_{rz}$$

$$e_{\theta z} = \frac{1+\sigma}{E}\tau_{\theta z} = \frac{1}{2\mu}\tau_{\theta z} = \frac{1}{2}\gamma_{\theta z}$$

(d) Spherical.

$$\tau_{rr} = \frac{E}{(1+\sigma)(1-2\sigma)}[(1-\sigma)e_{rr} + \sigma(e_{\theta\theta}+e_{\phi\phi})] \quad \mathbf{2.39}$$

$$\tau_{\theta\theta} = \frac{E}{(1+\sigma)(1-2\sigma)}[(1-\sigma)e_{\theta\theta} + \sigma(e_{rr}+e_{\phi\phi})]$$

$$\tau_{\phi\phi} = \frac{E}{(1+\sigma)(1-2\sigma)}[(1-\sigma)e_{\phi\phi} + \sigma(e_{rr}+e_{\theta\theta})]$$

$$\tau_{r\theta} = \frac{E}{1+\sigma}e_{r\theta} = 2\mu e_{r\theta} = \mu\gamma_{r\theta}$$

$$\tau_{\theta\phi} = \frac{E}{1+\sigma}e_{\theta\phi} = 2\mu e_{\theta\phi} = \mu\gamma_{\theta\phi}$$

$$\tau_{r\phi} = \frac{E}{1+\sigma}e_{r\phi} = 2\mu e_{r\phi} = \mu\gamma_{r\phi}$$

In terms of strain:

$$e_{rr} = \frac{1}{E}[\tau_{rr} - \sigma(\tau_{\theta\theta} + \tau_{\phi\phi})] \qquad \textbf{2.40}$$

$$e_{\theta\theta} = \frac{1}{E}[\tau_{\theta\theta} - \sigma(\tau_{rr} + \tau_{\phi\phi})]$$

$$e_{\phi\phi} = \frac{1}{E}[\tau_{\phi\phi} - \sigma(\tau_{rr} + \tau_{\theta\theta})]$$

$$e_{r\theta} = \frac{1+\sigma}{E}\tau_{r\theta} = \frac{1}{2\mu}\tau_{r\theta} = \frac{1}{2}\gamma_{r\theta}$$

$$e_{r\phi} = \frac{1+\sigma}{E}\tau_{r\phi} = \frac{1}{2\mu}\tau_{r\phi} = \frac{1}{2}\gamma_{r\phi}$$

$$e_{\theta\phi} = \frac{1+\sigma}{E}\tau_{\theta\phi} = \frac{1}{2\mu}\tau_{\theta\phi} = \frac{1}{2}\gamma_{\theta\phi}$$

(e) Plane Strain, Cartesian Coordinates.

$$\tau_{xx} = \frac{E}{(1+\sigma)(1-2\sigma)}[(1-\sigma)e_{xx} + \sigma e_{yy}] \qquad \textbf{2.41a}$$

$$\tau_{yy} = \frac{E}{(1+\sigma)(1-2\sigma)}[(1-\sigma)e_{yy} + \sigma e_{xx}]$$

$$\tau_{zz} = \frac{E\sigma}{(1+\sigma)(1-2\sigma)}[e_{xx} + e_{yy}]$$

$$\tau_{xy} = \frac{E}{(1+\sigma)}e_{xy} = 2\mu e_{xy} = \mu\gamma_{xy}$$

$$\tau_{yz} = \tau_{xz} = 0$$

In terms of strain:

$$e_{xx} = \frac{1+\sigma}{E}[(1-\sigma)\tau_{xx} - \sigma\tau_{yy}] \qquad \textbf{2.41b}$$

$$e_{yy} = \frac{1+\sigma}{E}[(1-\sigma)\tau_{yy} - \sigma\tau_{xx}]$$

$$e_{zz} = 0$$

$$e_{xy} = \frac{1+\sigma}{E}\tau_{xy} = \frac{1}{2\mu}\tau_{xy} = \frac{1}{2}\gamma_{xy}$$

$$e_{yz} = e_{xz} = 0$$

(f) Plane Strain, Polar Coordinates.

$$\tau_{rr} = \frac{E}{(1+\sigma)(1-2\sigma)}[(1-\sigma)e_{rr} + \sigma e_{\theta\theta}] \qquad \textbf{2.42}$$

$$\tau_{\theta\theta} = \frac{E}{(1+\sigma)(1-2\sigma)}[(1-\sigma)e_{\theta\theta} + \sigma e_{rr}]$$

$$\tau_{zz} = \frac{E\sigma}{(1+\sigma)(1-2\sigma)}[e_{rr} + e_{\theta\theta}]$$

$$\tau_{r\theta} = \frac{E}{1+\sigma} e_{r\theta} = 2\mu e_{r\theta} = \mu\gamma_{r\theta}$$

$$\tau_{rz} = \tau_{z\theta} = 0$$

In terms of strain:

$$e_{rr} = \frac{1+\sigma}{E}[(1-\sigma)\tau_{rr} - \sigma\tau_{\theta\theta}] \qquad \textbf{2.43}$$

$$e_{\theta\theta} = \frac{1+\sigma}{E}[(1-\sigma)\tau_{\theta\theta} - \sigma\tau_{rr}]$$

$$e_{zz} = 0$$

$$e_{r\theta} = \frac{1+\sigma}{E}\tau_{r\theta} = \frac{1}{2\mu}\tau_{r\theta} = \frac{1}{2}\gamma_{r\theta}$$

$$e_{rz} = e_{\theta z} = 0$$

(g) Plane Stress, Cartesian Coordinates.

$$\tau_{xx} = \frac{E}{1-\sigma^2}(e_{xx} + \sigma e_{yy}) \qquad \textbf{2.44}$$

$$\tau_{yy} = \frac{E}{1-\sigma^2}(e_{yy} + \sigma e_{xx})$$

$$\tau_{zz} = 0$$

$$\tau_{xy} = \frac{E}{1+\sigma} e_{xy} = 2\mu e_{xy} = \mu\gamma_{xy}$$

$$\tau_{yz} = \tau_{xz} = 0$$

In terms of strain:

$$e_{xx} = \frac{1}{E}(\tau_{xx} - \sigma\tau_{yy}) \qquad \textbf{2.45}$$

$$e_{yy} = \frac{1}{E}(\tau_{yy} - \sigma\tau_{xx})$$

$$e_{zz} = \frac{1}{E}(\tau_{xx} + \tau_{yy})$$

$$e_{xy} = \frac{1+\sigma}{E}\tau_{xy} = \frac{1}{2\mu}\tau_{xy} = \frac{1}{2}\gamma_{xy}$$

$$e_{yz} = e_{xz} = 0$$

(h) Plane Stress, Polar Coordinates.

$$\tau_{rr} = \frac{E}{1-\sigma^2}(e_{rr} + \sigma e_{\theta\theta}) \qquad \textbf{2.46}$$

$$\tau_{\theta\theta} = \frac{E}{1-\sigma^2}(e_{\theta\theta} + \sigma e_{rr})$$

$$\tau_{zz} = 0$$

$$\tau_{r\theta} = \frac{E}{1+\sigma} e_{r\theta} = 2\mu e_{r\theta} = \mu \gamma_{r\theta}$$

$$\tau_{rz} = \tau_{\theta z} = 0$$

In terms of strain:

$$e_{rr} = \frac{1}{E}(\tau_{rr} - \sigma\tau_{\theta\theta}) \qquad 2.47$$

$$e_{\theta\theta} = \frac{1}{E}(\tau_{\theta\theta} - \sigma\tau_{rr})$$

$$e_{zz} = \frac{1}{E}(\tau_{rr} + \tau_{\theta\theta})$$

$$e_{r\theta} = \frac{1+\sigma}{E}\tau_{r\theta} = \frac{1}{2\mu}\tau_{r\theta} = \frac{1}{2}\gamma_{r\theta}$$

$$e_{rz} = e_{\theta z} = 0$$

2.4 RELATIONSHIPS BETWEEN THE ELASTIC CONSTANTS

The following is a listing of the more common relationships between the elastic constants. E is the Young's modulus, and σ is the Poisson ratio. The Lamé constants are denoted by λ and μ. μ is sometimes called the modulus of rigidity, or shear modulus and is often written, especially in engineering work, as G. k is the bulk modulus.

$$E = \frac{\mu(3\lambda + 2\mu)}{\lambda + \mu} \qquad 2.48$$

$$E = \frac{\lambda(1+\sigma)(1-2\sigma)}{\sigma} \qquad 2.49$$

$$E = \frac{9k(k-\lambda)}{3k-\lambda} \qquad 2.50$$

$$E = 2\mu(1+\sigma) \qquad 2.51$$

$$E = \frac{9k\mu}{3k+\mu} \qquad 2.52$$

$$E = 3k(1-2\sigma) \qquad 2.53$$

$$\mu = \frac{\sqrt{(E+\lambda)^2 + 8\lambda^2} + (E-3\lambda)}{4} \qquad 2.54$$

$$\mu = \frac{\lambda(1-2\sigma)}{2\sigma} \qquad 2.55$$

$$\mu = \frac{3(k-\lambda)}{2} \qquad 2.56$$

$$\mu = \frac{E}{2(1+\sigma)} \qquad 2.57$$

$$\mu = \frac{3Ek}{9k-E} \qquad 2.58$$

$$\mu = \frac{3k(1-2\sigma)}{2(1+\sigma)} \tag{2.59}$$

$$\lambda = \frac{\mu(2\mu - E)}{E - 3\mu} \tag{2.60}$$

$$\lambda = \frac{2\mu\sigma}{1-2\sigma} \tag{2.61}$$

$$\lambda = \frac{3k - 2\mu}{3} \tag{2.62}$$

$$\lambda = \frac{\sigma E}{(1+\sigma)(1-2\sigma)} \tag{2.63}$$

$$\lambda = \frac{3k(3k-E)}{9k-E} \tag{2.64}$$

$$\lambda = \frac{3k\sigma}{1+\sigma} \tag{2.65}$$

$$\sigma = \frac{\lambda}{2(\lambda+\mu)} \tag{2.66}$$

$$\sigma = \frac{\sqrt{(E+\lambda)^2 + 8\lambda^2} - (E+\lambda)}{4\lambda} \tag{2.67}$$

$$\sigma = \frac{\lambda}{3k-\lambda} \tag{2.68}$$

$$\sigma = \frac{E - 2\mu}{2\mu} \tag{2.69}$$

$$\sigma = \frac{3k - 2\mu}{2(3k+\mu)} \tag{2.70}$$

$$\sigma = \frac{3k - E}{6k} \tag{2.71}$$

$$k = \frac{3\lambda + 2\mu}{3} \tag{2.72}$$

$$k = \frac{\sqrt{(E+\lambda)^2 + 8\lambda^2} + (3\lambda+E)}{6} \tag{2.73}$$

$$k = \frac{\lambda(1+\sigma)}{3\sigma} \tag{2.74}$$

$$k = \frac{\mu E}{3(3\mu - E)} \tag{2.75}$$

$$k = \frac{2\mu(1+\sigma)}{3(1-2\sigma)} \tag{2.76}$$

$$k = \frac{E}{3(1-2\sigma)} \tag{2.77}$$

2.5 EQUATIONS OF EQUILIBRIUM, HOMOGENEOUS ISOTROPIC MEDIA

The following equations, in various coordinates systems, express the conditions of static equilibrium in an elastic body. In dynamical situations acceleration terms must be added to the equations. Such dynamical situations are discussed in Section 2.11 of this chapter and in the chapter on Dynamics. τ_{ij} is the stress tensor, and F_i is an external body force.

(a) Cartesian Tensor.

$$\frac{\partial \tau_{ij}}{\partial x_j} + F_i = 0 \qquad \mathbf{2.78}$$

On a surface the equilibrium condition is given by:

$$T_i = \tau_{ij} n_j \qquad \mathbf{2.79}$$

where T_i is the stress vector on the surface and n_j is the outward normal vector.

(b) Cartesian.

$$\frac{\partial \tau_{xx}}{\partial x} + \frac{\partial \tau_{yx}}{\partial y} + \frac{\partial \tau_{zx}}{\partial z} + F_x = 0 \qquad \mathbf{2.80}$$

$$\frac{\partial \tau_{xy}}{\partial x} + \frac{\partial \tau_{yy}}{\partial y} + \frac{\partial \tau_{zy}}{\partial z} + F_y = 0$$

$$\frac{\partial \tau_{xz}}{\partial x} + \frac{\partial \tau_{yz}}{\partial y} + \frac{\partial \tau_{zz}}{\partial z} + F_z = 0$$

and on the surface:

$$T_x = l\tau_{xx} + m\tau_{yx} + n\tau_{zx} \qquad \mathbf{2.81}$$

$$T_y = l\tau_{xy} + m\tau_{yy} + n\tau_{zy}$$

$$T_z = l\tau_{xz} + m\tau_{yz} + n\tau_{zz}$$

where l, m, and n are the direction cosines of the surface normal vector $\mathbf{n}$ (see Fig. 2-2).

(c) Cylindrical.

$$\frac{\partial \tau_{rr}}{\partial r} + \frac{1}{r}\frac{\partial \tau_{r\theta}}{\partial \theta} + \frac{\partial \tau_{rz}}{\partial z} + \frac{\tau_{rr} - \tau_{\theta\theta}}{r} + F_r = 0 \qquad \mathbf{2.82}$$

$$\frac{\partial \tau_{r\theta}}{\partial r} + \frac{1}{r}\frac{\partial \tau_{\theta\theta}}{\partial \theta} + \frac{\partial \tau_{\theta z}}{\partial z} + \frac{2}{r}\tau_{r\theta} + F_\theta = 0$$

$$\frac{\partial \tau_{rz}}{\partial r} + \frac{1}{r}\frac{\partial \tau_{\theta z}}{\partial \theta} + \frac{\partial \tau_{zz}}{\partial z} + \frac{1}{r}\tau_{rz} + F_z = 0$$

(d) Spherical.

$$\frac{\partial \tau_{rr}}{\partial r} + \frac{1}{r\sin\theta}\frac{\partial \tau_{r\phi}}{\partial \phi} + \frac{1}{r}\frac{\partial \tau_{r\theta}}{\partial \theta} + \frac{2\tau_{rr} - \tau_{\phi\phi} - \tau_{\theta\theta} + \tau_{r\theta}\cot\theta}{r} + F_r = 0 \qquad \mathbf{2.83}$$

$$\frac{\partial \tau_{r\phi}}{\partial r} + \frac{1}{r\sin\theta}\frac{\partial \tau_{\phi\phi}}{\partial \phi} + \frac{1}{r}\frac{\partial \tau_{\theta\phi}}{\partial \theta} + \frac{3\tau_{r\phi} + 2\tau_{\phi\theta}\cot\theta}{r} + F_\phi = 0$$

$$\frac{\partial \tau_{r\theta}}{\partial r} + \frac{1}{r\sin\theta}\frac{\partial \tau_{\phi\theta}}{\partial \phi} + \frac{1}{r}\frac{\partial \tau_{\theta\theta}}{\partial \theta} + \frac{3\tau_{r\theta} + (\tau_{\theta\theta} - \tau_{\phi\phi})\cot\theta}{r} + F_\theta = 0$$

(e) Plane Stress, Cartesian Coordinates.

$$\frac{\partial \tau_{xx}}{\partial x} + \frac{\partial \tau_{yx}}{\partial y} + F_x = 0 \qquad \textbf{2.84}$$

$$\frac{\partial \tau_{xy}}{\partial x} + \frac{\partial \tau_{yy}}{\partial y} + F_y = 0$$

(f) Plane Stress, Polar Coordinates.

$$\frac{\partial \tau_{rr}}{\partial r} + \frac{1}{r}\frac{\partial \tau_{r\theta}}{\partial \theta} + \frac{\tau_{rr} - \tau_{\theta\theta}}{r} + F_r = 0 \qquad \textbf{2.85}$$

$$\frac{1}{r}\frac{\partial \tau_{\theta\theta}}{\partial \theta} + \frac{\partial \tau_{r\theta}}{\partial r} + \frac{2\tau_{r\theta}}{r} + F_\theta = 0$$

(g) Plane Strain, Cartesian Coordinates.

$$\frac{\partial \tau_{xx}}{\partial x} + \frac{\partial \tau_{yx}}{\partial y} + F_x = 0 \qquad \textbf{2.86}$$

$$\frac{\partial \tau_{xy}}{\partial x} + \frac{\partial \tau_{yy}}{\partial y} + F_y = 0$$

$$\frac{\partial \tau_{zz}}{\partial z} + F_z = 0$$

(h) Plane Strain, Polar Coordinates.

$$\frac{\partial \tau_{rr}}{\partial r} + \frac{1}{r}\frac{\partial \tau_{r\theta}}{\partial \theta} + \frac{\tau_{rr} - \tau_{\theta\theta}}{r} + F_r = 0 \qquad \textbf{2.87}$$

$$\frac{1}{r}\frac{\partial \tau_{\theta\theta}}{\partial \theta} + \frac{\partial \tau_{r\theta}}{\partial r} + \frac{2\tau_{r\theta}}{r} + F_\theta = 0$$

$$\frac{\partial \tau_{zz}}{\partial z} + F_z = 0$$

(i) Orthogonal Curvilinear.

Note. The summation convention of Cartesian tensor analysis is not used below.

$$\frac{\partial}{\partial x_i}(h_1 h_2 h_3 \tau_{ii}) - \frac{1}{2}\sum_{j=1}^{3} \frac{h_1 h_2 h_3}{h_j^2}\tau_{jj}\frac{\partial h_j^2}{\partial x_i} \qquad \textbf{2.88}$$

$$+ \sum_{j \neq i} \frac{\partial}{\partial x_j}\left(\frac{h_1 h_2 h_3 h_i^2 \tau_{ij}}{h_i h_j}\right) + (h_1 h_2 h_3) h_i \cdot F_i = 0$$

(j) Equilibrium in Terms of Displacement, Cartesian Tensor.

The Navier equilibrium equations in terms of displacement u_i can be written as:

$$\mu \frac{\partial^2 u_i}{\partial x_k \, \partial x_k} + (\lambda + \mu)\frac{\partial \phi}{\partial x_i} + F_i = 0 \qquad \textbf{2.89}$$

or in terms of rotation as:

$$(\lambda + 2\mu)\frac{\partial \phi}{\partial x_i} - 2\mu(\nabla \times \omega)_i + F_i = 0 \qquad \textbf{2.90}$$

where the dilatation $\phi = e_{11} + e_{22} + e_{33}$, and μ is the Lamé constant, sometimes called the shear modulus or modulus of rigidity. λ is the other Lamé constant.

(k) Equilibrium in Terms of Displacement, Vector Notation.

In the following, **u** is the displacement vector, $\boldsymbol{\omega}$ is the rotation vector (see Section 2.1), and λ and μ are the Lamé constants. μ is sometimes called the shear modulus or modulus of rigidity. ϕ is the dilatation, $\phi = \nabla \cdot \mathbf{u}$.

$$(\lambda + 2\mu)\nabla\phi - \mu\nabla \times (\nabla \times \mathbf{u}) + \mathbf{F} = 0 \qquad \textbf{2.91}$$

which can also be written as:

$$(\lambda + \mu)\nabla\phi + \mu\nabla^2\mathbf{u} + \mathbf{F} = 0$$

or equivalently:

$$\nabla^2\mathbf{u} + \frac{1}{1-2\sigma}\nabla(\nabla \cdot \mathbf{u}) + \frac{2(1+\sigma)}{E}\mathbf{F} = 0 \qquad \textbf{2.92}$$

or

$$\nabla^2\mathbf{u} + \frac{1}{1-2\sigma}\nabla(\nabla \cdot \mathbf{u}) + \frac{\mathbf{F}}{\mu} = 0$$

or in terms of the rotation vector:

$$(\lambda + 2\mu)\nabla\phi - 2\mu\nabla \times \boldsymbol{\omega} + \mathbf{F} = 0 \qquad \textbf{2.93}$$

(l) Equilibrium in Terms of Displacement, Orthogonal Curvilinear.

In the following ω_1, ω_2, and ω_3 are the three components of rotation in the three coordinate directions. λ and μ are the Lamé constants. μ is sometimes called the shear modulus or modulus of rigidity. ϕ is the dilatation which can be written:

$$\phi = \frac{1}{h_1h_2h_3}\left\{\frac{\partial}{\partial x_1}(u_1h_2h_3) + \frac{\partial}{\partial x_2}(u_2h_3h_1) + \frac{\partial}{\partial x_3}(u_3h_1h_2)\right\} \qquad \textbf{2.94}$$

The equilibrium equations can be written:

$$\frac{(\lambda+2\mu)}{h_1}\frac{\partial\phi}{\partial x_1} - \frac{2\mu}{h_2h_3}\frac{\partial}{\partial x_2}(h_3\omega_3) + \frac{2\mu}{h_2h_3}\frac{\partial}{\partial x_3}(h_2\omega_2) + F_1 = 0 \qquad \textbf{2.95}$$

$$\frac{(\lambda+2\mu)}{h_2}\frac{\partial\phi}{\partial x_2} - \frac{2\mu}{h_1h_3}\frac{\partial}{\partial x_3}(\omega_1h_1) + \frac{2\mu}{h_1h_3}\frac{\partial}{\partial x_1}(h_3\omega_3) + F_2 = 0$$

$$\frac{(\lambda+2\mu)}{h_3}\frac{\partial\phi}{\partial x_3} - \frac{2\mu}{h_1h_2}\frac{\partial}{\partial x_1}(\omega_2h_2) + \frac{2\mu}{h_1h_2}\frac{\partial}{\partial x_2}(\omega_1h_1) + F_3 = 0$$

(m) Equilibrium in Terms of Displacement, Cartesian Coordinates.

In the following u, v, and w are the displacements in the x, y, and z directions respectively. σ is the Poisson ratio. In the equations, use has been made of the relationship, $\dfrac{\lambda+\mu}{\mu} = \dfrac{1}{1-2\sigma}$ in order to simplify the equations. (λ and μ are the Lamé constants). The Laplacian is:

$$\nabla^2 = \frac{\partial^2}{\partial x^2} + \frac{\partial^2}{\partial y^2} + \frac{\partial^2}{\partial z^2}$$

The equilibrium equations are then:

$$\nabla^2 u + \frac{1}{1-2\sigma}\frac{\partial}{\partial x}\left(\frac{\partial u}{\partial x}+\frac{\partial v}{\partial y}+\frac{\partial w}{\partial z}\right) + \frac{F_x}{\mu} = 0 \qquad \textbf{2.96}$$

$$\nabla^2 v + \frac{1}{1-2\sigma}\frac{\partial}{\partial y}\left(\frac{\partial u}{\partial x}+\frac{\partial v}{\partial y}+\frac{\partial w}{\partial z}\right) + \frac{F_y}{\mu} = 0$$

$$\nabla^2 w + \frac{1}{1-2\sigma}\frac{\partial}{\partial z}\left(\frac{\partial u}{\partial x}+\frac{\partial v}{\partial y}+\frac{\partial w}{\partial z}\right) + \frac{F_z}{\mu} = 0$$

On the surfaces the boundary conditions take the form:

$$T_x = \lambda\phi l + \mu\left[2\frac{\partial u}{\partial x}l + \left(\frac{\partial u}{\partial y}+\frac{\partial v}{\partial x}\right)m + \left(\frac{\partial u}{\partial z}+\frac{\partial w}{\partial x}\right)n\right] \qquad \textbf{2.97}$$

$$T_y = \lambda\phi m + \mu\left[2\frac{\partial v}{\partial y}m + \left(\frac{\partial v}{\partial z}+\frac{\partial w}{\partial y}\right)n + \left(\frac{\partial v}{\partial x}+\frac{\partial u}{\partial y}\right)l\right]$$

$$T_z = \lambda\phi n + \mu\left[2\frac{\partial w}{\partial z}n + \left(\frac{\partial w}{\partial x}+\frac{\partial u}{\partial z}\right)l + \left(\frac{\partial w}{\partial y}+\frac{\partial v}{\partial z}\right)m\right]$$

where l, m, and n are the direction cosines of the normal vector **n**. T_x, T_y, and T_z are the components of the stress vector, and the dilatation

$$\phi = e_{xx} + e_{yy} + e_{zz} = \frac{\partial u}{\partial x} + \frac{\partial v}{\partial y} + \frac{\partial w}{\partial z}$$

(n) *Equilibrium in Terms of Displacement, Cylindrical Coordinates.*

In the following, u_r, u_θ, and u_z are the components of displacement in the r, θ, and z directions respectively. λ and μ are the Lamé constants. μ is sometimes called the shear modulus or modulus of rigidity. The Laplacian is:

$$\nabla^2 = \frac{\partial^2}{\partial r^2} + \frac{1}{r}\frac{\partial}{\partial r} + \frac{1}{r^2}\frac{\partial^2}{\partial \theta^2} + \frac{\partial^2}{\partial z^2}$$

The equilibrium equations are then:

$$(\lambda+\mu)\frac{\partial}{\partial r}\left[\frac{1}{r}\frac{\partial}{\partial r}(ru_r) + \frac{1}{r}\frac{\partial u_\theta}{\partial \theta} + \frac{\partial u_z}{\partial z}\right] + \mu\left[\nabla^2 u_r - \frac{u_r}{r^2} - \frac{2}{r^2}\frac{\partial u_\theta}{\partial \theta}\right] + F_r = 0 \qquad \textbf{2.98}$$

$$(\lambda+\mu)\frac{1}{r}\frac{\partial}{\partial \theta}\left[\frac{1}{r}\frac{\partial}{\partial r}(ru_r) + \frac{1}{r}\frac{\partial u_\theta}{\partial \theta} + \frac{\partial u_z}{\partial z}\right] + \mu\left[\nabla^2 u_\theta + \frac{2}{r^2}\frac{\partial u_r}{\partial \theta} - \frac{u_\theta}{r^2}\right] + F_\theta = 0$$

$$(\lambda+\mu)\frac{\partial}{\partial z}\left[\frac{1}{r}\frac{\partial}{\partial r}(ru_r) + \frac{1}{r}\frac{\partial u_\theta}{\partial \theta} + \frac{\partial u_z}{\partial z}\right] + \mu[\nabla^2 u_z] + F_z = 0$$

(o) *Equilibrium in Terms of Displacement, Spherical Coordinates.*

In the following, u_r, u_θ, and u_ϕ are the displacement components in the r, θ, and ϕ directions respectively. λ and μ are the Lamé constants. μ is sometimes called the modulus of rigidity or the shear modulus. The Laplacian in spherical coordinates is:

$$\nabla^2 = \frac{1}{r^2}\frac{\partial}{\partial r}\left(r^2\frac{\partial}{\partial r}\right) + \frac{1}{r^2\sin\theta}\frac{\partial}{\partial \theta}\left(\sin\theta\frac{\partial}{\partial \theta}\right) + \frac{1}{r^2\sin^2\theta}\frac{\partial^2}{\partial \phi^2}$$

The equilibrium equations are then:

$$(\lambda+\mu)\frac{\partial}{\partial r}\left[\frac{1}{r^2}\frac{\partial}{\partial r}(r^2u_r) + \frac{1}{r\sin\theta}\frac{\partial}{\partial\theta}(u_\theta\sin\theta) + \frac{1}{r\sin\theta}\frac{\partial u_\phi}{\partial\phi}\right]$$
$$+ \mu\left[\nabla^2 u_r - \frac{2u_r}{r^2} - \frac{2}{r^2}\frac{\partial u_\theta}{\partial\theta} - \frac{2u_\theta\cot\theta}{r^2} - \frac{2}{r^2\sin\theta}\frac{\partial u_\phi}{\partial\phi}\right] + F_r = 0 \qquad \textbf{2.99}$$

$$(\lambda+\mu)\frac{1}{r}\frac{\partial}{\partial\theta}\left[\frac{1}{r^2}\frac{\partial}{\partial r}(r^2u_r) + \frac{1}{r\sin\theta}\frac{\partial}{\partial\theta}(u_\theta\sin\theta) + \frac{1}{r\sin\theta}\frac{\partial u_\phi}{\partial\phi}\right]$$
$$+ \mu\left[\nabla^2 u_\theta + \frac{2}{r^2}\frac{\partial u_r}{\partial\theta} - \frac{u_\theta}{r^2\sin^2\theta} - \frac{2\cos\theta}{r^2\sin^2\theta}\frac{\partial u_\phi}{\partial\phi}\right] + F_\theta = 0$$

$$(\lambda+\mu)\frac{1}{r\sin\theta}\frac{\partial}{\partial\phi}\left[\frac{1}{r^2}\frac{\partial}{\partial r}(r^2u_r) + \frac{1}{r\sin\theta}\frac{\partial}{\partial\theta}(u_\theta\sin\theta) + \frac{1}{r\sin\theta}\frac{\partial u_\phi}{\partial\phi}\right]$$
$$+ \mu\left[\nabla^2 u_\phi - \frac{u_\phi}{r^2\sin^2\theta} + \frac{2}{r^2\sin^2\theta}\frac{\partial u_r}{\partial\phi} + \frac{2\cos\theta}{r^2\sin^2\theta}\frac{\partial u_\theta}{\partial\phi}\right] + F_\phi = 0$$

2.6 COMPATIBILITY EQUATIONS

The Compatibility equations are written out below in various coordinate systems. Of particular interest are the compatibility equations in terms of stress. The equations are written in their basic form in terms of strain; then various forms, of importance in analysis, are written out in terms of stress, implicit use having been made of the stress-strain relationships for homogeneous isotropic media.

(a) In Terms of Strain, Cartesian Tensor.

$$\frac{\partial^2 e_{ij}}{\partial x_k\,\partial x_l} + \frac{\partial^2 e_{kl}}{\partial x_i\,\partial x_j} - \frac{\partial^2 e_{ik}}{\partial x_j\,\partial x_l} - \frac{\partial^2 e_{jl}}{\partial x_i\,\partial x_k} = 0 \qquad \textbf{2.100}$$

(b) In Terms of Strain, Cartesian Coordinates.

$$\frac{\partial^2 e_{xx}}{\partial y\,\partial z} = \frac{\partial}{\partial x}\left(-\frac{\partial e_{yz}}{\partial x} + \frac{\partial e_{zx}}{\partial y} + \frac{\partial e_{xy}}{\partial z}\right) \qquad \textbf{2.101}$$

$$\frac{\partial^2 e_{yy}}{\partial z\,\partial x} = \frac{\partial}{\partial y}\left(-\frac{\partial e_{zx}}{\partial y} + \frac{\partial e_{yx}}{\partial z} + \frac{\partial e_{yz}}{\partial x}\right)$$

$$\frac{\partial^2 e_{zz}}{\partial x\,\partial y} = \frac{\partial}{\partial z}\left(-\frac{\partial e_{xy}}{\partial z} + \frac{\partial e_{yz}}{\partial x} + \frac{\partial e_{zx}}{\partial y}\right)$$

$$2\frac{\partial^2 e_{xy}}{\partial x\,\partial y} = \frac{\partial^2 e_{xx}}{\partial y^2} + \frac{\partial^2 e_{yy}}{\partial x^2}$$

$$2\frac{\partial^2 e_{yz}}{\partial y\,\partial z} = \frac{\partial^2 e_{yy}}{\partial z^2} + \frac{\partial^2 e_{zz}}{\partial y^2}$$

$$2\frac{\partial^2 e_{zx}}{\partial z\,\partial x} = \frac{\partial^2 e_{zz}}{\partial x^2} + \frac{\partial^2 e_{xx}}{\partial z^2}$$

(c) Plane Strain, in Terms of Strain.

Only one equation remains here and is written out in Cartesian form:

$$\frac{\partial^2 e_{xx}}{\partial y^2} + \frac{\partial^2 e_{yy}}{\partial x^2} = 2\frac{\partial^2 e_{xy}}{\partial x\,\partial y} \qquad 2.102$$

(d) Plane Stress, in Terms of Strain.

Written out in Cartesian form these are:

$$\frac{\partial^2 e_{yy}}{\partial z^2} + \frac{\partial^2 e_{zz}}{\partial y^2} = 0 \qquad 2.103$$

$$\frac{\partial^2 e_{zz}}{\partial x^2} + \frac{\partial^2 e_{xx}}{\partial z^2} = 0$$

$$\frac{\partial^2 e_{xx}}{\partial y^2} + \frac{\partial^2 e_{yy}}{\partial x^2} = 2\frac{\partial^2 e_{xy}}{\partial x\,\partial y}$$

$$\frac{\partial^2 e_{xx}}{\partial y\,\partial z} = \frac{\partial^2 e_{xy}}{\partial x\,\partial z}$$

$$\frac{\partial^2 e_{yy}}{\partial x\,\partial z} = \frac{\partial^2 e_{xy}}{\partial y\,\partial z}$$

$$\frac{\partial^2 e_{zz}}{\partial x\,\partial y} = -\frac{\partial^2 e_{xy}}{\partial z^2}$$

(e) The Beltrami-Michell Equations.

The Compatibility equations in terms of stresses are known as the Beltrami-Michell equations. These can be written in Cartesian tensor form as:

$$\nabla^2\tau_{ij} + \frac{1}{1+\sigma}\frac{\partial^2\theta}{\partial x_i\,\partial x_j} = -\frac{\sigma}{1-\sigma}\,\delta_{ij}\frac{\partial F_k}{\partial x_k} - \left(\frac{\partial F_i}{\partial x_j} + \frac{\partial F_j}{\partial x_i}\right) \qquad 2.104$$

where the stress invariant $\theta = \tau_{11} + \tau_{22} + \tau_{33}$. σ is the Poisson ratio, and δ_{ij} is the Kronecker delta. In Cartesian coordinates the Beltrami-Michell equations are:

$$\nabla^2\tau_{xx} + \frac{1}{1+\sigma}\frac{\partial^2\theta}{\partial x^2} = -\frac{\sigma}{1-\sigma}\nabla\cdot\mathbf{F} - 2\frac{\partial F_x}{\partial x} \qquad 2.105$$

$$\nabla^2\tau_{yy} + \frac{1}{1+\sigma}\frac{\partial^2\theta}{\partial y^2} = -\frac{\sigma}{1-\sigma}\nabla\cdot\mathbf{F} - 2\frac{\partial F_y}{\partial y}$$

$$\nabla^2\tau_{zz} + \frac{1}{1+\sigma}\frac{\partial^2\theta}{\partial z^2} = -\frac{\sigma}{1-\sigma}\nabla\cdot\mathbf{F} - 2\frac{\partial F_z}{\partial z}$$

$$\nabla^2\tau_{yz} + \frac{1}{1+\sigma}\frac{\partial^2\theta}{\partial y\,\partial z} = -\left(\frac{\partial F_y}{\partial z} + \frac{\partial F_z}{\partial y}\right)$$

$$\nabla^2\tau_{zx} + \frac{1}{1+\sigma}\frac{\partial^2\theta}{\partial z\,\partial x} = -\left(\frac{\partial F_z}{\partial x} + \frac{\partial F_x}{\partial z}\right)$$

$$\nabla^2\tau_{xy} + \frac{1}{1+\sigma}\frac{\partial^2\theta}{\partial x\,\partial y} = -\left(\frac{\partial F_x}{\partial y} + \frac{\partial F_y}{\partial x}\right)$$

where the stress invariant $\theta = \tau_{xx} + \tau_{yy} + \tau_{zz}$.

(f) Compatibility in Terms of Stress, Body Forces Conservative.

If the body force **F** is given in terms of a potential Ω as

$$\mathbf{F} = -\nabla\Omega$$

then the Beltrami-Michell equation becomes in Cartesian tensor form:

$$\nabla^2\tau_{ij} + \frac{1}{1+\sigma}\frac{\partial^2\theta}{\partial x_i\,\partial x_j} = \frac{\sigma}{1-\sigma}\delta_{ij}\nabla^2\Omega + 2\frac{\partial^2\Omega}{\partial x_j\,\partial x_i} \qquad \textbf{2.106}$$

where the stress invariant $\theta = \tau_{11} + \tau_{22} + \tau_{33}$.

If **F** is a constant, we get the equation of Beltrami:

$$\nabla^2\tau_{ij} + \frac{1}{1+\sigma}\frac{\partial^2\theta}{\partial x_i\,\partial x_j} = 0 \qquad \textbf{2.107}$$

in Cartesian tensor form.

Written out in Cartesian coordinates, these Beltrami equations become:

$$\nabla^2\tau_{xx} + \frac{1}{1+\sigma}\frac{\partial^2\theta}{\partial x^2} = 0 \qquad \textbf{2.108}$$

$$\nabla^2\tau_{yy} + \frac{1}{1+\sigma}\frac{\partial^2\theta}{\partial y^2} = 0$$

$$\nabla^2\tau_{zz} + \frac{1}{1+\sigma}\frac{\partial^2\theta}{\partial z^2} = 0$$

$$\nabla^2\tau_{xy} + \frac{1}{1+\sigma}\frac{\partial^2\theta}{\partial x\,\partial y} = 0$$

$$\nabla^2\tau_{xz} + \frac{1}{1+\sigma}\frac{\partial^2\theta}{\partial x\,\partial z} = 0$$

$$\nabla^2\tau_{yz} + \frac{1}{1+\sigma}\frac{\partial^2\theta}{\partial y\,\partial z} = 0$$

where ∇^2, the Laplacian, is $\nabla^2 = \dfrac{\partial^2}{\partial x^2} + \dfrac{\partial^2}{\partial y^2} + \dfrac{\partial^2}{\partial z^2}$.

In the case of constant **F**, the stress and strain invariants satisfy the following equation:

$$\nabla^2\theta = \nabla^2\phi = 0 \qquad \textbf{2.109}$$

and the stress and strain components all satisfy the biharmonic equation (if **F** is constant):

$$\nabla^4\tau_{ij} = 0 \qquad \textbf{2.110}$$

$$\nabla^4 e_{ij} = 0$$

(The biharmonic equation is written out in full in the appendix.)

In the case that **F** is not constant but is derivable from a potential function that is harmonic, equation 2.109 above is still valid.

2.7 STRESS FUNCTIONS IN TWO DIMENSIONS

(a) The Airy Stress Function.

The Airy stress function Φ is defined as:

$$\tau_{xx} = \Omega + \frac{\partial^2\Phi}{\partial y^2} \qquad \textbf{2.111}$$

$$\tau_{yy} = \Omega + \frac{\partial^2\Phi}{\partial x^2}$$

$$\tau_{xy} = -\frac{\partial^2\Phi}{\partial x\,\partial y}$$

where the body forces are determined from the potential function Ω as

$$F_x = -\frac{\partial\Omega}{\partial x}, \qquad F_y = -\frac{\partial\Omega}{\partial y}, \qquad \mathbf{F} = -\nabla\Omega$$

(b) Plain Strain, Cartesian Coordinates.

The Airy stress function in this case satisfies the equation:

$$\frac{\partial^4\Phi}{\partial x^4} + 2\frac{\partial^4\Phi}{\partial x^2\,\partial y^2} + \frac{\partial^4\Phi}{\partial y^4} + \frac{1-2\sigma}{1-\sigma}\left(\frac{\partial^2\Omega}{\partial x^2} + \frac{\partial^2\Omega}{\partial y^2}\right) = 0 \qquad \textbf{2.112}$$

where σ is the Poisson ratio. This equation may be written as:

$$\nabla^4\Phi + \frac{1-2\sigma}{1-\sigma}\nabla^2\Omega = 0 \qquad \textbf{2.113}$$

where Ω is the body force potential defined in part (a) above. In plain strain the stress τ_{zz} is given by $\tau_{zz} = f(x,y) + \text{constant}$, and τ_{xx}, τ_{yy} and τ_{xy} are given as in equation 2.111 above.

(c) Plain Strain, Polar Coordinates.

The Airy stress function satisfies the equation:

$$\nabla^4\Phi + \frac{1-2\sigma}{1-\sigma}\nabla^2\Omega = 0 \qquad \textbf{2.114}$$

which may be written out as:

$$\left(\frac{\partial^2}{\partial r^2} + \frac{1}{r}\frac{\partial}{\partial r} + \frac{1}{r^2}\frac{\partial^2}{\partial\theta^2}\right)\left(\frac{\partial^2\Phi}{\partial r^2} + \frac{1}{r}\frac{\partial\Phi}{\partial r} + \frac{1}{r^2}\frac{\partial^2\Phi}{\partial\theta^2}\right) \qquad \textbf{2.115}$$

$$+ \frac{1-2\sigma}{1-\sigma}\left(\frac{\partial^2\Omega}{\partial r^2} + \frac{1}{r}\frac{\partial\Omega}{\partial r} + \frac{1}{r^2}\frac{\partial^2\Omega}{\partial\theta^2}\right) = 0$$

The stresses are related to the stress function as:

$$\tau_{zz} = f(r,\theta) + \text{constant} \tag{2.116}$$

$$\tau_{rr} = \frac{1}{r}\frac{\partial\Phi}{\partial r} + \frac{1}{r^2}\frac{\partial^2\Phi}{\partial\theta^2} + \Omega$$

$$\tau_{\theta\theta} = \frac{\partial^2\Phi}{\partial r^2} + \Omega$$

$$\tau_{r\theta} = -\frac{\partial}{\partial r}\left(\frac{1}{r}\frac{\partial\Phi}{\partial\theta}\right)$$

(d) Plane Stress, Cartesian Coordinates.

The Airy stress function satisfies the equation:

$$\nabla^4\Phi + (1-\sigma)\nabla^2\Omega = 0 \tag{2.117}$$

or, written out:

$$\frac{\partial^4\Phi}{\partial x^4} + \frac{2\partial^4\Phi}{\partial x^2\,\partial y^2} + \frac{\partial^4\Phi}{\partial y^4} + (1-\sigma)\left(\frac{\partial^2\Omega}{\partial x^2} + \frac{\partial^2\Omega}{\partial y^2}\right) = 0 \tag{2.118}$$

where the stresses are related to the stress function as in part (*b*) above. Ω is the body force potential defined in part (*a*) above. $(\tau_{zz} = 0)$

(e) Plane Stress, Polar Coordinates.

The Airy stress function satisfies the equation:

$$\nabla^4\Phi + (1-\sigma)\nabla^2\Omega = 0 \tag{2.119}$$

or, written out:

$$\left(\frac{\partial^2}{\partial r^2} + \frac{1}{r}\frac{\partial}{\partial r} + \frac{1}{r^2}\frac{\partial^2}{\partial\theta^2}\right)\left(\frac{\partial^2\Phi}{\partial r^2} + \frac{1}{r}\frac{\partial\Phi}{\partial r} + \frac{1}{r^2}\frac{\partial^2\Phi}{\partial\theta^2}\right) \tag{2.120}$$

$$+ (1-\sigma)\left(\frac{\partial^2\Omega}{\partial r^2} + \frac{1}{r}\frac{\partial\Omega}{\partial r} + \frac{1}{r^2}\frac{\partial^2\Omega}{\partial\theta^2}\right) = 0$$

where the stresses are related to the stress function as in part (*c*) above. Ω is the body force potential defined in part (*a*) above. $(\tau_{zz} = 0)$

2.8 STRESS FUNCTIONS IN THREE DIMENSIONS

There are two commonly used systems of three dimensional stress functions, the Maxwell system and the Morera system.

(a) Maxwell's System.

In the absence of body forces the stress functions Φ_1, Φ_2, and Φ_3 are defined as:

$$\tau_{xx} = \frac{\partial^2\Phi_3}{\partial y^2} + \frac{\partial^2\Phi_2}{\partial z^2} \tag{2.121}$$

$$\tau_{yy} = \frac{\partial^2\Phi_1}{\partial z^2} + \frac{\partial^2\Phi_3}{\partial x^2}$$

$$\tau_{zz} = \frac{\partial^2\Phi_2}{\partial x^2} + \frac{\partial^2\Phi_1}{\partial y^2}$$

$$\tau_{xy} = -\frac{\partial^2\Phi_3}{\partial x\,\partial y}$$

$$\tau_{yz} = -\frac{\partial^2\Phi_1}{\partial y\,\partial z}$$

$$\tau_{zx} = -\frac{\partial^2\Phi_2}{\partial z\,\partial x}$$

The stress functions satisfy the following six equations where

$$\Phi = \Phi_1 + \Phi_2 + \Phi_3 \qquad \text{and} \qquad \Lambda = \frac{\partial^2\Phi_1}{\partial x^2} + \frac{\partial^2\Phi_2}{\partial y^2} + \frac{\partial^2\Phi_3}{\partial z^2}$$

$$(1+\sigma)\nabla^2\left[\frac{\partial^2\Phi_3}{\partial y^2} + \frac{\partial^2\Phi_2}{\partial z^2}\right] + \frac{\partial^2}{\partial x^2}(\nabla^2\Phi - \Lambda) = 0 \qquad \textbf{2.122}$$

$$(1+\sigma)\nabla^2\left[\frac{\partial^2\Phi_1}{\partial z^2} + \frac{\partial^2\Phi_3}{\partial x^2}\right] + \frac{\partial^2}{\partial y^2}(\nabla^2\Phi - \Lambda) = 0$$

$$(1+\sigma)\nabla^2\left[\frac{\partial^2\Phi_2}{\partial x^2} + \frac{\partial^2\Phi_1}{\partial y^2}\right] + \frac{\partial^2}{\partial z^2}(\nabla^2\Phi - \Lambda) = 0$$

$$\frac{\partial^2}{\partial x\,\partial y}[(1+\sigma)\nabla^2\Phi_3 - \nabla^2\Phi + \Lambda] = 0$$

$$\frac{\partial^2}{\partial y\,\partial z}[(1+\sigma)\nabla^2\Phi_1 - \nabla^2\Phi + \Lambda] = 0$$

$$\frac{\partial^2}{\partial z\,\partial x}[(1+\sigma)\nabla^2\Phi_2 - \nabla^2\Phi + \Lambda] = 0$$

(b) Morera's System.

The stress functions Φ_1, Φ_2, Φ_3 are defined in the absence of body forces as:

$$\tau_{xx} = \frac{\partial^2\Phi_1}{\partial y\,\partial z} \qquad \textbf{2.123}$$

$$\tau_{yy} = \frac{\partial^2\Phi_2}{\partial z\,\partial x}$$

$$\tau_{zz} = \frac{\partial^2\Phi_3}{\partial x\,\partial y}$$

$$\tau_{yz} = -\frac{1}{2}\frac{\partial}{\partial x}\left(-\frac{\partial\Phi_1}{\partial x} + \frac{\partial\Phi_2}{\partial y} + \frac{\partial\Phi_3}{\partial z}\right)$$

$$\tau_{zx} = -\frac{1}{2}\frac{\partial}{\partial y}\left(\frac{\partial\Phi_1}{\partial x} - \frac{\partial\Phi_2}{\partial y} + \frac{\partial\Phi_3}{\partial z}\right)$$

$$\tau_{xy} = -\frac{1}{2}\frac{\partial}{\partial z}\left(\frac{\partial\Phi_1}{\partial x} + \frac{\partial\Phi_2}{\partial y} - \frac{\partial\Phi_3}{\partial z}\right)$$

2.9 THERMAL STRESSES

The basic equations for stress and strain are the same as those in Sections 2.1 and 2.2. In the following equations α is the linear coefficient of thermal expansion, and T is the temperature excess above an arbitrary datum. E is Young's modulus, and σ is Poisson's ratio. The coefficient β is defined as: $\beta = \alpha(3\lambda + 2\mu) = 3\kappa\alpha$ where λ and μ are the Lamé constants and κ is the bulk modulus. μ is also known as the shear modulus and is sometimes denoted as G.

(a) Hooke's Law. (The shear relationships are unchanged.)

$$e_{xx} = \frac{1}{E}[\tau_{xx} - \sigma(\tau_{yy} + \tau_{zz})] + \alpha T \qquad \textbf{2.124}$$

$$e_{yy} = \frac{1}{E}[\tau_{yy} - \sigma(\tau_{xx} + \tau_{zz})] + \alpha T$$

$$e_{zz} = \frac{1}{E}[\tau_{zz} - \sigma(\tau_{xx} + \tau_{yy})] + \alpha T$$

or:

$$\tau_{xx} = \frac{E}{(1+\sigma)(1-2\sigma)}[(1-\sigma)e_{xx} + \sigma(e_{yy} + e_{zz})] - \beta T \qquad \textbf{2.125}$$

$$\tau_{yy} = \frac{E}{(1+\sigma)(1-2\sigma)}[(1-\sigma)e_{yy} + \sigma(e_{xx} + e_{zz})] - \beta T$$

$$\tau_{zz} = \frac{E}{(1+\sigma)(1-2\sigma)}[(1-\sigma)e_{zz} + \sigma(e_{xx} + e_{yy})] - \beta T$$

(b) Equilibrium.

In terms of stress the equilibrium equations are the same as those given in Section 2.5. In terms of strain or displacement the equilibrium equations take a different form. In terms of displacement in Cartesian Tensor notation:

$$\mu \nabla^2 u_i + (\lambda + \mu)\frac{\partial \phi}{\partial x_i} + F_i - \beta \nabla T = 0 \qquad \textbf{2.126}$$

or in vectors:

$$\frac{(1-\sigma)}{1+\sigma}\nabla(\nabla \cdot \mathbf{u}) - \frac{(1-2\sigma)}{2(1+\sigma)}\nabla \times \nabla \times \mathbf{u} + \frac{(1-2\sigma)\mathbf{F}}{E} - \alpha \nabla T = 0$$

where the dilatation $\phi = e_{11} + e_{22} + e_{33}$. λ and μ are the Lamé constants. F_i is the body force.

(c) Compatibility.

In terms of strain the equations are the same as in Section 2.6. In terms of stress the equations must be modified to:

$$\nabla^2\tau_{ij} + \frac{1}{1+\sigma}\frac{\partial^2\theta}{\partial x_i\,\partial x_j}$$

$$= -\frac{\sigma}{1-\sigma}\delta_{ij}\,\nabla\cdot\mathbf{F} - \left(\frac{\partial F_i}{\partial x_j} + \frac{\partial F_j}{\partial x_i}\right) - \frac{\sigma}{1-\sigma}\delta_{ij}\beta\nabla^2 T - \left(\beta\frac{\partial^2 T}{\partial x_i\,\partial x_j}\right) \qquad 2.127$$

which is written in Cartesian Tensor notation. σ is the Poisson ratio. $\mathbf{F}$ is the body force. β is defined above.

(d) The thermal stress problem can be stated as: The displacement in the body is the same as if the body were subjected to a body force (per unit volume) which is the gradient of a potential $-\beta T$, and to a normal surface pressure βT, in addition to the forces and surface tractions that are usually applied to it.

2.10 STRAIN ENERGY

In terms of strain, the strain energy U stored per unit volume can be written in the following fashion. Here λ and μ are the Lamé constants. μ is the shear modulus and is sometimes denoted by G. σ is the Poisson ratio. The equation holds not only in Cartesian formulation but is valid in general orthogonal coordinates, with x, y, and z replaced by x_1, x_2, and x_3 respectively.

$$\begin{aligned} U &= \tfrac{1}{2}(\lambda+2\mu)[e_{xx}^2 + e_{yy}^2 + e_{zz}^2] + 2\mu[e_{yx}^2 + e_{xz}^2 + e_{yz}^2] \\ &\quad + \lambda[e_{xx}e_{yy} + e_{zz}e_{xx} + e_{zz}e_{yy}] \\ &= \frac{(1-\sigma)\mu}{(1-2\sigma)}[e_{xx}^2 + e_{yy}^2 + e_{zz}^2] + \tfrac{1}{2}\mu[\gamma_{yx}^2 + \gamma_{xz}^2 + \gamma_{yz}^2] \\ &\quad + \lambda[e_{xx}e_{yy} + e_{zz}e_{xx} + e_{zz}e_{yy}] \end{aligned} \qquad 2.128$$

or in terms of stress:

$$\begin{aligned} U &= \frac{1}{2E}(\tau_{xx}^2 + \tau_{yy}^2 + \tau_{zz}^2) - \frac{\sigma}{E}(\tau_{xx}\tau_{yy} + \tau_{yy}\tau_{zz} + \tau_{xx}\tau_{zz}) \\ &\quad + \frac{1}{2\mu}(\tau_{xy}^2 + \tau_{xz}^2 + \tau_{yz}^2) \end{aligned} \qquad 2.129$$

2.11 WAVE PROPAGATION

In isotropic homogeneous media two independent wave equations can be written. A longitudinal wave equation and a shear or transverse wave equation are uncoupled. However, it must be remembered that in practice the two equations may become coupled at a boundary through the boundary conditions and that the waves exist alone as pure shear or longitudinal waves only if plane wave solutions are admissible.

(a) The Longitudinal Wave Equation.

$$(\lambda + 2\mu)\nabla^2\phi = \rho\frac{\partial^2\phi}{\partial t^2} \qquad \textbf{2.130}$$

where the dilatation $\phi = e_{11} + e_{22} + e_{33}$. ρ is mass density. λ and μ are the Lamé constants.

The longitudinal wave is often referred to as the dilatation wave.

(b) The Transverse or Shear Wave.

$$\mu\nabla^2\boldsymbol{\omega} = \rho\frac{\partial^2\boldsymbol{\omega}}{\partial t^2} \qquad \textbf{2.131}$$

where $\boldsymbol{\omega}$ is the rotation vector given in detail in Section 2.1. It should be remembered that the Laplacian operator operating on a vector is not the same as the operation on the individual scalar components. It is useful to replace $\nabla^2\boldsymbol{\omega}$ by the identity:

$$\nabla^2\boldsymbol{\omega} = \nabla(\nabla\cdot\boldsymbol{\omega}) - \nabla\times(\nabla\times\boldsymbol{\omega})$$

2.12 TORSION OF CYLINDERS

Fig. 2-3 below shows the cross section of a cylinder with an external torque M applied as shown. The angle of twist per unit length is α. $w(x,y)$ is the deformation in the z or axial direction due to warping. ϕ is the warping function defined so that $w = \alpha\phi$. The shear stresses on the cross sectional surface can be written then as:

$$\tau_{xz} = \mu\alpha\left(-y + \frac{\partial\phi}{\partial x}\right) \qquad \textbf{2.132}$$

$$\tau_{yz} = \mu\alpha\left(x + \frac{\partial\phi}{\partial y}\right)$$

and the warping function satisfies the harmonic equation:

$$\nabla^2\phi = 0 \qquad \textbf{2.133}$$

in the region R; and on the boundary C, ϕ satisfies the condition:

$$\left(-y + \frac{\partial\phi}{\partial x}\right)l + \left(x + \frac{\partial\phi}{\partial y}\right)m = 0$$

where l and m are the direction cosines of the outward normal to the curve C.

A function ψ may be defined such that $\dfrac{\partial\phi}{\partial n} = \dfrac{\partial\psi}{\partial s}$, and then ψ satisfies:

$$\nabla^2\psi = 0 \qquad \textbf{2.134}$$

in R, and on the curve C: $[\psi = \frac{1}{2}(x^2 + y^2) + \text{constant}]$.

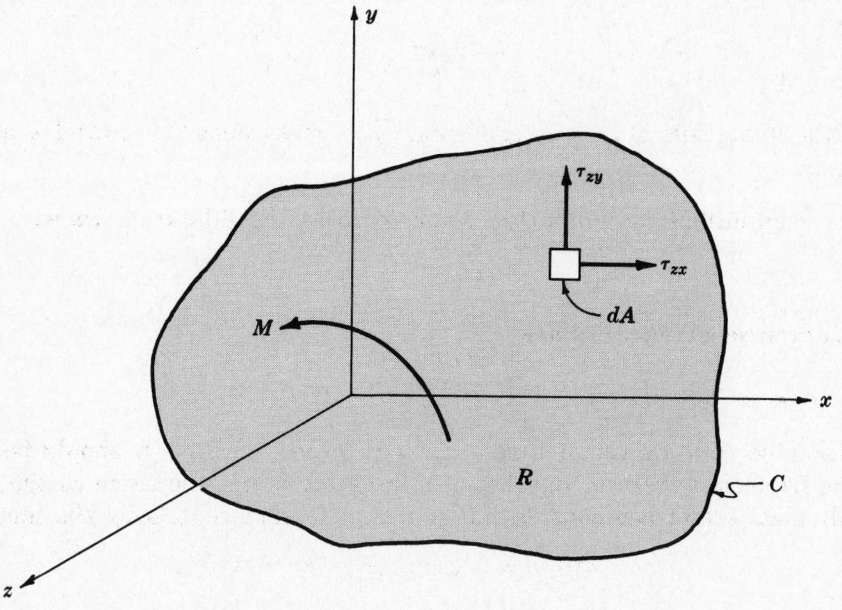

Fig. 2-3. Torsion of a Cylinder. Cross Section in the xy Plane.

The shear stresses in terms of ψ are:

$$\tau_{zx} = \mu\alpha\left(\frac{\partial\psi}{\partial y} - y\right) \qquad \textbf{2.135}$$

$$\tau_{zy} = -\mu\alpha\left(\frac{\partial\psi}{\partial x} - x\right)$$

A new function Ψ can be introduced such that:

$$\Psi = \psi - \tfrac{1}{2}(x^2+y^2) \qquad \text{and hence} \qquad \nabla^2\Psi = -2 \qquad \textbf{2.136}$$

in R, and $\Psi = 0$ on C. The stresses can be written:

$$\tau_{zx} = \mu\alpha\frac{\partial\Psi}{\partial y} \qquad \textbf{2.137}$$

$$\tau_{zy} = -\mu\alpha\frac{\partial\Psi}{\partial x}$$

and the angle of twist can be expressed as:

$$\alpha = \frac{M}{2\mu\int_R \Psi\,dA} \qquad \textbf{2.138}$$

in terms of the external moment M.

The torsional rigidity of the cross section is denoted as D and is defined as $M = D\alpha$. In terms of Ψ, D can be written:

$$D = -\mu\iint_R\left(x\frac{\partial\Psi}{\partial x} + y\frac{\partial\Psi}{\partial y}\right)dx\,dy \qquad \textbf{2.139}$$

$$= 2\mu\iint_R \Psi\,dx\,dy$$

2.13 THICK WALL CYLINDERS

Consider a thick wall cylinder of inner and outer radius a and b respectively. The inner pressure is P_i and the outer pressure is P_0. The stresses $\tau_{\theta\theta}$ and τ_{rr} can be written:

$$\tau_{\theta\theta} = \frac{a^2P_i - b^2P_0}{b^2 - a^2} + \frac{a^2b^2(P_i - P_0)}{r^2(b^2 - a^2)} \qquad \textbf{2.140}$$

$$\tau_{rr} = \frac{a^2P_i - b^2P_0}{b^2 - a^2} - \frac{a^2b^2(P_i - P_0)}{r^2(b^2 - a^2)} \qquad \textbf{2.141}$$

2.14 THICK WALL SPHERES

Consider a thick wall sphere with inner and outer radius a and b respectively. The inner pressure and outer pressure are P_i and P_0 respectively. The stresses are:

$$\tau_{rr} = P_i \frac{a^3}{r^3}\frac{(b^3 - r^3)}{(b^3 - a^3)} + P_0 \frac{b^3}{r^3}\frac{(r^3 - a^3)}{(b^3 - a^3)} \qquad \textbf{2.142}$$

$$\tau_{\theta\theta} = \tfrac{1}{2}P_i \frac{a^3}{r^3}\frac{(b^3 + 2r^3)}{(b^3 - a^3)} - \tfrac{1}{2}P_0 \frac{b^3}{r^3}\frac{(2r^3 + a^3)}{(b^3 - a^3)} \qquad \textbf{2.143}$$

2.15 THEORY OF THIN PLATES

We consider the theory of thin plates with small deformation. The deformation in the direction normal to the plate surface is denoted as w. The coordinate system is as shown in Fig. 2-4 below. The x and y axes lie in the surface of the plate. The z axis points downward to form a right handed system. D is the plate flexural rigidity defined as $D = \dfrac{Eh^3}{12(1 - \sigma^2)}$, where E is Young's nodulus, σ is Poisson's ratio, and h is the plate thickness. q is the transverse loading on the plate per unit area, measured positive in the positive z direction. M is the bending moment per unit length along the plate.

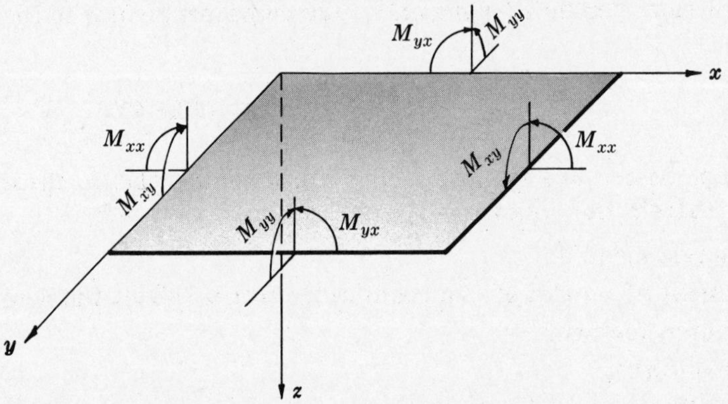

Fig. 2-4. Coordinates on the Thin Plate.
x and y lie in the plane of the plate.

The equation for the deflection w in the z direction for small deflections of thin plates is:

$$\nabla^4 w = q/D \tag{2.144}$$

The boundary conditions can be written as follows:

(a) Simply supported edge, along say, $y = 0$:

$$w|_{y=0} = 0$$

$$M_{yy}|_{y=0} = 0$$

or writing out the expression for M_{yy} and using the fact that $\left.\frac{\partial^2 w}{\partial x^2}\right|_{y=0} = 0$, we have:

$$w|_{y=0} = 0 \tag{2.145}$$

$$\left.\frac{\partial^2 w}{\partial y^2}\right|_{y=0} = 0$$

(b) Built-in edge, along say, $y = 0$:

$$w|_{y=0} = 0 \tag{2.146}$$

$$\left.\frac{\partial w}{\partial y}\right|_{y=0} = 0$$

(c) Free edge, along say, $x = a$:

The Kirchhoff boundary conditions are:

$$M_{xx}|_{x=a} = 0 \tag{2.147}$$

$$\left(Q_x - \frac{\partial M_{xy}}{\partial y}\right)_{x=a} = 0$$

which can be written:

$$\left(\frac{\partial^2 w}{\partial x^2} + \sigma\frac{\partial^2 w}{\partial y^2}\right)_{x=a} = 0 \tag{2.148}$$

$$\left[\frac{\partial^3 w}{\partial x^3} + (2-\sigma)\frac{\partial^3 w}{\partial x\,\partial y^2}\right]_{x=a} = 0$$

writing out the expressions for the moments M_{xx} and M_{xy}. The moment M_{ij} is the bending moment per unit length. The first subscript refers to the axis to which the plane on which the moment acts is perpendicular. The second subscript refers to the direction of the shear generating the moment. Refer to Fig. 2-4. Q_i is the shear force (in the z direction) per unit length on a surface perpendicular to the i axis.

2.16 SIMPLE BEAM THEORY

In engineering, beams are treated by an approximate elastic theory discussed below. In the ensuing analysis the following special symbols are used:

- E = Young's modulus.
- I = Moment of inertia of the beam cross section about the neutral axis.
- M = Bending moment.
- V = Shear force.
- x = Coordinate along the beam.
- y = Deflection of the beam, measured positively downward, or centroidal coordinate on the beam cross section.

(a) Deflection of Simple Beams.

Referring to Fig. 2-5, x is measured from the left end of the beam. y is measured positively downward and represents the deflection of the beam. Moments may be applied at the ends as shown. Positive moments tend to bend the beam concave upward as shown. The beam may be cut at any point, and the necessary shear and moment $M(x)$ determined in order to hold the beam in equilibrium, as shown in Fig. 2-6.

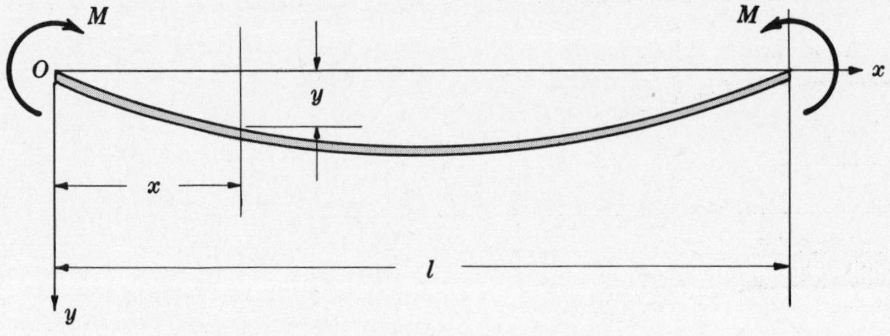

Fig. 2-5. The Simple Beam Coordinate System

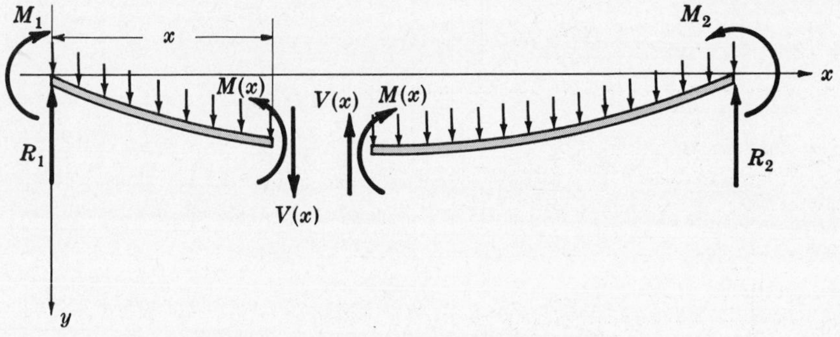

Fig. 2-6. Shears and Moments in a Beam

In Fig. 2-6 the shears and moments are all shown acting in a positive sense. In pure bending the top fibers compress and the bottom ones elongate. The axis through the beam which undergoes no strain is called the neutral axis. Consider the cross section of the beam in the yz plane, xyz forming a right handed system with the origin at the centroid. If the y or z axis is an axis of symmetry (so that the products of inertia of the yz sections are zero) then the neutral axis coincides with the z axis if the loading is in the xy plane as shown. The deflection will then be in the xy plane as shown. If loading also occurs in the xz plane, the deflection in the z direction can be linearly superposed on the y deflection.

If the z and y axes on the cross section are not principal axes, the principal axes can be found (in the yz plane) and these principal axes represent neutral axes for loading in the respective planes.

The equation for deflection is:

$$\frac{d^2y}{dx^2} = -\frac{M}{EI} \qquad \textbf{2.149}$$

where M is the moment in the beam, I is the moment of inertia of the cross section

Loading	Deflection	Maximum Deflection
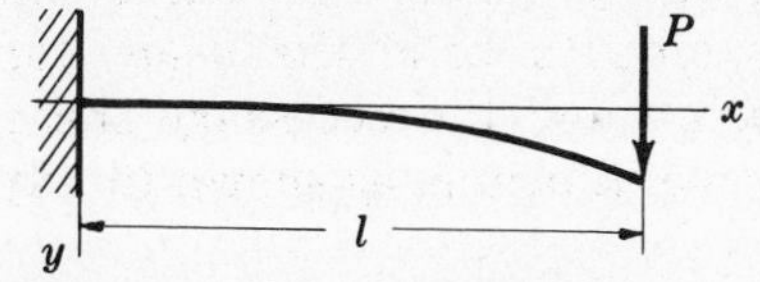	$y = \frac{Px^2}{6EI}(3l - x)$	$\delta = \frac{Pl^3}{3EI}$
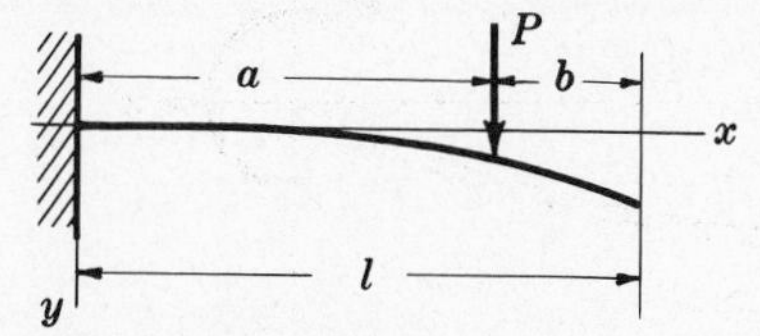	$y = \frac{Px^2}{6EI}(3a - x);\ 0 < x < a$ $y = \frac{Pa^2}{6EI}(3x - a);\ a < x < l$	$\delta = \frac{Pa^2}{6EI}(3l - a)$
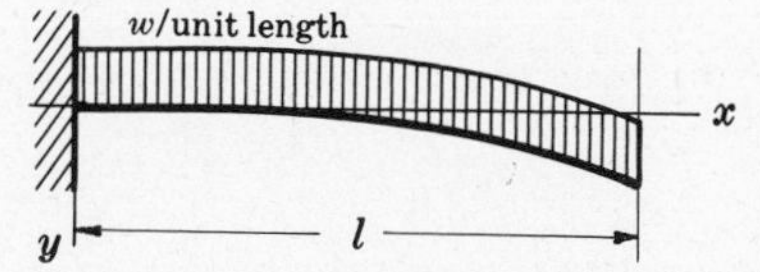	$y = \frac{wx^2}{24EI}(x^2 + 6l^2 - 4lx)$	$\delta = \frac{wl^4}{8EI}$
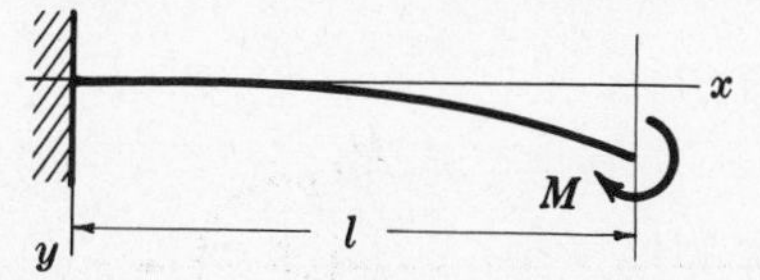	$y = \frac{Mx^2}{2EI}$	$\delta = \frac{wl^2}{2EI}$
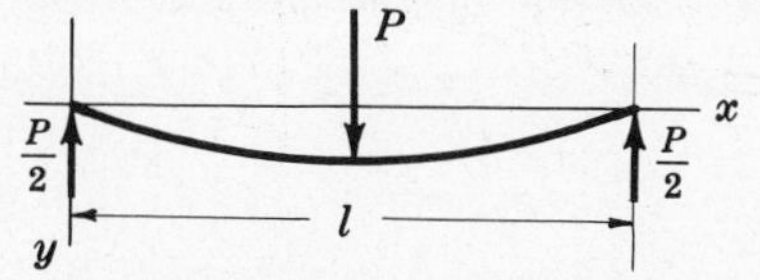	$y = \frac{Px}{12EI}\left(\frac{3l^2}{4} - x^2\right);\ 0 < x < \frac{l}{2}$	$\delta = \frac{Pl^3}{48EI}$
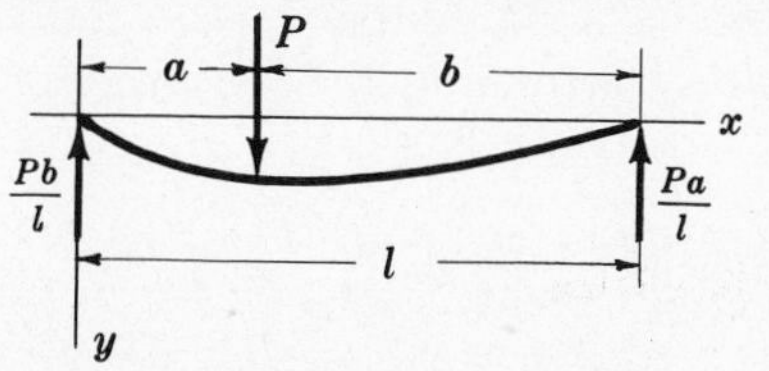	$y = \frac{Pbx}{6lEI}(l^2 - x^2 - b^2);\ 0 < x < a$ $y = \frac{Pb}{6lEI}\left[\frac{l}{b}(x - a)^3 + (l^2 - b^2)x - x^2\right];$ $a < x < b$	$\delta = \frac{Pb(l^2 - b^2)^{3/2}}{9\sqrt{3}\,lEI}$ at: $x = \sqrt{\frac{l^2 - b^2}{3}}$
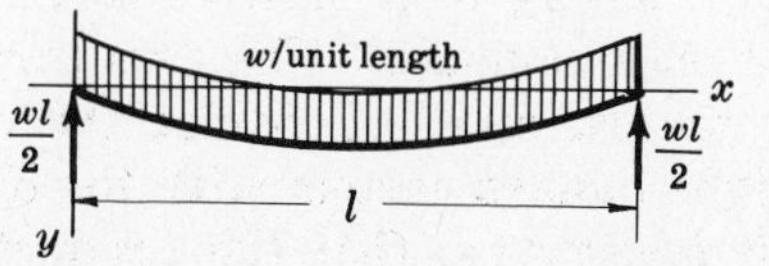	$y = \frac{wx}{24EI}(l^3 - 2lx^2 + x^3)$	$\delta = \frac{5wl^4}{384EI}$
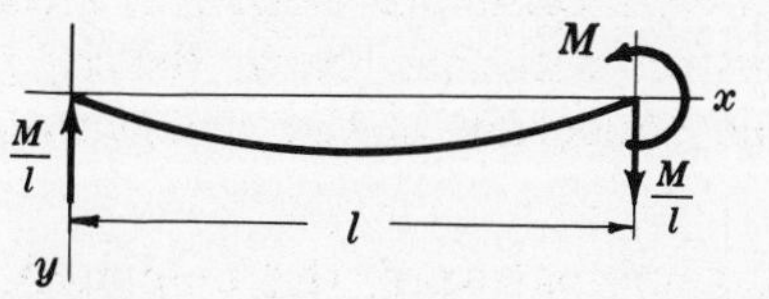	$y = \frac{Mlx}{6EI}\left(1 - \frac{x^2}{l^2}\right)$	$\delta = \frac{Ml^2}{9\sqrt{3}\,EI}$ at: $x = \frac{l}{\sqrt{3}}$
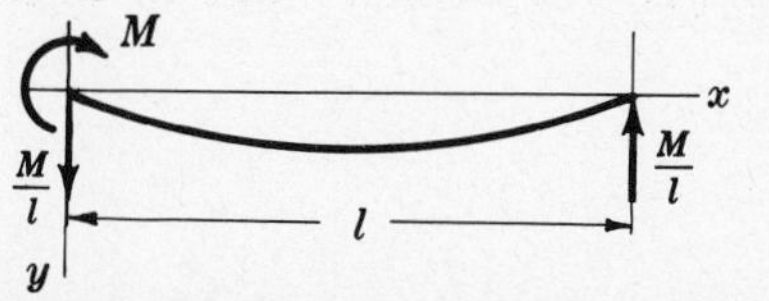	$y = \frac{Mx}{6lEI}(l - x)(2l - x)$	$\delta = \frac{Ml^3}{9\sqrt{3}\,EI}$ at: $x = \left(1 - \frac{1}{\sqrt{3}}\right)l$

Fig. 2-7. Table of Beam Deflections

about the z axis, and E is Young's modulus. Additional useful equations for small deflections are:

$$\frac{dM}{dx} = V \qquad 2.150a$$

and

$$\frac{d^2M}{dx^2} = -w \qquad 2.150b$$

where w is the loading per unit length of the beam. Hence:

$$\frac{d^3y}{dx^3} = -\frac{V}{EI} \qquad 2.151$$

$$\frac{d^4y}{dx^4} = \frac{w}{EI} \qquad 2.152$$

A table of beam deflections is given for reference in Fig. 2-7 above.

(b) *Stresses in Simple Beams.*

For a simple beam as shown in Fig. 2-6, the stresses consist of bending normal stresses acting on the cross section, and shear stresses acting on a cross section. For a symmetric cross section the bending stress is given by:

$$\tau_{xx} = \frac{My}{I} \qquad 2.153$$

where M is the bending moment at the value of x where the stress is computed, y is the distance from the neutral axis (not to be confused with deflection), and I is the moment of inertia about the z or neutral axis. It may be necessary to orient the yz axes so that they are the principal axes if they are not so originally. Equation 2.153 is only valid if the yz axes are principal axes. If moments and shears act in other than the xy plane, then the y axis may be considered as a neutral axis for the force and moment system in the xz plane and the two stress systems added linearly together. There results then a neutral point at the yz origin.

The general shear problem is not treated, but for most simple cross sections the shear stress is given by:

$$\tau_{xy} = \frac{VQ}{Ib} \qquad 2.154$$

Here V is the shear on the surface, Q is the first moment of the part of the cross section defined by a line through the point where the stress is determined (parallel to the neutral axis) and the outer extremity of the section. This first moment is taken about the neutral axis. b is the width of the section at the point where the shear stress is calculated, (width in the z direction). See Fig. 2-8.

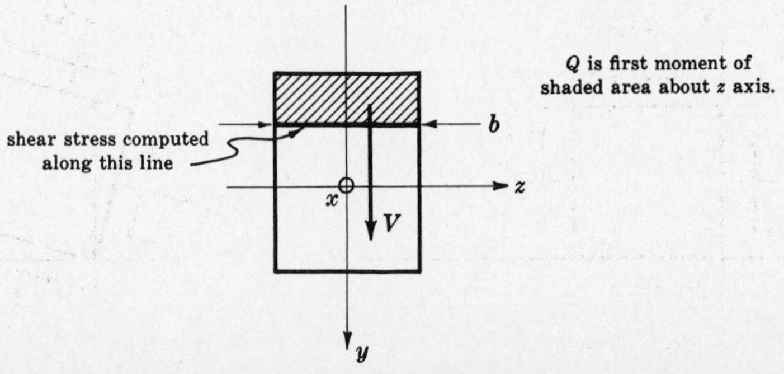

Fig. 2-8. Shear Stress in a Simple Beam.

2.17 SIMPLE COLUMN THEORY

Simple end loaded columns buckle under the Euler load, which we denote as P_{cr}. For various end conditions the critical loads can be given as listed below. I is the minimum moment of inertia about a centroidal axis. l is the length of the column.

(a) Both ends pinned.

$$P_{cr} = \frac{\pi^2 EI}{l^2} \qquad \textbf{2.155}$$

(b) One end pinned, one end built in.

$$P_{cr} = \frac{\pi^2 EI}{4l^2} \qquad \textbf{2.156a}$$

(c) Both ends built in but free to move vertically.

$$P_{cr} = \frac{4\pi^2 EI}{l^2} \qquad \textbf{2.156b}$$

The various situations are shown below in Fig. 2-9.

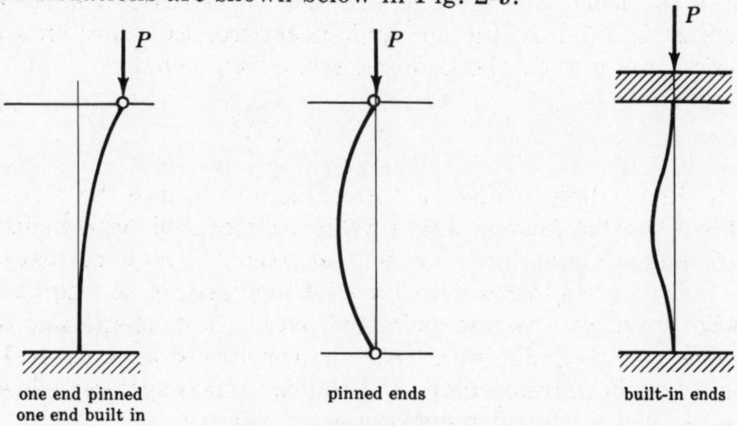

Fig. 2-9. Simple Columns.

2.18 COMBINED STRESSES IN TWO DIMENSIONS AND MOHR'S CIRCLE

In a two dimensional stress state, the principal stresses can be found for any orientation of the coordinate axes in a simple manner. A graphical method is known as Mohr's circle. Consider a stress state as shown in Fig. 2-10(a) below. What are the stresses on the faces of the square element when rotated into position (b)?

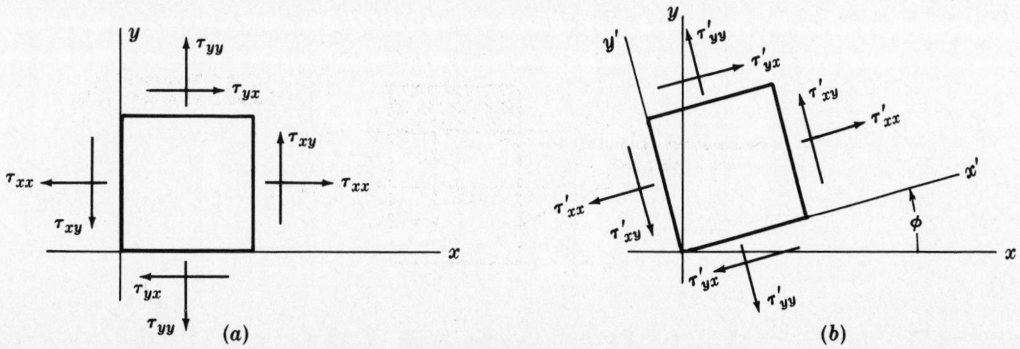

Fig. 2-10. Two Dimensional Stress State.

From equilibrium considerations the stresses on the surfaces of the element rotated through an angle ϕ in a counterclockwise direction are:

$$\tau'_{xx} = \frac{\tau_{xx} + \tau_{yy}}{2} + \frac{\tau_{xx} - \tau_{yy}}{2}\cos 2\phi + \tau_{xy}\sin 2\phi \qquad \textbf{2.157}$$

$$\tau'_{yy} = \frac{\tau_{xx} + \tau_{yy}}{2} - \frac{\tau_{xx} - \tau_{yy}}{2}\cos 2\phi - \tau_{xy}\sin 2\phi$$

$$\tau'_{xy} = \tau'_{yx} = \tau_{xy}\cos 2\phi - \frac{\tau_{xx} - \tau_{yy}}{2}\sin 2\phi$$

The principal stresses are given by:

$$\tau_x = \frac{\tau_{xx} + \tau_{yy}}{2} + \sqrt{\left(\frac{\tau_{xx} - \tau_{yy}}{2}\right)^2 + \tau_{xy}^2} \qquad \textbf{2.158}$$

$$\tau_y = \frac{\tau_{xx} + \tau_{yy}}{2} - \sqrt{\left(\frac{\tau_{xx} - \tau_{yy}}{2}\right)^2 + \tau_{xy}^2}$$

and occur on the element rotated through an angle ϕ_n given by:

$$\tan 2\phi_n = \frac{2\tau_{xy}}{\tau_{xx} - \tau_{yy}} \qquad \textbf{2.159}$$

The maximum shear stress is

$$(\tau'_{xy})_{\text{max.}} = \sqrt{\left(\frac{\tau_{xx} - \tau_{yy}}{2}\right)^2 + \tau_{xy}^2} \qquad \textbf{2.160}$$

and occurs at an angle ϕ_s given by

$$\tan 2\phi_s = -\left(\frac{\tau_{xx} - \tau_{yy}}{2\tau_{xy}}\right) \qquad \textbf{2.161}$$

The Mohr circle shows all these relationships graphically. As shown below in Fig. 2-11, the original stress state is plotted on the diagram, and the circle constructed. The stresses for any arbitrary orientation of the axes are given by inspection of the diagram.

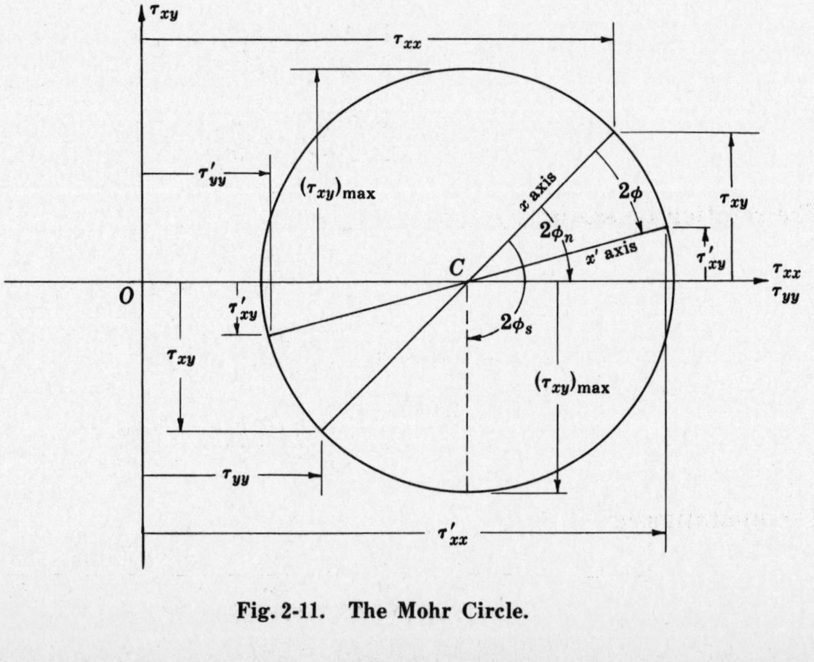

Fig. 2-11. The Mohr Circle.

2.19 MOHR'S CIRCLE FOR TWO DIMENSIONAL STRAIN

Analogous to the stress Mohr circle in the previous section, strains can be analyzed in the same manner. Consider the strain state shown in Fig. 2-12(*a*) below. The element may be rotated through an angle ϕ measured positive in the counterclockwise direction as shown in Fig. 2-12(*b*). The Mohr circle construction is shown below in Fig. 2-13.

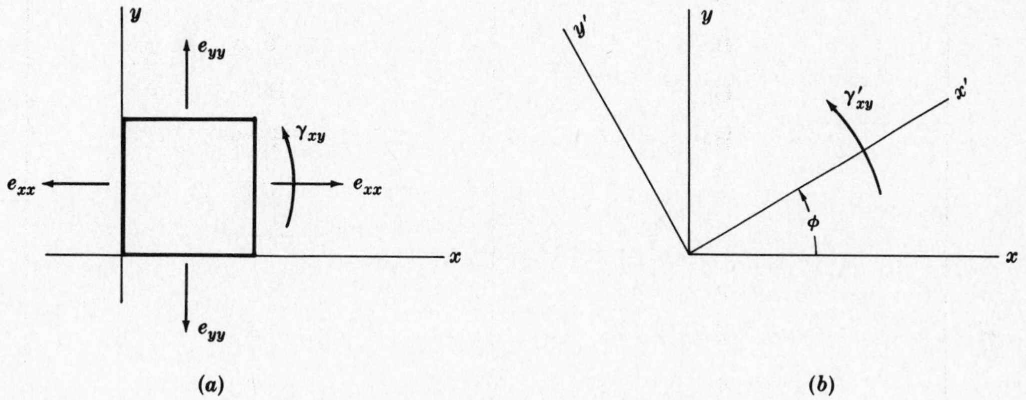

Fig. 2-12. Two Dimensional Strain State.

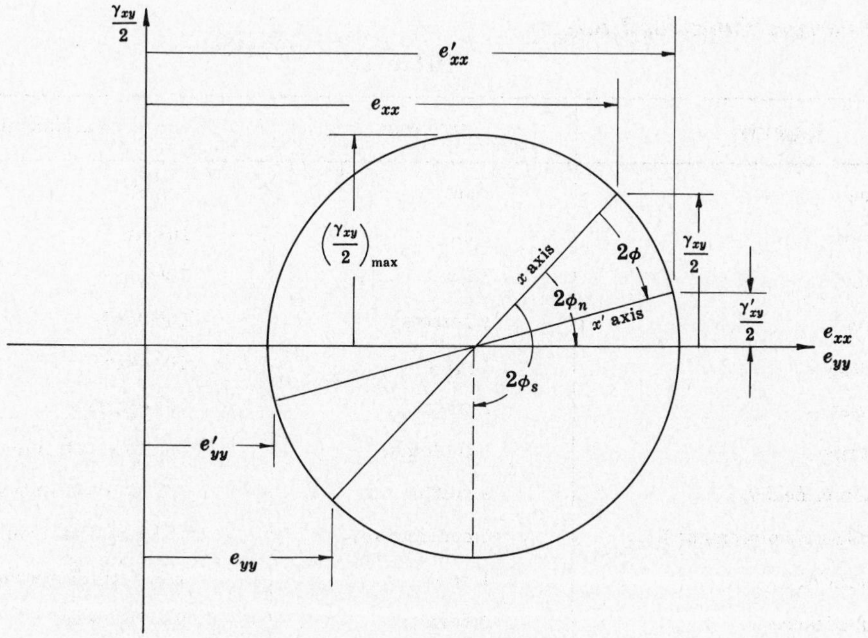

Fig. 2-13. The Strain Mohr Circle.

2.20 LIST OF SYMBOLS USED IN CHAPTER 2

Note. Other symbols were used in the text but were explained at the time. These represent the most frequently used symbols and correspond, in so far as possible, with current usage.

e_{ij} = Strain tensor.

E = Young's modulus.

$\mathbf{F}$ = Body Force.

h_i = Defined by line element for curvilinear coordinates.

k = Bulk modulus.

T = Temperature.

U = Strain energy per unit volume.

u = Component of displacement in x direction.

v = Component of displacement in y direction.

w = Component of displacement in z direction.

α = Linear thermal coefficient of expansion.

β = Defined as: $\alpha(3\lambda + 2\mu) = 3k\alpha = \beta$.

γ_{ij} = True strain matrix. $\gamma_{ij} = 2e_{ij}$, $i \neq j$; $\gamma_{ij} = e_{ij}$, $i = j$.

δ_{ij} = Kronecker delta.

θ = Stress invariant, $(\tau_{11} + \tau_{22} + \tau_{33})$.

λ = Lamé constant, $= \dfrac{2\mu\sigma}{1 - 2\sigma}$.

μ = Shear modulus, or modulus of rigidity, sometimes denoted as G in engineering literature.

ρ = Density.

σ = Poisson's ratio.

τ_{ij} = Stress tensor.

ϕ = Strain invariant or dilatation, $(e_{11} + e_{22} + e_{33})$.

Φ = Stress function.

Ω = Body force potential.

2.21 LIST OF REFERENCES

1. Biezano, C. B., and Grammel, R., *Engineering Dynamics, Vol. I, Theory of Elasticity*, Blackie and Sons Ltd., London, 1955
2. Borg, S. F., *Fundamentals of Engineering Elasticity*, Van Nostrand, 1946
3. Borg, S. F., *Matrix-Tensor Methods in Continuum Mechanics*, Van Nostrand, 1963
4. Durelli, A. J., Phillips, E. A., and Tsao, C. H., *Introduction to the Theoretical and Experimental Analysis of Stress and Strain*, McGraw-Hill, 1958
5. Eringen, A. C., *Nonlinear Theory of Continuous Media*, McGraw-Hill, 1962

6. Godfrey, D. E. R., *Theoretical Elasticity and Plasticity,* Thames and Hudson, London, 1962

7. Green, A. E., and Zerna, W., *Theoretical Elasticity,* Oxford University Press, 1954

8. Landau, L. D., and Lifshitz, E. M., *Theory of Elasticity,* Addison-Wesley, 1959

9. Love, A. E. H., *A Treatise on the Mathematical Theory of Elasticity,* Cambridge University Press, 1927. (Also Dover, 1954.)

10. Murnaghan, F. D., *Finite Deformations of an Elastic Solid,* John Wiley, 1951

11. Prescott, John, *Applied Elasticity,* Longmans, Green and Co., London, 1924

12. Sechler, Ernest E., *Elasticity in Engineering,* John Wiley, 1952

13. Sokolnikoff, I. S., *Mathematical Theory of Elasticity,* McGraw-Hill, 1946

14. Sommerfeld, A., *Mechanics of a Deformable Body,* Academic Press, 1950

15. Southwell, R. V., *An Introduction to the Theory of Elasticity,* Oxford University Press, 1936

16. Timoshenko, S., and Goodier, J. N., *Theory of Elasticity,* McGraw-Hill, 1951

17. Trefetz, E., Mechanik der Elastischen Körper, *Handbuch der Physik, Vol. 6*

18. Wang, Chi-Teh, A*pplied Elasticity,* McGraw-Hill, 1953

Chapter 3

Electromagnetic Theory

Several systems of units are used in electromagnetic theory. The two most commonly used systems are the mks and cgs systems, both of which may be either rationalized or unrationalized. A rational system of units is one that contains a factor 4π in the fundamental source relationships such as Coulomb's law, and hence does not contain the 4π factor in the Maxwell field equations.

The conversion from one system of units to another is indicated in the table below. In current engineering practice the rationalized mks system (referred to as RMKS) seems to be the most widely used. In this chapter the equations are given in both RMKS units and in unrationalized cgs (Gaussian) units, which are used extensively in scientific work.

The following conversion table is listed here for convenience. To convert from one system of units to another make the following substitution:

RMKS (Rationalized mks)	**Gaussian** (Unrationalized cgs)
$\mathbf{E}$	$\mathbf{E}$
$\mathbf{B}$	$\mathbf{B}/c$
$\mathbf{D}$	$\mathbf{D}/4\pi$
$\mathbf{H}$	$\mathbf{H}c/4\pi$
ϵ	$\epsilon/4\pi$
μ	$\mu 4\pi/c^2$
ρ	ρ
$\mathbf{J}$	$\mathbf{J}$
ϕ	ϕ
$\mathbf{A}$	$\mathbf{A}/c$

In Gaussian units the current density vector **J** may be measured in esu or emu. Usually esu is used and that is the system used in this chapter. However, the results listed here in esu can be converted to emu by multiplying the current density **J** (as it appears here) by c, the velocity of light.

Conventional symbols used for the field quantities are listed below.

A = Vector potential.

B = Magnetic induction field.

D = Displacement field.

E = Electric field.

H = Magnetic field.

J = Current density. (Conduction current unless otherwise stated.)

M = Magnetization.

P = Polarization.

ρ = Charge density.

ϵ = Dielectric constant or permittivity.

μ = Magnetic permeability.

ϕ = Scalar electric potential.

Other symbols are explained as they are used throughout the text, and a complete listing of symbols follows at the end of this chapter.

3.1 MAXWELL'S EQUATIONS

Maxwell's equations are listed below in various coordinate systems in RMKS and in Gaussian units. The detailed forms in various coordinate systems are given only in RMKS, but the forms in Gaussian follow from the vector forms. Other systems of units can be written using the table which appears in Section 3.24 of this chapter. The symbols for the field quantities have been defined immediately above in the introduction.

(a) Vector.

RMKS units:

$$\nabla \cdot \mathbf{D} = \rho \qquad \textbf{3.1}$$

$$\nabla \cdot \mathbf{B} = 0 \qquad \textbf{3.2}$$

$$\nabla \times \mathbf{E} = -\frac{\partial \mathbf{B}}{\partial t} \qquad \textbf{3.3}$$

$$\nabla \times \mathbf{H} = \mathbf{J} + \frac{\partial \mathbf{D}}{\partial t} \qquad \textbf{3.4}$$

Gaussian units:

$$\nabla \cdot \mathbf{D} = 4\pi\rho \qquad \textbf{3.5}$$

$$\nabla \cdot \mathbf{B} = 0 \qquad \textbf{3.6}$$

$$\nabla \times \mathbf{E} = -\frac{1}{c}\frac{\partial \mathbf{B}}{\partial t} \qquad \textbf{3.7}$$

$$\nabla \times \mathbf{H} = \frac{4\pi\mathbf{J}}{c} + \frac{1}{c}\frac{\partial \mathbf{D}}{\partial t} \qquad \textbf{3.8}$$

In the above, ρ is true charge density. **J** is conduction current.

(b) Cartesian, RMKS:

$$\frac{\partial D_x}{\partial x} + \frac{\partial D_y}{\partial y} + \frac{\partial D_z}{\partial z} = \rho \qquad 3.9$$

$$\frac{\partial B_x}{\partial x} + \frac{\partial B_y}{\partial y} + \frac{\partial B_z}{\partial z} = 0 \qquad 3.10$$

$$\left.\begin{aligned} \frac{\partial E_z}{\partial y} - \frac{\partial E_y}{\partial z} &= -\frac{\partial B_x}{\partial t} \\ \frac{\partial E_x}{\partial z} - \frac{\partial E_z}{\partial x} &= -\frac{\partial B_y}{\partial t} \\ \frac{\partial E_y}{\partial x} - \frac{\partial E_x}{\partial y} &= -\frac{\partial B_z}{\partial t} \end{aligned}\right\} \qquad 3.11$$

$$\left.\begin{aligned} \frac{\partial H_z}{\partial y} - \frac{\partial H_y}{\partial z} &= J_x + \frac{\partial D_x}{\partial t} \\ \frac{\partial H_x}{\partial z} - \frac{\partial H_z}{\partial x} &= J_y + \frac{\partial D_y}{\partial t} \\ \frac{\partial H_y}{\partial x} - \frac{\partial H_x}{\partial y} &= J_z + \frac{\partial D_z}{\partial t} \end{aligned}\right\} \qquad 3.12$$

(c) Cylindrical, RMKS:

$$\frac{1}{r}\frac{\partial}{\partial r}(rD_r) + \frac{1}{r}\frac{\partial D_\theta}{\partial \theta} + \frac{\partial D_z}{\partial z} = \rho \qquad 3.13$$

$$\frac{1}{r}\frac{\partial}{\partial r}(rB_r) + \frac{1}{r}\frac{\partial B_\theta}{\partial \theta} + \frac{\partial B_z}{\partial z} = 0 \qquad 3.14$$

$$\left.\begin{aligned} \frac{1}{r}\frac{\partial E_z}{\partial \theta} - \frac{\partial E_\theta}{\partial z} &= -\frac{\partial B_r}{\partial t} \\ \frac{\partial E_r}{\partial z} - \frac{\partial E_z}{\partial r} &= -\frac{\partial B_\theta}{\partial t} \\ \frac{1}{r}\left[\frac{\partial}{\partial r}(rE_\theta) - \frac{\partial E_r}{\partial \theta}\right] &= -\frac{\partial B_z}{\partial t} \end{aligned}\right\} \qquad 3.15$$

$$\left.\begin{aligned} \frac{1}{r}\frac{\partial H_z}{\partial \theta} - \frac{\partial H_\theta}{\partial z} &= J_r + \frac{\partial D_r}{\partial t} \\ \frac{\partial H_r}{\partial z} - \frac{\partial H_z}{\partial r} &= J_\theta + \frac{\partial D_\theta}{\partial t} \\ \frac{1}{r}\left[\frac{\partial (rH_\theta)}{\partial r} - \frac{\partial H_r}{\partial \theta}\right] &= J_z + \frac{\partial D_z}{\partial t} \end{aligned}\right\} \qquad 3.16$$

(d) Spherical, RMKS:

$$\frac{1}{r^2}\frac{\partial}{\partial r}(r^2 D_r) + \frac{1}{r\sin\theta}\frac{\partial}{\partial\theta}(D_\theta \sin\theta) + \frac{1}{r\sin\theta}\frac{\partial D_\phi}{\partial\phi} = \rho \qquad \textbf{3.17}$$

$$\frac{1}{r^2}\frac{\partial}{\partial r}(r^2 B_r) + \frac{1}{r\sin\theta}\frac{\partial}{\partial\theta}(B_\theta \sin\theta) + \frac{1}{r\sin\theta}\frac{\partial B_\phi}{\partial\phi} = 0 \qquad \textbf{3.18}$$

$$\left.\begin{aligned} \frac{1}{r\sin\theta}\left[\frac{\partial}{\partial\theta}(E_\phi \sin\theta) - \frac{\partial E_\theta}{\partial\phi}\right] &= -\frac{\partial B_r}{\partial t} \\ \frac{1}{r\sin\theta}\frac{\partial E_r}{\partial\phi} - \frac{1}{r}\frac{\partial}{\partial r}(rE_\phi) &= -\frac{\partial B_\theta}{\partial t} \\ \frac{1}{r}\left[\frac{\partial}{\partial r}(rE_\theta) - \frac{\partial E_r}{\partial\theta}\right] &= -\frac{\partial B_\phi}{\partial t} \end{aligned}\right\} \qquad \textbf{3.19}$$

$$\left.\begin{aligned} \frac{1}{r\sin\theta}\left[\frac{\partial}{\partial\theta}(H_\phi \sin\theta) - \frac{\partial H_\theta}{\partial\phi}\right] &= J_r + \frac{\partial D_r}{\partial t} \\ \frac{1}{r\sin\theta}\frac{\partial H_r}{\partial\phi} - \frac{1}{r}\frac{\partial}{\partial r}(rH_\phi) &= J_\theta + \frac{\partial D_\theta}{\partial t} \\ \frac{1}{r}\left[\frac{\partial}{\partial r}(rH_\theta) - \frac{\partial H_r}{\partial\theta}\right] &= J_\phi + \frac{\partial D_\phi}{\partial t} \end{aligned}\right\} \qquad \textbf{3.20}$$

(e) Orthogonal Curvilinear, RMKS:

In the following, h_1, h_2, and h_3 are defined by the line element, (see Appendix). The subscripts refer to the field quantity component in the coordinate direction.

$$\frac{1}{h_1h_2h_3}\left[\frac{\partial(h_2h_3D_1)}{\partial x_1} + \frac{\partial(h_3h_1D_2)}{\partial x_2} + \frac{\partial(h_1h_2D_3)}{\partial x_3}\right] = \rho \qquad \textbf{3.21a}$$

$$\frac{1}{h_1h_2h_3}\left[\frac{\partial(h_2h_3B_1)}{\partial x_1} + \frac{\partial(h_3h_1B_2)}{\partial x_2} + \frac{\partial(h_1h_2B_3)}{\partial x_3}\right] = 0 \qquad \textbf{3.21b}$$

$$\left.\begin{aligned} \frac{1}{h_2h_3}\left[\frac{\partial(h_3E_3)}{\partial x_2} - \frac{\partial(h_2E_2)}{\partial x_3}\right] &= -\frac{\partial B_1}{\partial t} \\ \frac{1}{h_1h_3}\left[\frac{\partial(h_1E_1)}{\partial x_3} - \frac{\partial(h_3E_3)}{\partial x_1}\right] &= -\frac{\partial B_2}{\partial t} \\ \frac{1}{h_1h_2}\left[\frac{\partial(h_2E_2)}{\partial x_1} - \frac{\partial(h_1E_1)}{\partial x_2}\right] &= -\frac{\partial B_3}{\partial t} \end{aligned}\right\} \qquad \textbf{3.22}$$

$$\left.\begin{aligned} \frac{1}{h_2h_3}\left[\frac{\partial(h_3H_3)}{\partial x_2} - \frac{\partial(h_2H_2)}{\partial x_3}\right] &= J_1 + \frac{\partial D_1}{\partial t} \\ \frac{1}{h_1h_3}\left[\frac{\partial(h_1H_1)}{\partial x_3} - \frac{\partial(h_3H_3)}{\partial x_1}\right] &= J_2 + \frac{\partial D_2}{\partial t} \\ \frac{1}{h_1h_2}\left[\frac{\partial(h_2H_2)}{\partial x_1} - \frac{\partial(h_1H_1)}{\partial x_2}\right] &= J_3 + \frac{\partial D_3}{\partial t} \end{aligned}\right\} \qquad \textbf{3.23}$$

3.2 CONSTITUTIVE EQUATIONS

(a) In general the following equations can be written:

RMKS

$$\mathbf{D} = \epsilon_0\mathbf{E} + \mathbf{P} \qquad \mathbf{3.24}$$

$$\mathbf{B} = \mu_0(\mathbf{H} + \mathbf{M})$$

where **P** and **M** are the polarization and magnetization fields.

Gaussian

$$\mathbf{P} = \frac{1}{4\pi}(\mathbf{D} - \mathbf{E}) \qquad \mathbf{3.25}$$

$$\mathbf{M} = \frac{1}{4\pi}(\mathbf{B} - \mathbf{H})$$

(b) For a linear medium the following equations can be written in the rest frame. The rest frame of reference is that frame at rest with respect to the material medium. Because of the covariant character of Maxwell's equations, they are valid in any frame of reference. However, the constitutive equations, being phenomenological, can be written only in the rest frame (unless the field quantities are all transformed to another frame as is done later for moving media).

RMKS

$$\mathbf{D} = \epsilon\mathbf{E} = \epsilon_0\kappa\mathbf{E} = \epsilon_0(1 + \chi)\mathbf{E} \qquad \mathbf{3.26}$$

$$\mathbf{B} = \mu\mathbf{H} = \mu_0\kappa_m\mathbf{H} = \mu_0(1 + \chi_m)\mathbf{H}$$

Gaussian

$$\mathbf{D} = \epsilon\mathbf{E} = \kappa\mathbf{E} = (1 + \chi)\mathbf{E} \qquad \mathbf{3.27}$$

$$\mathbf{B} = \mu\mathbf{H} = \kappa_m\mathbf{H} = (1 + \chi_m)\mathbf{H}$$

ϵ and μ are the dielectric constant and magnetic permeability respectively. κ and κ_m are the relative dielectric constant, or relative permittivity, and relative permeability respectively. χ and χ_m are the electric and magnetic susceptibilities respectively.

In Gaussian units, ϵ and μ are simply equal to κ and κ_m respectively. Hence, in free space, we can write:

$$\mathbf{D} = \epsilon_0\mathbf{E}, \qquad \mathbf{B} = \mu_0\mathbf{H} \qquad \mathbf{3.28}$$

in RMKS, and

$$\mathbf{D} = \mathbf{E}, \qquad \mathbf{B} = \mathbf{H} \qquad \mathbf{3.29}$$

in Gaussian units.

The value of ϵ_0 and μ_0 in RMKS units are:

$$\epsilon_0 = 10^7/4\pi c^2 = 8.854 \times 10^{-12} \text{ farad/meter}, \qquad \mu_0 = 4\pi \times 10^{-7} \text{ henry/meter}$$

(c) ***Anisotropic Media.***

In anisotropic media, in the rest frame the constitutive equations can be written as:

$$D_i = \epsilon_{ij}E_j, \qquad B_i = \mu_{ij}H_j \qquad \mathbf{3.30}$$

if the dielectric constant and permeability can be written as tensors. The summation convention for Cartesian Tensors is used above.

3.3 OHM'S LAW AND CURRENTS

These equations, as the other constitutive equations, hold only in the rest frame. The generalization to moving media will be discussed later. **J** is the conduction current density, **E** is the electric field, and σ is the conductivity. Ohm's law holds in any system of units as it is written below.

(a) Scalar Conductivity.

$$\mathbf{J} = \sigma \mathbf{E} \qquad \textbf{3.31}$$

(b) Tensor Conductivity.

$$J_i = \sigma_{ij} E_j \qquad \textbf{3.32}$$

(c) Total Current.

The total current $\mathbf{J}_t$ can be written in terms of the polarization **P** and magnetization **M** as (in any system of units):

$$\mathbf{J}_t = \mathbf{J} + \frac{\partial \mathbf{P}}{\partial t} + \nabla \times \mathbf{M} \qquad \textbf{3.33}$$

The polarization current $\mathbf{J}_p$ is:

$$\mathbf{J}_p = \frac{\partial \mathbf{P}}{\partial t} \qquad \textbf{3.34}$$

The magnetization current $\mathbf{J}_m$ is:

$$\mathbf{J}_m = \nabla \times \mathbf{M} \qquad \textbf{3.35}$$

(d) Conservation of Current and Charge.

In any system of units:

$$\nabla \cdot \mathbf{J} + \frac{\partial \rho}{\partial t} = 0 \qquad \textbf{3.36}$$

This equation is not independent of Maxwell's equations and follows directly from them.

3.4 POTENTIALS

(a) Scalar Potential.

The scalar potential ϕ, for an irrotational electric field is defined as:

$$\mathbf{E} = -\nabla \phi \qquad \textbf{3.37}$$

in any system of units.

(b) Vector Potential.

The vector potential **A** for the magnetic field can be written:

$$\mathbf{B} = \nabla \times \mathbf{A} \qquad \textbf{3.38}$$

in any system of units.

In general,

RMKS

$$\mathbf{E} = -\nabla\phi - \frac{\partial \mathbf{A}}{\partial t} \qquad 3.39$$

Gaussian

$$\mathbf{E} = -\nabla\phi - \frac{1}{c}\frac{\partial \mathbf{A}}{\partial t} \qquad 3.40$$

(c) The electric potential satisfies the Poisson equation in static situations.

RMKS

$$\nabla^2\phi = -\frac{\rho}{\epsilon} \qquad 3.41$$

Gaussian

$$\nabla^2\phi = -\frac{4\pi\rho}{\epsilon} \qquad 3.42$$

3.5 WAVE EQUATIONS

In the following, κ and κ_m denote the relative dielectric constant and permeability respectively, σ is the conductivity, and c is the velocity of light.

(a) In a region of no true charge or sources of electromotive force:

RMKS

$$\nabla^2\mathbf{E} - \frac{\kappa\kappa_m}{c^2}\frac{\partial^2 \mathbf{E}}{\partial t^2} - \mu\sigma\frac{\partial \mathbf{E}}{\partial t} = 0 \qquad 3.43$$

$$\nabla^2\mathbf{B} - \frac{\kappa\kappa_m}{c^2}\frac{\partial^2 \mathbf{B}}{\partial t^2} - \mu\sigma\frac{\partial \mathbf{B}}{\partial t} = 0 \qquad 3.44$$

Gaussian

$$\nabla^2\mathbf{E} - \frac{\epsilon\mu}{c^2}\frac{\partial^2 \mathbf{E}}{\partial t^2} - \frac{4\pi\mu\sigma}{c^2}\frac{\partial \mathbf{E}}{\partial t} = 0 \qquad 3.45$$

$$\nabla^2\mathbf{B} - \frac{\epsilon\mu}{c^2}\frac{\partial^2 \mathbf{B}}{\partial t^2} - \frac{4\pi\mu\sigma}{c^2}\frac{\partial \mathbf{B}}{\partial t} = 0 \qquad 3.46$$

In free space, (in vacuum), the homogeneous wave equation becomes (in either RMKS or Gaussian):

$$\nabla^2\mathbf{E} - \frac{1}{c^2}\frac{\partial^2 \mathbf{E}}{\partial t^2} = 0 \qquad 3.47$$

$$\nabla^2\mathbf{B} - \frac{1}{c^2}\frac{\partial^2 \mathbf{B}}{\partial t^2} = 0$$

(b) Inhomogeneous wave equations in regions where true charge and electromotive force exist.

RMKS

$$\nabla^2\mathbf{A} - \mu\epsilon\frac{\partial^2 \mathbf{A}}{\partial t^2} - \mu\sigma\frac{\partial \mathbf{A}}{\partial t} = -\mu\mathbf{J}' \qquad 3.48$$

$$\nabla^2\phi - \mu\epsilon\frac{\partial^2 \phi}{\partial t^2} - \mu\sigma\frac{\partial \phi}{\partial t} = -\frac{\rho}{\epsilon} \qquad 3.49$$

Gaussian

$$\nabla^2\mathbf{A} - \frac{\mu\epsilon}{c^2}\frac{\partial^2\mathbf{A}}{\partial t^2} - \frac{4\pi\mu\sigma}{c^2}\frac{\partial\mathbf{A}}{\partial t} = -\frac{4\pi\mu\mathbf{J}'}{c} \qquad \textbf{3.50}$$

$$\nabla^2\phi - \frac{\mu\epsilon}{c^2}\frac{\partial^2\phi}{\partial t^2} - \frac{4\pi\mu\sigma}{c^2}\frac{\partial\phi}{\partial t} = -\frac{4\pi\rho}{\epsilon} \qquad \textbf{3.51}$$

where $\mathbf{J}'$ is the current produced by external electromotive forces. The following relationships are useful in the above equations:

$$\frac{\kappa\kappa_m}{c^2} = \mu\epsilon, \qquad \frac{1}{c^2} = \mu_0\epsilon_0 \qquad \textbf{3.52}$$

Note that in the wave equations the following vector identity is useful

$$\nabla^2\mathbf{A} = \nabla(\nabla\cdot\mathbf{A}) - \nabla\times(\nabla\times\mathbf{A})$$

∇^2 operating on a vector is not the same as ∇^2 operating on a scalar component except in Cartesian coordinates.

3.6 BOUNDARY CONDITIONS

(a) At an interface between two adjoining media we can write (RMKS) in vector form:

$$\mathbf{n}\times(\mathbf{E}_2-\mathbf{E}_1) = 0 \qquad \textbf{3.53}$$

$$\mathbf{n}\times(\mathbf{H}_2-\mathbf{H}_1) = \mathbf{J}_s \qquad \textbf{3.54}$$

$$\mathbf{n}\cdot(\mathbf{D}_2-\mathbf{D}_1) = \rho_s \qquad \textbf{3.55}$$

$$\mathbf{n}\cdot(\mathbf{B}_2-\mathbf{B}_1) = 0 \qquad \textbf{3.56}$$

In Gaussian units the equations become:

$$\mathbf{n}\times(\mathbf{E}_2-\mathbf{E}_1) = 0 \qquad \textbf{3.57}$$

$$\mathbf{n}\times(\mathbf{H}_2-\mathbf{H}_1) = \frac{4\pi\mathbf{J}_s}{c} \qquad \textbf{3.58}$$

$$\mathbf{n}\cdot(\mathbf{D}_2-\mathbf{D}_1) = 4\pi\rho_s \qquad \textbf{3.59}$$

$$\mathbf{n}\cdot(\mathbf{B}_2-\mathbf{B}_1) = 0 \qquad \textbf{3.60}$$

In the above equations $\mathbf{n}$ is the unit normal vector measured positive from medium 1 into medium 2. $\mathbf{J}_s$ is the true surface current on the interface, and ρ_s is the surface charge density.

(b) Moving Media.

For moving media in situations where a tangential velocity discontinuity exists at an interface, the above boundary conditions all hold if the field quantities are all measured in any one frame of reference which moves parallel to the interface. For a general motion the Lorentz transformations may be applied to the above equations. Fig. 3-1 below shows the orientation of the normal vector.

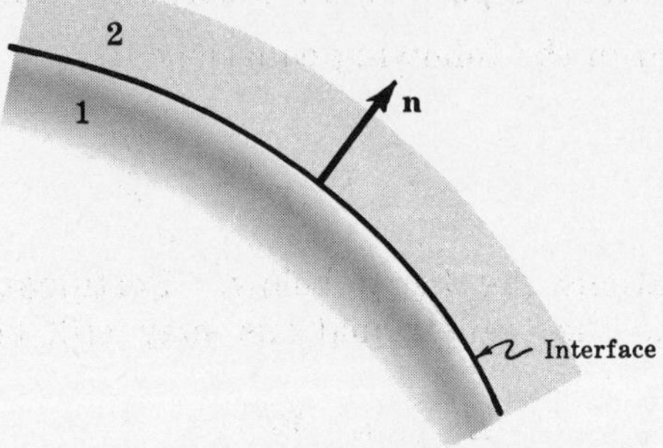

Fig. 3-1. Adjoining Media for Boundary Conditions.

3.7 MAXWELL'S EQUATIONS FOR MOVING MEDIA

Since Maxwell's equations are covariant, they take the same form in any frame of reference. Consider a coordinate frame S' attached to the medium which is moving with velocity $\mathbf{V}$ with respect to the laboratory coordinate system. The field quantities measured in the frame attached to the medium (the rest frame S') are denoted by a prime, while those quantities measured in the laboratory frame are unprimed. Maxwell's equations can be written in either frame of reference. In each case the field quantities and coordinates are those with respect to the observer writing the equations. The transformations of the fields will be discussed in the next section. Hence:

RMKS

$$\nabla' \cdot \mathbf{D}' = \rho' \qquad \nabla \cdot \mathbf{D} = \rho \tag{3.61}$$

$$\nabla' \cdot \mathbf{B}' = 0 \qquad \nabla \cdot \mathbf{B} = 0$$

$$\nabla' \times \mathbf{E}' = -\frac{\partial \mathbf{B}'}{\partial t'} \qquad \nabla \times \mathbf{E} = -\frac{\partial \mathbf{B}}{\partial t}$$

$$\nabla' \times \mathbf{H}' = \mathbf{J}' + \frac{\partial \mathbf{D}'}{\partial t'} \qquad \nabla \times \mathbf{H} = \mathbf{J} + \frac{\partial \mathbf{D}}{\partial t}$$

Gaussian

$$\nabla' \cdot \mathbf{D}' = 4\pi\rho' \qquad \nabla \cdot \mathbf{D} = 4\pi\rho \tag{3.62}$$

$$\nabla' \cdot \mathbf{B}' = 0 \qquad \nabla \cdot \mathbf{B} = 0$$

$$\nabla' \times \mathbf{E}' = -\frac{1}{c}\frac{\partial \mathbf{B}'}{\partial t'} \qquad \nabla \times \mathbf{E} = -\frac{1}{c}\frac{\partial \mathbf{B}}{\partial t}$$

$$\nabla' \times \mathbf{H}' = \frac{4\pi \mathbf{J}'}{c} + \frac{1}{c}\frac{\partial \mathbf{D}'}{\partial t'} \qquad \nabla \times \mathbf{H} = \frac{4\pi \mathbf{J}}{c} + \frac{1}{c}\frac{\partial \mathbf{D}}{\partial t}$$

3.8 LORENTZ TRANSFORMATIONS

The field quantities as measured by observers in the rest frame and laboratory frame are related by the Lorentz transformations. In the following equations the primed quantities denote those measured in the rest frame, and the unprimed quantities are those measured in the laboratory frame. The rest frame is at rest with the frame S' which is moving with velocity $\mathbf{V}$ with respect to the laboratory frame S.

The symbol γ, as used in the following equations, is:

$$\gamma = \sqrt{1 - \frac{|\mathbf{V}|^2}{c^2}} \qquad 3.63$$

The general transformations are listed below. Rectilinear motion is assumed, but for most practical situations the transformations may still be used for accelerated motion.

$$\mathbf{E}'_{\parallel} = \mathbf{E}_{\parallel} \qquad 3.64$$

$$\mathbf{E}'_{\perp} = \frac{1}{\gamma}(\mathbf{E} + \mathbf{V} \times \mathbf{B})_{\perp} \qquad 3.65$$

$$\mathbf{D}'_{\parallel} = \mathbf{D}_{\parallel} \qquad 3.66$$

$$\mathbf{D}'_{\perp} = \frac{1}{\gamma}\left(\mathbf{D} + \frac{\mathbf{V} \times \mathbf{H}}{c^2}\right)_{\perp} \qquad 3.67$$

$$\mathbf{H}'_{\parallel} = \mathbf{H}_{\parallel} \qquad 3.68$$

$$\mathbf{H}'_{\perp} = \frac{1}{\gamma}(\mathbf{H} - \mathbf{V} \times \mathbf{D})_{\perp} \qquad 3.69$$

$$\mathbf{B}'_{\parallel} = \mathbf{B}_{\parallel} \qquad 3.70$$

$$\mathbf{B}'_{\perp} = \frac{1}{\gamma}\left(\mathbf{B} - \frac{\mathbf{V} \times \mathbf{E}}{c^2}\right)_{\perp} \qquad 3.71$$

$$\mathbf{J}'_{\parallel} = \frac{1}{\gamma}(\mathbf{J} - \rho\mathbf{V})_{\parallel} \qquad 3.72$$

$$\mathbf{J}'_{\perp} = \mathbf{J}_{\perp} \qquad 3.73$$

$$\rho' = \frac{1}{\gamma}\left(\rho - \frac{\mathbf{V} \cdot \mathbf{J}}{c^2}\right) \qquad 3.74$$

$$\mathbf{P}'_{\parallel} = \mathbf{P}_{\parallel} \qquad 3.75$$

$$\mathbf{P}'_{\perp} = \frac{1}{\gamma}\left(\mathbf{P} - \frac{\mathbf{V} \times \mathbf{M}}{c^2}\right)_{\perp} \qquad 3.76$$

$$\mathbf{M}'_{\parallel} = \mathbf{M}_{\parallel} \qquad 3.77$$

$$\mathbf{M}'_{\perp} = \frac{1}{\gamma}(\mathbf{M} + \mathbf{V} \times \mathbf{P})_{\perp} \qquad 3.78$$

3.9 LORENTZ TRANSFORMATIONS FOR VELOCITIES SMALL COMPARED TO THAT OF LIGHT

For velocities small compared to that of light, ($|\mathbf{V}|^2 \ll c^2$), γ can be assumed equal to unity and the above transformations simplify to the following forms.

$$\mathbf{E}' = \mathbf{E} + \mathbf{V} \times \mathbf{B} \tag{3.79}$$

$$\mathbf{D}' = \mathbf{D} + \frac{\mathbf{V} \times \mathbf{H}}{c^2} \tag{3.80}$$

$$\mathbf{B}' = \mathbf{B} - \frac{\mathbf{V} \times \mathbf{E}}{c^2} \tag{3.81}$$

$$\mathbf{H}' = \mathbf{H} - \mathbf{V} \times \mathbf{D} \tag{3.82}$$

$$\mathbf{J}' = \mathbf{J} - \rho\mathbf{V} \tag{3.83}$$

$$\rho' = \rho - \frac{\mathbf{V} \cdot \mathbf{J}}{c^2} \tag{3.84}$$

$$\mathbf{P}' = \mathbf{P} - \frac{\mathbf{V} \times \mathbf{M}}{c^2} \tag{3.85}$$

$$\mathbf{M}' = \mathbf{M} + \mathbf{V} \times \mathbf{P} \tag{3.86}$$

Note that for nonmagnetic material ($\mu = \mu_0$), $\mathbf{P} = \mathbf{P}'$; and for nonpolarizable material, $\mathbf{M} = \mathbf{M}'$. In some of the above equations, factors of c^2 are retained. This retention is necessary even for low velocity because of the relative magnitude of the terms in the expressions, and may under some conditions be important.

3.10 CONSTITUTIVE EQUATIONS IN MOVING MEDIA

Constitutive equations can only be written in the rest frame of material media. (The distinction between the frames of reference has been made in the preceding two sections). The rest frame is a frame of reference at rest with respect to the material media. If the material is moving at a velocity **V** with respect to the laboratory frame of reference, the observer in the laboratory must transform the rest frame constitutive equations into the laboratory frame if he is to write constitutive equations in terms of field quantities measured in the laboratory.

Equations 3.24 through 3.30 express the constitutive equations in the rest frame. The following equations are written for the laboratory frame:

(a) General expressions (valid in any frame):

<u>RMKS</u>

$$\mathbf{D} = \epsilon_0\mathbf{E} + \mathbf{P} \tag{3.87}$$

$$\mathbf{B} = \mu_0(\mathbf{H} + \mathbf{M}) \tag{3.88}$$

<u>Gaussian</u>

$$\mathbf{D} = 4\pi\mathbf{P} + \mathbf{E} \tag{3.89}$$

$$\mathbf{B} = 4\pi\mathbf{M} + \mathbf{H} \tag{3.90}$$

(b) In free space, (vacuum) in any frame:

RMKS

$$\mathbf{D} = \epsilon_0 \mathbf{E} \tag{3.91}$$

$$\mathbf{B} = \mu_0 \mathbf{H} \tag{3.92}$$

Gaussian

$$\mathbf{D} = \mathbf{E} \tag{3.93}$$

$$\mathbf{B} = \mathbf{H} \tag{3.94}$$

(c) The following general expressions can be obtained by substituting the Lorentz transformations into the rest frame equations. These equations hold only for linear media with a scalar permittivity and permeability (RMKS or Gaussian).

$$\mathbf{D} = \epsilon[\mathbf{E} + \mathbf{V} \times \mathbf{B}] - \frac{1}{c^2}\mathbf{V} \times \mathbf{H} \tag{3.95}$$

$$\mathbf{B} = \mu[\mathbf{H} - \mathbf{V} \times \mathbf{D}] + \frac{1}{c^2}\mathbf{V} \times \mathbf{E} \tag{3.96}$$

For velocities small compared to light ($|\mathbf{V}|^2 \ll c^2$), these equations become:

$$\mathbf{D} = \epsilon\left[\mathbf{E} + \left(1 - \frac{1}{\kappa\kappa_m}\right)\mathbf{V} \times \mathbf{B}\right] \tag{3.97}$$

$$\mathbf{B} = \mu\left[\mathbf{H} - \left(1 - \frac{1}{\kappa\kappa_m}\right)\mathbf{V} \times \mathbf{D}\right] \tag{3.98}$$

3.11 OHM'S LAW FOR MOVING MEDIA

In the rest frame (at rest with respect to the material medium) Ohm's law can be written (for a scalar conductivity) as: $\mathbf{J}' = \sigma\mathbf{E}'$. This expression can be transformed into the laboratory frame and thus be written in terms of variables as measured in the laboratory frame. The rest frame is assumed to move with velocity $\mathbf{V}$ with respect to the laboratory frame. u, v, and w are the x, y, and z components of $\mathbf{V}$ in Cartesian coordinates.

The equations are written with the assumption that $|\mathbf{V}|^2 \ll c^2$. Ohm's law written thusly is valid in either RMKS or Gaussian units.

(a) Vector.

$$\mathbf{J} = \sigma(\mathbf{E} + \mathbf{V} \times \mathbf{B}) + \rho\mathbf{V} \tag{3.99}$$

(b) Cartesian.

$$\begin{aligned} J_x &= \sigma(E_x + vB_z - wB_y) + \rho V_x \\ J_y &= \sigma(E_y - uB_z + wB_x) + \rho V_y \\ J_z &= \sigma(E_z + uB_y - vB_x) + \rho V_z \end{aligned} \tag{3.100}$$

(c) Cylindrical.

v_r, v_θ, and v_z are the velocities in the r, θ, and z directions respectively.

$$J_r = \sigma(E_r + v_\theta B_z - v_z B_\theta) + \rho V_r \qquad \textbf{3.101}$$
$$J_\theta = \sigma(E_\theta + v_z B_r - v_r B_z) + \rho V_\theta$$
$$J_z = \sigma(E_z + v_r B_\theta - v_\theta B_r) + \rho V_z$$

(d) Spherical.

v_r, v_θ, and v_ϕ are the velocities in the r, θ, and ϕ directions respectively.

$$J_r = \sigma(E_r + v_\theta B_\phi - v_\phi B_\theta) + \rho V_r \qquad \textbf{3.102}$$
$$J_\theta = \sigma(E_\theta + v_\phi B_r - v_r B_\phi) + \rho V_\theta$$
$$J_\phi = \sigma(E_\phi + v_r B_\theta - v_\theta B_r) + \rho V_\phi$$

3.12 LORENTZ FORCE ON A CHARGED PARTICLE

The Lorentz force on a charged particle, **F**, transforms according to the Lorentz transformations for force. In the rest frame of the particle the force can be written as:

$$\mathbf{F}' = q\mathbf{E}' \qquad \textbf{3.103}$$

where q is the charge on the particle, and $\mathbf{E}'$ is the local electric field seen by the particle. By transforming the force according to the transformation:

$$\mathbf{F}'_{\parallel} = \mathbf{F}_{\parallel}, \qquad \mathbf{F}'_{\perp} = \frac{1}{\sqrt{1 - \dfrac{|\mathbf{V}|^2}{c^2}}}\,\mathbf{F}_{\perp} = \frac{1}{\gamma}\mathbf{F}_{\perp} \qquad \textbf{3.104}$$

(where **V** is the velocity of the particle with respect to the laboratory frame of reference, and the parallel and perpendicular components refer to the components parallel and perpendicular to the velocity vector **V**), and transforming the fields accordingly, there results (in RMKS):

$$\mathbf{F} = q(\mathbf{E} + \mathbf{V} \times \mathbf{B}) \qquad \textbf{3.105}$$

which is a covariant expression and holds in any frame of reference. In Gaussian units, equation 3.105 is:

$$\mathbf{F} = q\left(\mathbf{E} + \frac{\mathbf{V} \times \mathbf{B}}{c}\right) \qquad \textbf{3.106}$$

For velocities **V** small compared to that of light, c, we can write:

$$\mathbf{F}' = \mathbf{F} \qquad \textbf{3.107}$$

The force density **f**, (per unit volume), can be written in the rest frame as:

$$\mathbf{f}' = \rho'\mathbf{E} \qquad \textbf{3.108}$$

where ρ' is the charge density. From the Lorentz transformation for volume, $\delta V = \gamma\,\delta V'$, it follows directly from equation 3.104 that (RMKS):

$$\mathbf{f} = \rho(\mathbf{E} + \mathbf{V} \times \mathbf{B}) \qquad \textbf{3.109}$$

which is valid in any frame of reference. The force density then transforms as:

$$\mathbf{f}'_{\perp} = \mathbf{f}_{\perp}, \qquad \mathbf{f}'_{\parallel} = \sqrt{1 - \frac{|\mathbf{V}|^2}{c^2}}\,\mathbf{f}_{\parallel} = \gamma \mathbf{f}_{\parallel} \tag{3.110}$$

In Gaussian units, equation 3.109 becomes:

$$\mathbf{f} = \rho\left(\mathbf{E} + \frac{\mathbf{V}\times\mathbf{B}}{c}\right) \tag{3.111}$$

3.13 BODY FORCE IN MATERIAL MEDIA (STATIONARY)

In the rest frame the body force can be written in the following manner. This expression is valid only for quasi-static situations and is not a covariant expression. General expressions valid for any frame of reference will be given in subsequent sections. Assuming a linear, isotropic medium, then:

RMKS

$$\mathbf{f} = \rho\mathbf{E} + \mathbf{J}\times\mathbf{B} - \frac{\epsilon_0}{2}E^2\nabla\kappa - \frac{\mu_0}{2}H^2\nabla\kappa_m + \frac{\epsilon_0}{2}\nabla\left(E^2\frac{\partial\kappa}{\partial\rho_m}\rho_m\right) + \frac{\mu_0}{2}\nabla\left(H^2\frac{\partial\kappa_m}{\partial\rho_m}\rho_m\right) \tag{3.112}$$

Gaussian

$$\mathbf{f} = \rho\mathbf{E} + \frac{\mathbf{J}\times\mathbf{B}}{c} - \frac{E^2}{8\pi}\nabla\kappa - \frac{H^2}{8\pi}\nabla\kappa_m + \frac{1}{8\pi}\nabla\left(E^2\frac{\partial\kappa}{\partial\rho_m}\rho_m\right) + \frac{1}{8\pi}\nabla\left(H^2\frac{\partial\kappa_m}{\partial\rho_m}\rho_m\right) \tag{3.113}$$

where ρ_m is the mechanical density of the medium.

The individual terms have the following physical interpretation:

Electrostatic:

$$\rho\mathbf{E} \tag{3.114}$$

Current field interaction:

RMKS

$$\mathbf{J}\times\mathbf{B} \tag{3.115}$$

Gaussian

$$\frac{\mathbf{J}\times\mathbf{B}}{c} \tag{3.116}$$

Inhomogeneity in the magnetic permeability or permittivity:

RMKS

$$-\frac{\epsilon_0}{2}E^2\nabla\kappa - \frac{\mu_0}{2}H^2\nabla\kappa_m \tag{3.117}$$

Gaussian

$$-\frac{E^2}{8\pi}\nabla\kappa - \frac{H^2}{8\pi}\nabla\kappa_m \tag{3.118}$$

Electrostriction:

RMKS

$$\frac{\epsilon_0}{2}\nabla\left(E^2\frac{\partial\kappa}{\partial\rho_m}\rho_m\right) \tag{3.119}$$

Gaussian

$$\frac{1}{8\pi}\nabla\left(E^2\frac{\partial\kappa}{\partial\rho_m}\rho_m\right) \tag{3.120}$$

Magnetostriction:

RMKS
$$\frac{\mu_0}{2}\nabla\left(H^2\frac{\partial\kappa_m}{\partial\rho_m}\rho_m\right) \tag{3.121}$$

Gaussian
$$\frac{1}{8\pi}\nabla\left(H^2\frac{\partial\kappa_m}{\partial\rho_m}\rho_m\right) \tag{3.122}$$

3.14 MAXWELL STRESS TENSOR (REST FRAME ONLY)

In general, in any frame of reference the body force in material media can be written:

$$f_i = \frac{\partial T_{ij}}{\partial x_j} - \frac{\partial g_i}{\partial t} \tag{3.123}$$

where g_i is the electromagnetic momentum density. The Maxwell stress tensor T_{ij} can be given in covariant fashion, but we write out below an expression valid only in the rest frame because the constitutive equations have been implicitly used. The stress tensor actually has physical significance only in terms of its tensor divergence and hence body force. The stresses themselves do not always have significance, and one must be careful in their interpretation as actual stresses. In fact the stress tensor is defined only to within an arbitrary function whose tensor divergence is zero. Including striction effects, the stress tensor can be written in the rest frame as:

RMKS

$$T_{ij} = -\frac{1}{2}\left[\mathbf{D}\cdot\mathbf{E} + \mathbf{B}\cdot\mathbf{H} - E^2\rho_m\frac{\partial\epsilon}{\partial\rho_m} - H^2\rho_m\frac{\partial\mu}{\partial\rho_m}\right]\delta_{ij} + D_iE_j + B_iH_j \tag{3.124}$$

Gaussian

$$T_{ij} = -\left[\frac{\mathbf{D}\cdot\mathbf{E}}{8\pi} + \frac{\mathbf{B}\cdot\mathbf{H}}{8\pi} - \frac{E^2}{8\pi}\rho_m\frac{\partial\epsilon}{\partial\rho_m} - \frac{H^2}{8\pi}\rho_m\frac{\partial\mu}{\partial\rho_m}\right]\delta_{ij} + \frac{D_iE_j}{4\pi} + \frac{B_iH_j}{4\pi} \tag{3.125}$$

For reference, the stress tensor is written out in full in RMKS units below, with the constitutive equations for a linear, isotropic medium having been applied.

$$T_{ij} = \tag{3.126}$$

$$\begin{bmatrix} \left\{\begin{matrix}\frac{1}{2}\epsilon[E_x^2 - E_y^2 - E_z^2] + \frac{1}{2}\rho_m E^2\frac{\partial\epsilon}{\partial\rho_m} \\ + \frac{1}{2}\mu[H_x^2 - H_y^2 - H_z^2] + \frac{1}{2}\rho_m H^2\frac{\partial\mu}{\partial\rho_m}\end{matrix}\right\} & (\epsilon E_xE_y + \mu H_xH_y) & (\epsilon E_xE_z + \mu H_xH_z) \\ (\epsilon E_xE_y + \mu H_xH_y) & \left\{\begin{matrix}\frac{1}{2}\epsilon[E_y^2 - E_z^2 - E_x^2] + \frac{1}{2}\rho_m E^2\frac{\partial\epsilon}{\partial\rho_m} \\ + \frac{1}{2}\mu[H_y^2 - H_z^2 - H_x^2] + \frac{1}{2}\rho_m H^2\frac{\partial\mu}{\partial\rho_m}\end{matrix}\right\} & (\epsilon E_yE_z + \mu H_yH_z) \\ (\epsilon E_xE_z + \mu H_xH_z) & (\epsilon E_yE_z + \mu H_yH_z) & \left\{\begin{matrix}\frac{1}{2}\epsilon[E_z^2 - E_x^2 - E_y^2] + \frac{1}{2}\rho_m E^2\frac{\partial\epsilon}{\partial\rho_m} \\ + \frac{1}{2}\mu[H_z^2 - H_x^2 - H_y^2] + \frac{1}{2}\rho_m H^2\frac{\partial\mu}{\partial\rho_m}\end{matrix}\right\} \end{bmatrix}$$

An important consideration is the diagonalizing of the stress tensor, that is, the determination of the principal stresses. Although these stresses do not always have physical significance, the stress state and consequent body force which it generates is particularly easy to visualize in terms of the principal stresses.

We denote the principal stresses as λ_1, λ_2, and λ_3, oriented along the principal axes $\mathbf{A}_1$, $\mathbf{A}_2$, and $\mathbf{A}_3$ respectively. The secular determinant for these stresses is:

$$|T_{ij} - \lambda\delta_{ij}| = 0 \qquad 3.127$$

and the vectors **A** are given by:

$$[T_{ij} - \lambda\delta_{ij}][A_j] = 0 \qquad 3.128$$

It is convenient to split the stress tensor into an electric and magnetic part and then add, linearly, the resultant stresses. Hence we will solve for the electric principal stress state, and the magnetic principal stress state separately. We can write then:

$$|T^e_{ij} - \lambda^e\delta_{ij}| = 0 \qquad 3.129$$

$$[T^e_{ij} - \lambda^e\delta_{ij}][A^e_j] = 0$$

and

$$|T^m_{ij} - \lambda^m\delta_{ij}| = 0 \qquad 3.130$$

$$[T^m_{ij} - \lambda^m\delta_{ij}][A^m_j] = 0$$

The results for the principal stresses and directions of the principal axes are given below for the case in which the striction effects are neglected.

In RMKS units:

$$\lambda^e_1 = \frac{\mathbf{E}\cdot\mathbf{D}}{2}, \qquad \lambda^e_2 = \lambda^e_3 = -\frac{\mathbf{E}\cdot\mathbf{D}}{2} \qquad 3.131$$

λ^e_1 is oriented along the electric field **E**, and λ^e_2 and λ^e_3 are oriented normal to the **E** vector. Hence the stress state is one of tension along the **E** vector, and hydrostatic compression normal to it. If the **E** and **D** vectors are not collinear, then the situation is more complicated and one must work directly from equation 3.124 or 3.125 since these results above are based on isotropy.

In Gaussian units the stresses are:

$$\lambda^e_1 = \frac{\mathbf{E}\cdot\mathbf{D}}{8\pi}, \qquad \lambda^e_2 = \lambda^e_3 = -\frac{\mathbf{E}\cdot\mathbf{D}}{8\pi} \qquad 3.132$$

The principal magnetic stresses are given as:

<u>RMKS</u>

$$\lambda^m_1 = \frac{\mathbf{H}\cdot\mathbf{B}}{2}, \qquad \lambda^m_2 = \lambda^m_3 = -\frac{\mathbf{H}\cdot\mathbf{B}}{2} \qquad 3.133$$

<u>Gaussian</u>

$$\lambda^m_1 = \frac{\mathbf{H}\cdot\mathbf{B}}{8\pi}, \qquad \lambda^m_2 = \lambda^m_3 = \frac{\mathbf{H}\cdot\mathbf{B}}{8\pi} \qquad 3.134$$

Analogous to the electric stresses the orientation of λ^m_1 is along the **H** vector, and λ^m_2 and λ^m_3 normal to the **H** vector. Hence the stress state is one of tension along **H** and compression normal to it. The same observations about isotropy apply here as were made above about the electric stresses.

An alternative interpretation of the principal stresses is as follows. The stress state can be interpreted as a state of pure hydrostatic compression of value:

$$-\lambda \;=\; \frac{\mathbf{E}\cdot\mathbf{D}}{2}+\frac{\mathbf{H}\cdot\mathbf{B}}{2} \tag{3.135}$$

in RMKS, and

$$-\lambda \;=\; \frac{\mathbf{E}\cdot\mathbf{D}}{8\pi}+\frac{\mathbf{H}\cdot\mathbf{B}}{8\pi} \tag{3.136}$$

in Gaussian, with an added tension along the electric field $\mathbf{E}$ of $\mathbf{E}\cdot\mathbf{D}$ (RMKS, or $\frac{\mathbf{E}\cdot\mathbf{D}}{4\pi}$ in Gaussian) and a tension of $\mathbf{H}\cdot\mathbf{B}$ along the magnetic field $\mathbf{H}$ (or $\frac{\mathbf{H}\cdot\mathbf{B}}{4\pi}$ in Gaussian), hence the origin of the so-called electromagnetic pressure. One must remember that these stresses and pressures act together with the mechanical stress tensor, and in a state of equilibrium the mechanical stresses are equal in magnitude and opposite in sign to the electromagnetic stresses.

The striction effects can very easily be included in the principal stress determination. The striction effect is one of electromagnetic hydrostatic tension, and hence λ_1, λ_2 and λ_3 must be modified by the addition of the term

$$\frac{1}{2}\rho_m E^2\frac{\partial\epsilon}{\partial\rho_m}+\frac{1}{2}\rho_m H^2\frac{\partial\mu}{\partial\rho_m}$$

in RMKS units, so that

$$\lambda_1^e \;=\; \frac{\mathbf{E}\cdot\mathbf{D}}{2}+\frac{1}{2}\rho_m E^2\frac{\partial\epsilon}{\partial\rho_m}, \qquad \lambda_2^e \;=\; \lambda_3^e \;=\; -\frac{\mathbf{E}\cdot\mathbf{D}}{2}+\frac{1}{2}\rho_m E^2\frac{\partial\epsilon}{\partial\rho_m} \tag{3.137}$$

and

$$\lambda_1^m \;=\; \frac{\mathbf{H}\cdot\mathbf{B}}{2}+\frac{1}{2}\rho_m H^2\frac{\partial\mu}{\partial\rho_m}, \qquad \lambda_2^m \;=\; \lambda_3^m \;=\; -\frac{\mathbf{H}\cdot\mathbf{B}}{2}+\frac{1}{2}\rho_m H^2\frac{\partial\mu}{\partial\rho_m} \tag{3.138}$$

In the alternative formulation given above by equations 3.135 and 3.136, the hydrostatic pressure term becomes:

$$-\lambda \;=\; \frac{\mathbf{E}\cdot\mathbf{D}}{2}+\frac{\mathbf{H}\cdot\mathbf{B}}{2}-\frac{1}{2}\rho_m E^2\frac{\partial\epsilon}{\partial\rho_m}-\frac{1}{2}\rho_m H^2\frac{\partial\mu}{\partial\rho_m} \tag{3.139}$$

in RMKS, and

$$-\lambda \;=\; \frac{\mathbf{E}\cdot\mathbf{D}}{8\pi}+\frac{\mathbf{H}\cdot\mathbf{B}}{8\pi}-\frac{1}{8\pi}\rho_m E^2\frac{\partial\kappa}{\partial\rho_m}-\frac{1}{8\pi}\rho_m H^2\frac{\partial\kappa_m}{\partial\rho_m}$$

in Gaussian. The tensions along the $\mathbf{E}$ and $\mathbf{H}$ vectors remain as stated above.

The form of the momentum density g_i which was discussed above is still in dispute, but the two commonly accepted forms appear below. The Minkowski expression for the momentum, which is the same in any frame of reference, is:

$$g_i \;=\; (\mathbf{D}\times\mathbf{B})_i \tag{3.140}$$

in RMKS, and

$$g_i \;=\; \frac{(\mathbf{D}\times\mathbf{B})_i}{4\pi c} \tag{3.141}$$

in Gaussian. The Abraham expression for g_i, which is written here only in its rest frame form, is:

$$g_i = \frac{1}{c^2}(\mathbf{E} \times \mathbf{H})_i \qquad 3.142$$

in RMKS, and

$$g_i = \frac{(\mathbf{E} \times \mathbf{H})_i}{4\pi c} \qquad 3.143$$

in Gaussian.

By combining one of these forms of the momentum with the stress tensor in equation 3.123, the force density can be obtained. In the rest frame this force is identical to equation 3.112 for quasi-static situations. If the Minkowski momentum is used the expression for force density is the same as equation 3.112 (in the rest frame) even for time varying fields. However, if the Abraham momentum is used, there is an additional force of

$$\frac{1}{c^2}(\kappa\kappa_m - 1)\frac{\partial}{\partial t}(\mathbf{E} \times \mathbf{H}) \qquad 3.144$$

in RMKS units in the rest frame. Current usage tends to indicate that the Abraham tensor should be used, although until a few years ago the Minkowski momentum was accepted.

3.15 FORCE IN MOVING MEDIA

The Lorentz force transforms according to the Lorentz transformation as indicated in Section 3.12, equation 3.110. That is:

$$\mathbf{f}'_\perp = \mathbf{f}_\perp, \qquad \mathbf{f}'_{\parallel} = \sqrt{1 - \frac{|\mathbf{V}|^2}{c^2}}\,\mathbf{f}_{\parallel} = \gamma \mathbf{f}_{\parallel} \qquad 3.145$$

where $\mathbf{f}$ is the body force density, and the primes indicate the values as measured in the rest frame. The unprimed quantities are those measured in the laboratory frame with respect to which the material media is moving. For velocities small compared to that of light, the force is numerically the same in any frame of reference. For high velocities the rest frame value of force as calculated by the equations presented previously may be transformed into the laboratory frame as indicated above in equation 3.145.

Alternatively, the force can be calculated directly in the laboratory frame. For forces on charge distributions, equations 3.109 or 3.111 may be used. In general, however, the covariant form of the stress tensor must be used. The general form, neglecting striction effects, is written out below. In tensor form, before constitutive equations are applied, this tensor is the same as the Maxwell stress tensor. In obtaining the tensor divergence of the stress tensor and finding the force, the constitutive equations are useful in simplifying the resulting expression. Care must be taken if the constitutive equations are applied in the laboratory frame, and the reader is referred to Section 3.10 of this chapter.

The principal stresses in the laboratory frame (in covariant form) are the same as those given by equations 3.127 through 3.136, since the constitutive equations have not been applied in these equations and they are derived from the covariant form of the stress tensor.

The covariant form of the stress tensor can then be written:

$$T_{ij} = -\tfrac{1}{2}[\mathbf{D}\cdot\mathbf{E} + \mathbf{H}\cdot\mathbf{B}]\delta_{ij} + D_iE_j + B_iH_j \qquad 3.146$$

3.16 FORCE ON A CONTROL VOLUME OR BODY

The total force can be obtained by integrating the force density throughout the body, or by integrating the stresses over the body. By Gauss' theorem it follows that:

$$F_i = \int_V f_i \, dV = \int_A T_{ij} \, dA_j \qquad 3.147$$

where F_i is the total force on the body.

3.17 POYNTING'S THEOREM

From Maxwell's equations it follows that in any frame of reference:

RMKS

$$-\nabla \cdot (\mathbf{E} \times \mathbf{H}) = \mathbf{E} \cdot \mathbf{J} + \mathbf{H} \cdot \frac{\partial \mathbf{B}}{\partial t} + \mathbf{E} \cdot \frac{\partial \mathbf{D}}{\partial t} \qquad 3.148$$

Gaussian

$$-\nabla \cdot (\mathbf{E} \times \mathbf{H}) = \mathbf{E} \cdot \mathbf{J} + \frac{1}{c}\left[\mathbf{H} \cdot \frac{\partial \mathbf{B}}{\partial t} + \mathbf{E} \cdot \frac{\partial \mathbf{D}}{\partial t}\right] \qquad 3.149$$

If the constitutive equations are linear the theorem takes the following form in the rest frame of the material medium:

RMKS

$$-\nabla \cdot (\mathbf{E} \times \mathbf{H}) = \mathbf{E} \cdot \mathbf{J} + \frac{1}{2}\frac{\partial}{\partial t}(\mathbf{H} \cdot \mathbf{B} + \mathbf{E} \cdot \mathbf{D}) \qquad 3.150$$

Gaussian

$$-\nabla \cdot (\mathbf{E} \times \mathbf{H}) = \mathbf{E} \cdot \mathbf{J} + \frac{1}{2c}\frac{\partial}{\partial t}(\mathbf{H} \cdot \mathbf{B} + \mathbf{E} \cdot \mathbf{D}) \qquad 3.151$$

In equation 3.150 the left hand side represents the energy flux, $\mathbf{E} \times \mathbf{H}$ (RMKS) or $\frac{c}{4\pi}(\mathbf{E} \times \mathbf{H})$ (Gaussian) being the Poynting vector. On the RHS, $\mathbf{E} \cdot \mathbf{J}$ is the Joulean dissipation, and the $\frac{1}{2}\frac{\partial}{\partial t}(\mathbf{H} \cdot \mathbf{B} + \mathbf{E} \cdot \mathbf{D})$ term is the rate of increase of the free energy of the fields. Equation 3.150 or 3.151 is not a covariant expression since the constitutive equations have been used.

However, for the special case of free space properties of the material, $\mu = \mu_0$ and $\epsilon = \epsilon_0$, the above equations, 3.150 or 3.151, are covariant and hold in any frame of reference, and can be given a simple interpretation in the laboratory frame, with respect to which the material is moving with velocity $\mathbf{V}$. In the laboratory frame then:

RMKS

$$-\nabla \cdot (\mathbf{E} \times \mathbf{H}) = \mathbf{E} \cdot \mathbf{J} + \frac{1}{2}\frac{\partial}{\partial t}(\mu_0 H^2 + \epsilon_0 E^2) \qquad 3.152$$

Gaussian

$$-\nabla \cdot (\mathbf{E} \times \mathbf{H}) = \mathbf{E} \cdot \mathbf{J} + \frac{1}{2c}\frac{\partial}{\partial t}(\mu_0 H^2 + \epsilon_0 E^2) \qquad 3.153$$

The left hand side term is the energy flux. The RHS term $\mathbf{E} \cdot \mathbf{J}$ represents the Joulean dissipation plus work done on the media by body forces, and the last term on the RHS represents rate of energy increase. This interpretation can be seen by expanding the $\mathbf{E} \cdot \mathbf{J}$ term as (RMKS):

$$\mathbf{E}\cdot\mathbf{J} \quad = \quad \frac{\mathbf{E}'\cdot\mathbf{J}'}{\gamma} + \frac{\mathbf{V}}{\gamma}\cdot(\mathbf{E}'\rho' + \mathbf{J}'\times\mathbf{B}') \qquad \textbf{3.154}$$

The primes represent quantities measured in the rest frame. The appearance of the factor γ is to be expected due to the volume change because of the Lorentz transformation. The above interpretation is seen to be valid then if the force is simply $(\rho\mathbf{E} + \mathbf{J}\times\mathbf{B})$ (RMKS), which is the case for ϵ_0 and μ_0. In more complicated situations where the constitutive equations must be used in their complete laboratory frame formulation, the force is not so simple and the energy change is not easy to determine.

3.18 COMPLEX FORM OF POYNTING'S THEOREM

For A.C. problems Poynting's theorem can be expressed as (RMKS)

$$-\nabla\cdot(\mathbf{E}\times\mathbf{H}^*) \quad = \quad \mathbf{E}\cdot\mathbf{J}^* + j\omega(\mu\mathbf{H}\cdot\mathbf{H}^* - \epsilon\mathbf{E}\cdot\mathbf{E}^*) \qquad \textbf{3.155}$$

where the quantities denoted as $(\ )^*$ represent the complex conjugate. All the field quantities here are RMS values. ω is frequency, and $j = \sqrt{-1}$. The above form holds only in the rest frame since the constitutive equations have been applied. In general, μ and ϵ can be complex quantities if hysteresis or internal losses occur.

3.19 INTEGRAL FORM OF MAXWELL'S EQUATIONS

RMKS units:

$$\oint \mathbf{E}\cdot d\mathbf{l} \quad = \quad -\int_S \frac{\partial\mathbf{B}}{\partial t}\cdot d\mathbf{S} \quad = \quad \int_S (\nabla\times\mathbf{E})\cdot d\mathbf{S} \qquad \textbf{3.156}$$

$$\int_S \mathbf{D}\cdot d\mathbf{S} \quad = \quad \int_V \rho\, dV \quad = \quad q$$

$$\oint \mathbf{H}\cdot d\mathbf{l} \quad = \quad \int_S \left(\mathbf{J} + \frac{\partial\mathbf{D}}{\partial t}\right)\cdot d\mathbf{S}$$

$$\int_S \mathbf{B}\cdot d\mathbf{S} \quad = \quad 0$$

Gaussian units:

$$\oint \mathbf{E}\cdot d\mathbf{l} \quad = \quad -\frac{1}{c}\int_S \frac{\partial\mathbf{B}}{\partial t}\cdot d\mathbf{S} \quad = \quad \int_S (\nabla\times\mathbf{E})\cdot d\mathbf{S} \qquad \textbf{3.157}$$

$$\int_S \mathbf{D}\cdot d\mathbf{S} \quad = \quad 4\pi\int_V \rho\, dV \quad = \quad 4\pi q$$

$$\oint \mathbf{H}\cdot d\mathbf{l} \quad = \quad \int_S \left(\frac{4\pi\mathbf{J}}{c} + \frac{1}{c}\frac{\partial\mathbf{D}}{\partial t}\right)\cdot d\mathbf{S}$$

$$\int_S \mathbf{B}\cdot d\mathbf{S} \quad = \quad 0$$

In the above equations, q is the total true charge within the volume defined by the surface S.

3.20 COVARIANT (FOUR DIMENSIONAL) FORMULATION OF MAXWELL'S EQUATIONS

In the following formulation the metric tensor g_{ij} is assumed to be of the form:

$$g_{ij} = g^{ij} = \begin{bmatrix} -1 & 0 & 0 & 0 \\ 0 & -1 & 0 & 0 \\ 0 & 0 & -1 & 0 \\ 0 & 0 & 0 & +1 \end{bmatrix} \qquad \textbf{3.158}$$

where the coordinates are x^1, x^2, x^3, ct. c is the velocity of light. The following relationships between tensors are useful:

$$F_{ij} = F^{ij}, \qquad i,j = 1,2,3 \qquad \textbf{3.159}$$
$$F_{ij} = -F^{ij}, \qquad i,j = 4$$

The following field tensors can now be defined (in RMKS):

$$F_{ij} = \begin{bmatrix} 0 & -cB_z & cB_y & -E_x \\ cB_z & 0 & -cB_x & -E_y \\ -cB_y & cB_x & 0 & -E_z \\ E_x & E_y & E_z & 0 \end{bmatrix} \qquad \textbf{3.160}$$

$$H_{ij} = \begin{bmatrix} 0 & \frac{-H_z}{c} & \frac{H_y}{c} & -D_x \\ \frac{H_z}{c} & 0 & \frac{-H_x}{c} & -D_y \\ \frac{-H_y}{c} & \frac{H_x}{c} & 0 & -D_z \\ D_x & D_y & D_z & 0 \end{bmatrix} \qquad \textbf{3.161}$$

$$J^i = \left(\frac{\mathbf{J}}{c}, \rho\right) \qquad \textbf{3.162}$$

Maxwell's equations can then be written:

$$\frac{\partial F_{ij}}{\partial x^k} + \frac{\partial F_{jk}}{\partial x^i} + \frac{\partial F_{ki}}{\partial x^j} = 0 \qquad \textbf{3.163}$$

$$\frac{\partial H^{ji}}{\partial x^j} = J^i \qquad \textbf{3.164}$$

In Gaussian units, the field tensors are defined as:

$$F_{ij} = \begin{bmatrix} 0 & -B_z & B_y & -E_x \\ B_z & 0 & -B_x & -E_y \\ -B_y & B_x & 0 & -E_z \\ E_x & E_y & E_z & 0 \end{bmatrix} \qquad \textbf{3.165}$$

$$H_{ij} = \begin{bmatrix} 0 & \frac{-H_z}{4\pi} & \frac{H_y}{4\pi} & \frac{-D_x}{4\pi} \\ \frac{H_z}{4\pi} & 0 & \frac{-H_x}{4\pi} & \frac{-D_y}{4\pi} \\ \frac{-H_y}{4\pi} & \frac{H_x}{4\pi} & 0 & \frac{-D_z}{4\pi} \\ \frac{D_x}{4\pi} & \frac{D_y}{4\pi} & \frac{D_z}{4\pi} & 0 \end{bmatrix} \qquad 3.166$$

$$J^i = \left(\frac{\mathbf{J}}{c}, \rho\right) \qquad 3.167$$

and the Maxwell equations become the same as equations 3.163 and 3.164 in terms of the Gaussian field variables. Sometimes the field tensors are defined differently, but then the forms of the Maxwell equations are different for different systems of units.

3.21 ENERGY RELATIONSHIPS OF THE ELECTROMAGNETIC FIELD

For a linear medium $[\epsilon = \epsilon(\rho,T),\ \mu = \mu(\rho,T)]$ and fields measured in the rest frame, the reversible work done on the material per unit mass is:

$$dW_r = -P_T\, d\left(\frac{1}{\rho}\right) + \mathbf{H}\cdot d\left(\frac{\mathbf{B}}{\rho}\right) + \mathbf{E}\cdot d\left(\frac{\mathbf{D}}{\rho}\right) \qquad 3.168$$

where P_T is the total pressure including the mechanical pressure and electromagnetic pressure. The total pressure can be written:

$$P_T = P + \frac{1}{2}(\mathbf{B}\cdot\mathbf{H} + \mathbf{D}\cdot\mathbf{E}) - \frac{1}{2}\left(\rho H^2 \frac{\partial\mu}{\partial\rho} + \rho E^2 \frac{\partial\epsilon}{\partial\rho}\right) \qquad 3.169$$

where P is the mechanical pressure (which occurs in the gas law and which is the normal component of the mechanical stress tensor). The following thermodynamical relationships can be written:

$$dA_T = dU_T - T\, dS_T - S_T\, dT \qquad 3.170$$

$$dU_T = dW_r + T\, dS_T \qquad 3.171$$

$$\mathbf{H} = \rho \frac{\partial A_T}{\partial \mathbf{B}}\bigg|_{\rho,T,\mathbf{D}} = \rho \frac{\partial U_T}{\partial \mathbf{B}}\bigg|_{S_T,\rho,\mathbf{D}} \qquad 3.172$$

$$\mathbf{E} = \rho \frac{\partial A_T}{\partial \mathbf{D}}\bigg|_{\rho,T,\mathbf{B}} = \rho \frac{\partial U_T}{\partial \mathbf{D}}\bigg|_{S_T,\rho,\mathbf{B}} \qquad 3.173$$

$$S_T = -\frac{\partial A_T}{\partial T}\bigg|_{\rho,\mathbf{D},\mathbf{B}} \qquad 3.174$$

$$U_T = \frac{\mathbf{E}\cdot\mathbf{D}}{2\rho}\left(1 + \frac{T}{\epsilon}\frac{\partial\epsilon}{\partial T}\right) + \frac{\mathbf{H}\cdot\mathbf{B}}{2\rho}\left(1 + \frac{T}{\mu}\frac{\partial\mu}{\partial T}\right) + U_0(\rho, T) \qquad 3.175$$

$$A_T = \frac{\mathbf{E}\cdot\mathbf{D}}{2\rho} + \frac{\mathbf{H}\cdot\mathbf{B}}{2\rho} + A_0(\rho, T) \qquad 3.176$$

$$S_T = \frac{\mathbf{E}\cdot\mathbf{D}}{2\rho\epsilon}\frac{\partial\epsilon}{\partial T} + \frac{\mathbf{H}\cdot\mathbf{B}}{2\rho\mu}\frac{\partial\mu}{\partial T} + S_0(\rho, T) \qquad 3.177$$

The subscript T indicates total thermodynamic properties associated with the mechanical and electromagnetic effects. Equations 3.175 through 3.177 follow directly from integration of equations 3.172 through 3.174. U_T, A_T, and S_T are the specific (per unit mass) internal energy, free energy, and entropy respectively.

For media in which ϵ and μ are not functions of temperature, we obtain:

$$U_T = \frac{\mathbf{E}\cdot\mathbf{D}}{2\rho} + \frac{\mathbf{H}\cdot\mathbf{B}}{2\rho} + U_0(\rho, T) \qquad 3.178$$

If the density ρ is constant the above equations are all valid and the expression for reversible work simplifies to:

$$dW_r = \frac{1}{\rho}(\mathbf{H}\cdot d\mathbf{B} + \mathbf{E}\cdot d\mathbf{D}) \qquad 3.179$$

which is consistent with Poynting's theorem. The right hand side of 3.179 represents the work rate per unit volume in setting up the fields.

It should be remembered that the entire analysis above is valid only in the rest frame since constitutive equations were used in the simple form: $\mathbf{D} = \epsilon\mathbf{E}$, $\mathbf{B} = \mu\mathbf{H}$.

3.22 MAGNETOHYDRODYNAMICS

The basic equations of magnetohydrodynamics or MHD are the equations of electrodynamics for moving media and the fluid dynamics equations with the electromagnetic body force included. All these equations have been discussed in previous sections and it is merely a matter of combining them in an appropriate form. For convenience the basic equations are repeated here in vector form, in the RMKS system of units. The detailed forms of the equations in various coordinate systems are not written out here but reference can be made to previous sections of this chapter and to the chapter on fluid mechanics.

In MHD, relativistic effects are usually neglected and the body force is usually assumed to have the simple form $(\rho\mathbf{E} + \mathbf{J}\times\mathbf{B})$. Under these assumptions the equations take the forms below. The symbol ρ is used for charge density and ρ_m for fluid density.

(a) Maxwell's Equations.

$$\nabla\cdot\mathbf{D} = \rho \qquad \nabla'\cdot\mathbf{D}' = \rho' \qquad 3.180$$

$$\nabla\times\mathbf{E} = -\frac{\partial\mathbf{B}}{\partial t} \qquad \nabla'\times\mathbf{E}' = -\frac{\partial\mathbf{B}'}{\partial t'}$$

$$\nabla\times\mathbf{H} = \mathbf{J} + \frac{\partial\mathbf{D}}{\partial t} \qquad \nabla'\times\mathbf{H}' = \mathbf{J}' + \frac{\partial\mathbf{D}'}{\partial t'}$$

$$\nabla\cdot\mathbf{B} = 0 \qquad \nabla'\cdot\mathbf{B}' = 0$$

These equations hold in any frame of reference, the fields and coordinates being measured in a particular frame. Primes are used to denote quantities as measured in the rest frame of the fluid. The fluid is assumed to have velocity $\mathbf{V}$ (locally) with respect to the laboratory frame of reference. Unprimed quantities refer to values as measured in the laboratory frame of reference.

The equation $\nabla \cdot \mathbf{D} = \rho$ is not particularly useful and can lead to difficulties unless the appropriate Lorentz transformation between ρ and ρ' is carefully observed. Usually, as in conductors, the charge density ρ' will be zero in the rest frame, but there will be a small amount of induced charge in the laboratory frame. This induced charge may be neglected in the current equations, Ohm's law, etc., but must be retained in the equation $\nabla \cdot \mathbf{D} = \rho$. It is best to avoid this equation if possible and use instead the current conservation equation:

$$\nabla \cdot \mathbf{J} + \frac{\partial \rho}{\partial t} = 0 \tag{3.181}$$

which is simply:

$$\nabla \cdot \mathbf{J} = 0 \tag{3.182}$$

in steady state. The equation $\nabla \cdot \mathbf{D} = \rho$ must be used however, if the charge density is calculated from the **D** field. The charge density in the laboratory frame can also be found by transforming ρ'. Equations 3.181 or 3.182 are not independent of Maxwell's equations and its use makes the equation $\nabla \cdot \mathbf{D} = \rho$ redundant and unnecessary in most MHD problems.

(b) *Ohm's Law.*

$$\mathbf{J} = \sigma(\mathbf{E} + \mathbf{V} \times \mathbf{B}) + \rho \mathbf{V} = \sigma \mathbf{E}' \tag{3.183}$$

In gaseous conductors there may exist space charge in time-varying situations, such as wave motion, but in metallic conductors this term is neglected compared to the conduction current and Ohm's law can be written as:

$$\mathbf{J} = \sigma \mathbf{E}' = \sigma(\mathbf{E} + \mathbf{V} \times \mathbf{B}) \tag{3.184}$$

(c) *Constitutive Equations.*

In the rest frame (for a linear medium):

$$\mathbf{D}' = \epsilon \mathbf{E}' = \epsilon_0 \mathbf{E}' + \mathbf{P}' \tag{3.185}$$

$$\mathbf{B}' = \mu \mathbf{H}' = \mu_0(\mathbf{H}' + \mathbf{M}')$$

In general in any frame:

$$\mathbf{D} = \epsilon_0 \mathbf{E} + \mathbf{P} \tag{3.186}$$

$$\mathbf{B} = \mu_0(\mathbf{H} + \mathbf{M})$$

The fields must be transformed into the laboratory frame in order to obtain the equations in that frame. However, if the material medium has the properties of free space, then the constitutive equations take the following form in any frame:

$$\mathbf{D} = \epsilon_0 \mathbf{E} \tag{3.187}$$

$$\mathbf{B} = \mu_0 \mathbf{H}$$

For a more complete discussion, see Section 3.10.

(d) *Lorentz Transformations.*

The low velocity (compared to that of light) approximation can usually be made in magnetohydrodynamics so that the Lorentz transformations become:

$$\mathbf{E}' = \mathbf{E} + \mathbf{V}\times\mathbf{B} \qquad \textbf{3.188}$$

$$\mathbf{D}' = \mathbf{D} + \frac{\mathbf{V}\times\mathbf{H}}{c^2}$$

$$\mathbf{B}' = \mathbf{B}$$

$$\mathbf{H}' = \mathbf{H}$$

$$\mathbf{J}' = \mathbf{J} - \rho\mathbf{V}$$

$$\rho' = \rho - \frac{\mathbf{V}\cdot\mathbf{J}}{c^2}$$

In most MHD work the magnetic field and induction field can be considered the same in any frame.

(e) Fluid Continuity.

The fluid continuity equation is unchanged and is then:

$$\frac{\partial\rho_m}{\partial t} + \nabla\cdot(\rho_m\mathbf{V}) = 0 \qquad \textbf{3.189}$$

(f) The Fluid Equations of Motion.

The equations are identical to those of Chapter I with the appropriate electromagnetic body force written in. In vector form:

$$\rho_m\left[\frac{\partial\mathbf{V}}{\partial t} + \nabla\left(\frac{V^2}{2}\right) - \mathbf{V}\times(\nabla\times\mathbf{V})\right] \qquad \textbf{3.190}$$

$$= -\nabla P + \rho_m\nu\nabla^2\mathbf{V} + (\zeta + \tfrac{1}{3}\rho_m\nu)\nabla(\nabla\cdot\mathbf{V}) + (\rho\mathbf{E} + \mathbf{J}\times\mathbf{B})$$

where ν is the kinematic viscosity, and ζ is the second coefficient of viscosity.

(g) Energy Equation.

The exact form of the energy equation is unsettled, but for most problems in MHD (at least where there are no changes of μ or ϵ with temperature) the ordinary fluid energy equation is valid if the Joulean dissipation is included. The Joulean dissipation is $\mathbf{E}'\cdot\mathbf{J}'$. (Note that this quantity is a product of rest frame values).

$$\rho_m\frac{De}{Dt} + P\nabla\cdot\mathbf{V} = \Phi + \mathbf{E}'\cdot\mathbf{J}' + \nabla\cdot(k\nabla T) \qquad \textbf{3.191}$$

Here k is the thermal conductivity, e is the specific internal energy, and Φ is the mechanical dissipation function. From Ohm's law, the electrical dissipation can be written:

$$\mathbf{E}'\cdot\mathbf{J}' = \frac{J'^2}{\sigma} = \sigma|\mathbf{E} + \mathbf{V}\times\mathbf{B}|^2 \qquad \textbf{3.192}$$

See Section 3.21 for relevant thermodynamical relationships.

(h) In addition to the above equations, additional equations such as the equation of state, viscosity variations with temperature, etc., may be necessary. These equations are essentially unaffected by the electromagnetic fields to the MHD approximation.

3.23 PLASMA DYNAMICS

The two component fluid model will be discussed here. It is assumed that the gas consists of ions and electrons and is electrically neutral. The gas is assumed completely ionized. (RMKS units are used in the following presentation.)

The equation of motion for the ions is:

$$n_i m_i \left[\frac{\partial \mathbf{V}_i}{\partial t} + (\mathbf{V}_i \cdot \nabla)\mathbf{V}_i\right] = n_i Z e(\mathbf{E} + \mathbf{V}_i \times \mathbf{B}) + \nabla \cdot \tau_i - n_i m_i \nabla\phi + P_{ie} \qquad \textbf{3.193}$$

Continuity for the ions is:

$$\frac{\partial n_i}{\partial t} + \nabla \cdot (n_i \mathbf{V}_i) = 0 \qquad \textbf{3.194}$$

The equation of motion for the electrons is:

$$n_e m_e \left[\frac{\partial \mathbf{V}_e}{\partial t} + (\mathbf{V}_e \cdot \nabla)\mathbf{V}_e\right] = -n_e e(\mathbf{E} + \mathbf{V}_e \times \mathbf{B}) + \nabla \cdot \tau_e - n_e m_e \nabla\phi + P_{ei} \qquad \textbf{3.195}$$

Continuity for the electrons is:

$$\frac{\partial n_e}{\partial t} + \nabla \cdot (n_e \mathbf{V}_e) = 0 \qquad \textbf{3.196}$$

The following symbols have been used:

e = electronic charge. (The charge on the electron is $-e$.)

n_i = ion particle number density.

n_e = electron particle number density.

m_i = ion mass.

m_e = electron mass.

Z = number of electronic charges per ion.

ϕ = gravitational potential.

P_{ie} = interaction force due to collisions; force of electrons on ions. $P_{ie} = -P_{ei}$. (Per unit volume.)

P_{ei} = interaction force due to collisions, ions on electrons.

τ = stress tensor.

By defining certain auxiliary functions, the equations of motion can be put into various forms. Commonly defined are the terms:

$$\mathbf{V} = \frac{1}{\rho_m}(n_i m_i \mathbf{V}_i + n_e m_e \mathbf{V}_e) \qquad \textbf{3.197}$$

$$\mathbf{J} = e(n_i Z \mathbf{V}_i - n_e \mathbf{V}_e) \qquad \textbf{3.198}$$

$$\rho_m = n_i m_i + n_e m_e \qquad \textbf{3.199}$$

$$P = P_i + P_e \qquad \textbf{3.200}$$

where P_i and P_e are the ion and electron partial pressures respectively, and are the diagonal parts of the respective stress tensors. P is the total pressure. $\mathbf{V}$ is the average bulk velocity of the fluid, $\mathbf{J}$ is the current density vector, and ρ_m is the fluid density.

If the following assumptions are made, the equations of motion can be greatly simplified. These assumptions are valid for certain situations, but must be used with care. Assume, then:

1. Quadratic terms in **V** and **J** and their derivatives are neglected.
2. Electrical neutrality is assumed, e.g., $n_i Z = n_e$.
3. Throughout, the term m_e/m_i is ignored compared to unity.
4. Zm_eP_i/m_i is neglected compared to P_e.
5. The viscous stresses are neglected and the stress tensor is replaced by a scalar pressure, so that $-\nabla P_i = \nabla \cdot \tau_i$ and $-\nabla P_e = \nabla \cdot \tau_e$.

Under these assumptions the following equations can be derived. Adding the equations of motion, there results

$$\rho_m \frac{\partial \mathbf{V}}{\partial t} = \mathbf{J} \times \mathbf{B} - \nabla P - \rho_m \nabla \phi \qquad \textbf{3.201}$$

which is the linearized bulk equation of motion for the plasma. By subtracting the equations of motion, there results a form of Ohm's law

$$\frac{m_e}{n_e e^2} \frac{\partial \mathbf{J}}{\partial t} = \mathbf{E} + \mathbf{V} \times \mathbf{B} + \frac{\nabla P_e}{e n_e} - \frac{1}{e n_e} \mathbf{J} \times \mathbf{B} - \eta \mathbf{J} \qquad \textbf{3.202}$$

where the η term is essentially a resistivity and is given by

$$\eta = \frac{P_{ei}}{e n_e |\mathbf{J}|} \qquad \textbf{3.203}$$

3.24 THE BASIC EQUATIONS IN VARIOUS SYSTEMS OF UNITS

The units used in this chapter have been RMKS and Gaussian. For ready reference, we now list the basic equations in these units and others. We list the vacuum equations, the equations for material media, and finally the conversion method from RMKS to Gaussian.

(a) Vacuum Equations.

Table I

RMKS	Gaussian (cgs)	Heaviside-Lorentz (cgs)	Natural (Rationalized, $c = 1$)
	(In the cgs systems, **J** is measured in esu. If **J** is measured in emu, **J** in the following equations must be multiplied by c.)		
$\mathbf{B} = \mu_0 \mathbf{H}$	$\mathbf{B} = \mathbf{H}$	$\mathbf{B} = \mathbf{H}$	$\mathbf{B} = \mathbf{H}$
$\mathbf{D} = \epsilon_0 \mathbf{E}$	$\mathbf{D} = \mathbf{E}$	$\mathbf{D} = \mathbf{E}$	$\mathbf{D} = \mathbf{E}$
$\nabla \cdot \mathbf{E} = \frac{\rho}{\epsilon_0}$	$\nabla \cdot \mathbf{E} = 4\pi\rho$	$\nabla \cdot \mathbf{E} = \rho$	$\nabla \cdot \mathbf{E} = \rho$
$\nabla \times \mathbf{E} = -\frac{\partial \mathbf{B}}{\partial t}$	$\nabla \times \mathbf{E} = -\frac{1}{c}\frac{\partial \mathbf{B}}{\partial t}$	$\nabla \times \mathbf{E} = -\frac{1}{c}\frac{\partial \mathbf{B}}{\partial t}$	$\nabla \times \mathbf{E} = -\frac{\partial \mathbf{B}}{\partial t}$
$\nabla \cdot \mathbf{B} = 0$	$\nabla \cdot \mathbf{B} = 0$	$\nabla \cdot \mathbf{B} = 0$	$\nabla \cdot \mathbf{B} = 0$

Table I (cont.)

RMKS	Gaussian (cgs)	Heaviside-Lorentz (cgs)	Natural (Rationalized, $c = 1$)
	(In the cgs systems, **J** is measured in esu. If **J** is measured in emu, **J** in the following equations must be multiplied by c.)		
$\nabla \cdot \mathbf{J} + \frac{\partial \rho}{\partial t} = 0$	$\nabla \cdot \mathbf{J} + \frac{\partial \rho}{\partial t} = 0$	$\nabla \cdot \mathbf{J} + \frac{\partial \rho}{\partial t} = 0$	$\nabla \cdot \mathbf{J} + \frac{\partial \rho}{\partial t} = 0$
$\mathbf{B} = \nabla \times \mathbf{A}$	$\mathbf{B} = \nabla \times \mathbf{A}$	$\mathbf{B} = \nabla \times \mathbf{A}$	$\mathbf{B} = \nabla \times \mathbf{A}$
$\mathbf{E} = -\nabla\phi - \frac{\partial \mathbf{A}}{\partial t}$	$\mathbf{E} = -\nabla\phi - \frac{1}{c}\frac{\partial \mathbf{A}}{\partial t}$	$\mathbf{E} = -\nabla\phi - \frac{1}{c}\frac{\partial \mathbf{A}}{\partial t}$	$\mathbf{E} = -\nabla\phi - \frac{\partial \mathbf{A}}{\partial t}$
$\nabla \times \mathbf{B} = \mu_0\left(\mathbf{J} + \epsilon_0 \frac{\partial \mathbf{E}}{\partial t}\right)$	$\nabla \times \mathbf{B} = \frac{4\pi}{c}\mathbf{J} + \frac{1}{c}\frac{\partial \mathbf{E}}{\partial t}$	$\nabla \times \mathbf{B} = \frac{\mathbf{J}}{c} + \frac{1}{c}\frac{\partial \mathbf{E}}{\partial t}$	$\nabla \times \mathbf{B} = \mathbf{J} + \frac{\partial \mathbf{E}}{\partial t}$
$\mathbf{F} = q(\mathbf{E} + \mathbf{V} \times \mathbf{B})$	$\mathbf{F} = q\left(\mathbf{E} + \frac{\mathbf{V} \times \mathbf{B}}{c}\right)$	$\mathbf{F} = q\left(\mathbf{E} + \frac{\mathbf{V} \times \mathbf{B}}{c}\right)$	$\mathbf{F} = q(\mathbf{E} + \mathbf{V} \times \mathbf{B})$
$\mathbf{E} = \frac{1}{4\pi\epsilon_0}\int_V \frac{\rho\mathbf{r}}{r^3}\,dV$	$\mathbf{E} = \int_V \frac{\rho\mathbf{r}}{r^3}\,dV$	$\mathbf{E} = \frac{1}{4\pi}\int_V \frac{\rho\mathbf{r}}{r^3}\,dV$	$\mathbf{E} = \frac{1}{4\pi}\int_V \frac{\rho\mathbf{r}}{r^3}\,dV$
$\mathbf{B} = \frac{\mu_0}{4\pi}\int_V \frac{\left(\mathbf{J} + \epsilon_0 \frac{\partial \mathbf{E}}{\partial t}\right) \times \mathbf{r}}{r^3}\,dV$	$\mathbf{B} = \frac{1}{c}\int_V \frac{\left(\mathbf{J} + \frac{1}{4\pi}\frac{\partial \mathbf{E}}{\partial t}\right) \times \mathbf{r}}{r^3}\,dV$	$\mathbf{B} = \frac{1}{4\pi c}\int_V \frac{\left(\mathbf{J} + \frac{\partial \mathbf{E}}{\partial t}\right) \times \mathbf{r}}{r^3}\,dV$	$\mathbf{B} = \frac{1}{4\pi}\int_V \frac{\left(\mathbf{J} + \frac{\partial \mathbf{E}}{\partial t}\right) \times \mathbf{r}}{r^3}\,dV$

(b) Equations for Material Media.

Table II

RMKS	Gaussian (cgs)	Heaviside-Lorentz (cgs)	Natural (Rationalized, $c = 1$)
	(In the cgs systems, **J** is measured in esu. If **J** is measured in emu, **J** in the following equations must be multiplied by c.)		
$\nabla \cdot \mathbf{D} = \rho$	$\nabla \cdot \mathbf{D} = 4\pi\rho$	$\nabla \cdot \mathbf{D} = \rho$	$\nabla \cdot \mathbf{D} = \rho$
$\nabla \times \mathbf{E} = -\frac{\partial \mathbf{B}}{\partial t}$	$\nabla \times \mathbf{E} = -\frac{1}{c}\frac{\partial \mathbf{B}}{\partial t}$	$\nabla \times \mathbf{E} = -\frac{1}{c}\frac{\partial \mathbf{B}}{\partial t}$	$\nabla \times \mathbf{E} = -\frac{\partial \mathbf{B}}{\partial t}$
$\nabla \cdot \mathbf{B} = 0$	$\nabla \cdot \mathbf{B} = 0$	$\nabla \cdot \mathbf{B} = 0$	$\nabla \cdot \mathbf{B} = 0$
$\nabla \times \mathbf{H} = \mathbf{J} + \frac{\partial \mathbf{D}}{\partial t}$	$\nabla \times \mathbf{H} = \frac{4\pi\mathbf{J}}{c} + \frac{1}{c}\frac{\partial \mathbf{D}}{\partial t}$	$\nabla \times \mathbf{H} = \frac{\mathbf{J}}{c} + \frac{1}{c}\frac{\partial \mathbf{D}}{\partial t}$	$\nabla \times \mathbf{H} = \mathbf{J} + \frac{\partial \mathbf{D}}{\partial t}$
$\mathbf{D} = \epsilon\mathbf{E} = \epsilon_0\kappa\mathbf{E}$	$\mathbf{D} = \kappa\mathbf{E}$	$\mathbf{D} = \kappa\mathbf{E}$	$\mathbf{D} = \kappa\mathbf{E}$
$\mathbf{B} = \mu\mathbf{H} = \mu_0\kappa_m\mathbf{H}$	$\mathbf{B} = \kappa_m\mathbf{H}$	$\mathbf{B} = \kappa_m\mathbf{H}$	$\mathbf{B} = \kappa_m\mathbf{H}$
$\mathbf{F} = \rho\mathbf{E} + \mathbf{J} \times \mathbf{B}$	$\mathbf{F} = \rho\mathbf{E} + \frac{\mathbf{J} \times \mathbf{B}}{c}$	$\mathbf{F} = \rho\mathbf{E} + \frac{\mathbf{J} \times \mathbf{B}}{c}$	$\mathbf{F} = \rho\mathbf{E} + \mathbf{J} \times \mathbf{B}$

(c) To convert from RMKS to Gaussian or vice-versa, the following table is useful. The substitution indicated in the table should be made.

Table III

RMKS (Rationalized mks)	Gaussian (Unrationalized cgs)
$\mathbf{E}$	$\mathbf{E}$
$\mathbf{B}$	$\mathbf{B}/c$
$\mathbf{D}$	$\mathbf{D}/4\pi$
$\mathbf{H}$	$\mathbf{H}c/4\pi$
ϵ	$\epsilon/4\pi$
μ	$\mu 4\pi/c^2$
ρ	ρ
$\mathbf{J}$	$\mathbf{J}$
ϕ	ϕ
$\mathbf{A}$	$\mathbf{A}/c$

(d) Conversion Table for Units.

Table IV

Quantity	mks unit	Gaussian unit
time	1 sec	1 sec
length	1 m	10^2 cm
mass	1 kg	10^3 gm
force	1 newton	10^5 dynes
energy	1 joule	10^7 ergs
power	1 watt	10^7 ergs/sec
charge	1 coulomb	3×10^9 statcoulombs
electric field **E**	1 volt/m	$1/3 \times 10^{-4}$ statvolt/cm
electric displacement **D**	1 coulomb/m^2	$12\pi \times 10^5$ statcoulombs/cm^2
potential	1 volt	$1/3 \times 10^{-2}$ statvolt
capacitance	1 farad	9×10^{11} cm
current	1 amp	3×10^9 statamperes
resistance	1 ohm	$1/9 \times 10^{-11}$ statohm
magnetic field **H**	1 amp-turn/m	$4\pi \times 10^{-3}$ oersted
magnetic induction **B**	1 weber/m^2	10^4 gausses
magnetic flux $\mathbf{B} \cdot d\mathbf{S}$	1 weber	10^8 maxwells
inductance	1 henry	10^9 abhenrys

(e) The Fundamental Constants of Electromagnetic Theory.

Table V

Constant	mks	Gaussian
permittivity in vacuum, ϵ_0	8.854×10^{-12} farad/m	1
permeability in vacuum, μ_0	$4\pi \times 10^{-7}$ henry/m	1
velocity of light, c	2.998×10^{8} m/sec	2.998×10^{10} cm/sec
electronic charge, e	1.602×10^{-19} coulomb	4.803×10^{-10} statcoulomb
mass of the electron, m_e	9.108×10^{-31} kg	9.108×10^{-28} gm

3.25 LIST OF SYMBOLS USED IN CHAPTER 3

A = Free energy of the electromagnetic field.

$\mathbf{A}$ = Vector potential.

$\mathbf{B}$ = Magnetic induction.

c = Velocity of light.

$\mathbf{D}$ = Electric displacement.

$\mathbf{E}$ = Electric field.

F^{ij} = Field tensor.

$\mathbf{F}$ = Force.

$\mathbf{f}$ = Force density.

g_i = Electromagnetic momentum.

$\mathbf{H}$ = Magnetic field.

H^{ij} = Field tensor.

$\mathbf{J}$ = Current density.

$\mathbf{M}$ = Magnetization.

$\mathbf{P}$ = Polarization.

P = Pressure.

S = Entropy.

T_{ij} = Stress tensor.

u, v, w = Cartesian components of velocity.

U = Internal energy of the electromagnetic field.

$\mathbf{V}$ = Velocity.

γ = $\sqrt{1 - |\mathbf{V}|^2/c^2}$

ϵ_0 = Permittivity of free space.

ϵ = Permittivity or dielectric constant.

κ = Relative permittivity.

κ_m = Relative permeability.

μ_0 = Permeability of free space.

μ = Permeability.

ν = Kinematic viscosity.

ρ = Charge density.

ρ_m = Material density.

σ = Electrical conductivity.

ϕ = Scalar electric potential. Also used as gravitational potential in section on plasma theory.

Φ = Mechanical dissipation function.

τ = Mechanical stress tensor.

3.26 LIST OF REFERENCES

1. Abraham, M., and Becker, R., *The Classical Theory of Electricity and Magnetism,* Blackie and Sons, London, 1932
2. Becker, R., *Theorie der Elektrizität,* Band II, G. G. Teubner, Berlin, 1933
3. Cowling, T. G., *Magnetohydrodynamics,* Interscience, 1957
4. Delcroix, J. L., *Introduction to the Theory of Ionized Gases,* Interscience, 1960
5. Ferraro, V. C. A., and Plumpton, C., *An Introduction to Magneto-Fluid-Dynamics,* Oxford, 1961
6. Jeans, Sir J. H., *The Mathematical Theory of Electricity and Magnetism,* 5th edition, Cambridge, 1925
7. Landau, L. D., and Lifshitz, E. M., *Electrodynamics of Continuous Media,* Addison-Wesley, 1960
8. Menzel, D. H., *Fundamental Formulas of Physics,* Vol. I, Dover, 1960
9. Møller, C., *The Theory of Relativity,* Oxford, 1952
10. Pai, S. I., *Magnetogasdynamics and Plasma Dynamics,* Prentice Hall, 1962
11. Panofsky, W., and Phillips, M., *Classical Electricity and Magnetism,* Addison-Wesley, 1957
12. Smythe, W. R., *Static and Dynamic Electricity,* McGraw-Hill, 1950
13. Sommerfeld, A., *Electrodynamics,* Academic Press, 1952
14. Spitzer, L., *Physics of Fully Ionized Gases,* Interscience, 1956
15. Stratton, J. A., *Electromagnetic Theory,* McGraw-Hill, 1941
16. Thompson, W. B., *An Introduction to Plasma Physics,* Addison-Wesley, 1962
17. Tolman, R., *Relativity, Thermodynamics, and Cosmology,* Oxford, 1934

Chapter 4

Dynamics

4.1 KINEMATICS

(a) Vectors.

The right-handed triad of unit vectors is three mutually perpendicular vectors of unit length, defined as ($\mathbf{i}$, $\mathbf{j}$, and $\mathbf{k}$) such that their vector products are $\mathbf{i}\times\mathbf{j} = \mathbf{k}$, $\mathbf{j}\times\mathbf{k} = \mathbf{i}$, $\mathbf{k}\times\mathbf{i} = \mathbf{j}$. Other forms of notation are: for Cartesian coordinates, $(\mathbf{e}_1, \mathbf{e}_2, \mathbf{e}_3)$ or $(\hat{x}, \hat{y}, \hat{z})$; for cylindrical coordinates, $(\mathbf{e}_r, \mathbf{e}_\theta, \mathbf{e}_z)$; for spherical coordinates, $(\mathbf{e}_r, \mathbf{e}_\theta, \mathbf{e}_\phi)$.

The position vector is denoted as $\mathbf{r}$. In Cartesian coordinates $\mathbf{r} = x\mathbf{i} + y\mathbf{j} + z\mathbf{k}$ or $\mathbf{r} = \mathbf{e}_1 x + \mathbf{e}_2 y + \mathbf{e}_3 z$ which can be written more compactly in tensor form as $\mathbf{r} = \mathbf{e}_i x^i$.

(b) Generalized Coordinates.

A Cartesian component of a vector $\mathbf{r}$ can be expressed as

$$x^i = x^i(q^1, q^2, q^3, t) \qquad \textbf{4.1}$$

or conversely

$$q^m = q^m(x^1, x^2, x^3, t) \qquad \textbf{4.2}$$

where q^m is the generalized coordinate and t is time.

Determination of q^m from x^i: A necessary condition for solving for q^m, given $x^i = x^i(q^1, q^2, q^3)$, follows from the linear equations $\delta x^i = \dfrac{\partial x^i}{\partial q^m}\delta q^m$ which leads to the Jacobian determinant

$$\left|\frac{\partial x^i}{\partial q^m}\right| \neq 0 \qquad \textbf{4.3}$$

or

$$\begin{vmatrix} \dfrac{\partial x^1}{\partial q^1} & \dfrac{\partial x^1}{\partial q^2} & \dfrac{\partial x^1}{\partial q^3} \\ \dfrac{\partial x^2}{\partial q^1} & \dfrac{\partial x^2}{\partial q^2} & \dfrac{\partial x^2}{\partial q^3} \\ \dfrac{\partial x^3}{\partial q^1} & \dfrac{\partial x^3}{\partial q^2} & \dfrac{\partial x^3}{\partial q^3} \end{vmatrix} \neq 0$$

For a system of N particles the generalized coordinates can be expressed as (for the pth particle)

$$x_p^i = x_p^i(q^1, q^2, \ldots, q^f, t) \qquad \textbf{4.4}$$

where f = the $3N$ coordinates. If the Jacobian determinant is not zero, i.e.,

$$\left|\frac{\partial(x_1^1, \ldots, x_N^3)}{\partial(q^1, \cdots, q^f)}\right| \neq 0$$

then

$$q^m = q^m(x_1^1, \ldots, x_N^3) \qquad \textbf{4.5}$$

(c) Constraints.

If constraints are present, they are holonomic if they can be expressed in the form

$$\phi^s(x_1^1, \ldots, x_N^3, t) = 0, \qquad (s = 1, 2, \ldots, K) \qquad \textbf{4.6}$$

If the time t is involved in the above expression, it is a moving constraint. If time is not involved, it is a fixed or workless constraint.

In terms of generalized coordinates the equations for K constraints are

$$\tilde{q}^s = \phi^s(x_1^1, \ldots, x_N^3, t) \qquad \textbf{4.7}$$

where $s = 1, 2, \ldots, K$.

The other equations are: $q^m = q^m(x_1^1, \ldots, x_N^3, t)$, $m = 1, 2, \ldots, (3N - K)$. By proper choice of generalized coordinates, the constraints may become trivial, giving $\tilde{q}^s = 0$.

(d) Velocity and Acceleration in Generalized Coordinates.

For a system of N particles with equations of constraint removed

$$x_p^i = x_p^i(q^1, \ldots, q^f, t), \qquad p = 1, \ldots, N$$

The velocity is then

$$\dot{x}_p^i = \frac{\partial x_p^i}{\partial q^m}\dot{q}^m + \frac{\partial x_p^i}{\partial t} \qquad \textbf{4.8}$$

and the acceleration is

$$\ddot{x}_p^i = \frac{\partial x_p^i}{\partial q^m}\ddot{q}^m + \frac{\partial^2 x_p^i}{\partial q^m \partial q^n}\dot{q}^m \dot{q}^n + \frac{2\partial^2 x_p^i}{\partial q^m \partial t}\dot{q}^m + \frac{\partial^2 x_i^p}{\partial t^2} \qquad \textbf{4.9}$$

(e) Transformation Laws between Coordinates.

1. Contravariant components of a vector transform according to

$$\bar{\lambda}^n = \frac{\partial \bar{q}^n}{\partial q^m}\lambda^m \qquad \textbf{4.10}$$

2. Covariant components of a vector transform as

$$\bar{\lambda}_n = \frac{\partial q^m}{\partial \bar{q}^n}\lambda_m \qquad \textbf{4.11}$$

3. Scalar invariants of the contravariant and covariant components of two vectors:

If λ_m and μ^m are respectively the covariant and contravariant components of two vectors, then the quantity $\lambda_m \mu^m$ is a scalar invariant, that is,

$$\bar{\lambda}_n \bar{\mu}^n = \lambda_m \mu^m$$

(f) *Metric Tensor and Christoffel Symbols.*

The length of a vector in generalized coordinates is given by the metric tensor g_{mn}.

$$ds^2 = g_{mn}\, dq^m\, dq^n$$

where

$$g_{mn} = \frac{\partial x^1}{\partial q^m}\frac{\partial x^1}{\partial q^n} + \frac{\partial x^2}{\partial q^m}\frac{\partial x^2}{\partial q^n} + \frac{\partial x^3}{\partial q^m}\frac{\partial x^3}{\partial q^n} \qquad \textbf{4.12}$$

Christoffel symbol of the first kind:

$$[mn, r] = \frac{1}{2}\left[\frac{\partial g_{rm}}{\partial q^n} + \frac{\partial g_{nr}}{\partial q^m} - \frac{\partial g_{mn}}{\partial q^r}\right] \qquad \textbf{4.13}$$

Christoffel symbol of the second kind:

$$\left\{ {s \atop mn} \right\} = g^{sr}[mn, r] = \frac{1}{2} g^{sr}\left[\frac{\partial g_{rm}}{\partial q^n} + \frac{\partial g_{nr}}{\partial q^m} - \frac{\partial g_{mn}}{\partial q^r}\right] \qquad \textbf{4.14}$$

In Cartesian coordinates the Christoffel symbols are zero. In terms of Christoffel symbols, acceleration transforms as

$$\overline{\ddot{q}^k + \left\{ {k \atop mn} \right\} \dot{q}^m\, \dot{q}^n} = (\ddot{q}^l + \left\{ {l \atop rs} \right\} \dot{q}^r\, \dot{q}^s)\frac{\partial \bar{q}^k}{\partial q^l} \qquad \textbf{4.15}$$

and for Cartesian coordinates the Christoffel symbol of the second kind determines the components of acceleration as

$$\ddot{x}^k = (\ddot{q}^l + \left\{ {l \atop rs} \right\} \dot{q}^r\, \dot{q}^s)\frac{\partial x^k}{\partial q^l} \qquad \textbf{4.16}$$

(g) *Components of Velocity and Acceleration in Cylindrical Coordinates.*

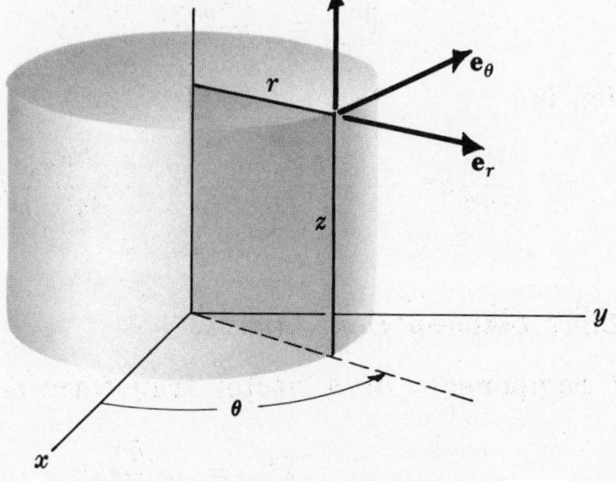

Fig. 4-1. Cylindrical Coordinates.

$$x = r\cos\theta, \quad y = r\sin\theta, \quad z = z$$

$$r = \sqrt{x^2 + y^2}, \quad \theta = \tan^{-1} y/x$$

The velocity is

$$\dot{x} = \dot{r}\cos\theta - r\dot{\theta}\sin\theta \qquad \textbf{4.17}$$

$$\dot{y} = \dot{r}\sin\theta + r\dot{\theta}\cos\theta$$

$$\dot{r} = \frac{\dot{x}x + \dot{y}y}{\sqrt{x^2+y^2}}$$

$$\dot{\theta} = \frac{x\dot{y} - y\dot{x}}{x^2+y^2}$$

The acceleration is

$$\ddot{x} = (\ddot{r} - r\dot{\theta}^2)\cos\theta - (r\ddot{\theta} + 2\dot{r}\dot{\theta})\sin\theta \qquad \textbf{4.18}$$

$$\ddot{y} = (\ddot{r} - r\dot{\theta}^2)\sin\theta + (r\ddot{\theta} + 2\dot{r}\dot{\theta})\cos\theta$$

The radial and transverse direction components are:

Velocity:

$$\mathbf{v} = \dot{r}\mathbf{e}_r + r\dot{\theta}\mathbf{e}_\theta + \dot{z}\mathbf{e}_z \qquad \textbf{4.19}$$

Acceleration:

$$\mathbf{a} = (\ddot{r} - r\dot{\theta}^2)\mathbf{e}_r + (r\ddot{\theta} + 2\dot{r}\dot{\theta})\mathbf{e}_\theta + \ddot{z}\mathbf{e}_z \qquad \textbf{4.20}$$

(h) Components of Velocity and Acceleration in Spherical Coordinates.

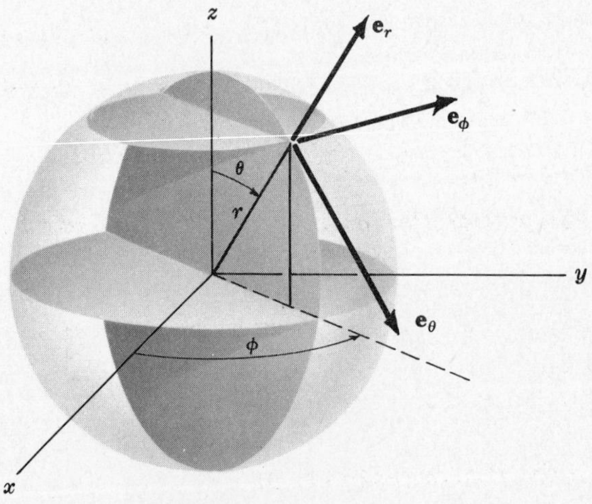

Fig. 4-2. Spherical Coordinates.

$$r = \sqrt{x^2+y^2+z^2}, \qquad \theta = \cot^{-1}\frac{z}{\sqrt{x^2+y^2}}, \qquad \phi = \tan^{-1}\frac{y}{x}$$

$$x = r\sin\theta\cos\phi, \qquad y = r\sin\theta\sin\phi, \qquad z = r\cos\theta$$

The velocity is then

$$\dot{x} = \dot{r}\sin\theta\cos\phi + r\dot{\theta}\cos\theta\cos\phi - r\dot{\phi}\sin\theta\sin\phi \qquad \textbf{4.21}$$

$$\dot{y} = \dot{r}\sin\theta\sin\phi + r\dot{\theta}\cos\theta\sin\phi + r\dot{\phi}\sin\theta\cos\phi$$

$$\dot{z} = \dot{r}\cos\theta - r\dot{\theta}\sin\theta$$

$$\dot{r} = \frac{x\dot{x} + y\dot{y} + z\dot{z}}{\sqrt{x^2 + y^2 + z^2}}$$

$$\dot{\theta} = \frac{(x\dot{x} + y\dot{y})z - \dot{z}(x^2 + y^2)}{\sqrt{x^2 + y^2}\,(x^2 + y^2 + z^2)}$$

$$\dot{\phi} = \frac{x\dot{y} - y\dot{x}}{x^2 + y^2}$$

The acceleration is

$$\begin{aligned} \ddot{x} &= (\ddot{r} - r\dot{\theta}^2 - r\dot{\phi}^2) \sin\theta \cos\phi + (2\dot{r}\dot{\theta} + r\ddot{\theta}) \cos\theta \cos\phi \\ &\quad - (r\ddot{\phi} + 2\dot{r}\dot{\phi}) \sin\theta \sin\phi - 2r\dot{\theta}\dot{\phi} \cos\theta \sin\phi \\ \ddot{y} &= (\ddot{r} - r\dot{\theta}^2 - r\dot{\phi}^2) \sin\theta \sin\phi + (2\dot{r}\dot{\theta} + r\ddot{\theta}) \cos\theta \sin\phi \\ &\quad + (r\ddot{\phi} + 2\dot{r}\dot{\phi}) \sin\theta \cos\phi + 2r\dot{\theta}\dot{\phi} \cos\theta \cos\phi \\ \ddot{z} &= (\ddot{r} - r\dot{\theta}^2) \cos\theta - (r\ddot{\theta} + 2\dot{r}\dot{\theta}) \sin\theta \end{aligned} \qquad \textbf{4.22}$$

In terms of $\mathbf{e}_r, \mathbf{e}_\theta, \mathbf{e}_\phi$ the equations can be written:

Velocity:

$$\mathbf{v} = \dot{r}\mathbf{e}_r + r\dot{\theta}\mathbf{e}_\theta + r \sin\theta\dot{\phi}\mathbf{e}_\phi \qquad \textbf{4.23}$$

Acceleration:

$$\begin{aligned} \mathbf{a} &= (\ddot{r} - r\dot{\theta}^2 - r\dot{\phi}^2 \sin^2\theta)\mathbf{e}_r \\ &\quad + (r\ddot{\theta} + 2\dot{r}\dot{\theta} - r\dot{\phi}^2 \sin\theta \cos\theta)\mathbf{e}_\theta \\ &\quad + (r \sin\phi\ddot{\phi} + 2\dot{r} \sin\theta\dot{\phi} + 2r \cos\theta\dot{\theta}\dot{\phi})\mathbf{e}_\phi \end{aligned} \qquad \textbf{4.24}$$

(i) Normal Tangential Coordinates in the Osculating Plane.

Velocity:

$$\mathbf{v} = q\mathbf{e}_t, \qquad q = \frac{ds}{dt} \qquad \textbf{4.25}$$

Acceleration:

$$\mathbf{a} = \dot{q}\mathbf{e}_t + \frac{q^2}{\rho}\mathbf{e}_n \qquad \textbf{4.26}$$

where ρ = the radius of curvature.

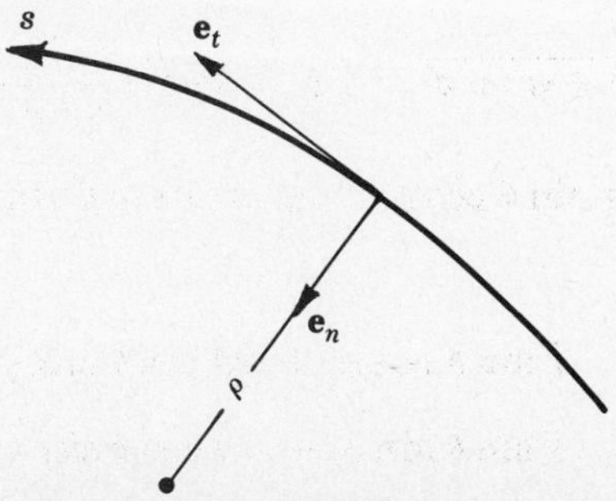

Fig. 4-3. The Osculating Plane.

4.2 ORTHOGONAL TRANSFORMATIONS OF COORDINATES

(a) Rotation.

Given a set of orthogonal unit vectors $\mathbf{e}_1, \mathbf{e}_2, \mathbf{e}_3$ and a new set $\bar{\mathbf{e}}_1, \bar{\mathbf{e}}_2, \bar{\mathbf{e}}_3$, then an orthogonal transformation, S_{ji}, is defined by $\mathbf{e}_i = \bar{\mathbf{e}}_j S_{ji}$. S_{ji} are the elements of an orthogonal matrix $\mathbf{S}$ which has the following properties:

1. Inverse of $\mathbf{S}$ is equal to the transpose of $\mathbf{S}$, $\mathbf{S}^{-1} = \mathbf{S}'$. Hence $\mathbf{SS}' = \mathbf{I}$, the identity matrix, or $S'_{ik} S_{kj} = \delta_{ij}$.
2. The determinant of $\mathbf{S}$ is equal to ± 1, $|\mathbf{S}| = \pm 1$.

An example is the rotation of two unit vectors in a plane. The unit vectors $\mathbf{e}_1$ and $\mathbf{e}_2$ are rotated through an angle θ to form unit vectors $\bar{\mathbf{e}}_1$ and $\bar{\mathbf{e}}_2$. Referring to Fig. 4-4, the transformation matrix for this rotation may be written:

$$\mathbf{S} = \begin{pmatrix} \cos\theta & \sin\theta \\ -\sin\theta & \cos\theta \end{pmatrix} \qquad 4.27$$

$$\mathbf{S}' = \begin{pmatrix} \cos\theta & -\sin\theta \\ \sin\theta & \cos\theta \end{pmatrix} = \mathbf{S}^{-1} \qquad 4.28$$

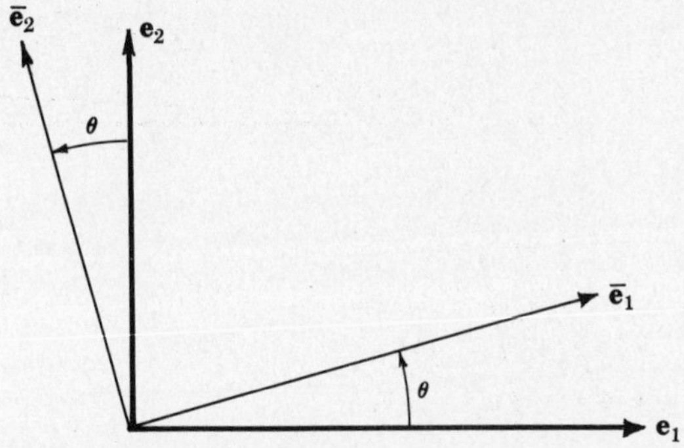

Fig. 4-4. Rotation of Two Unit Vectors in a Plane.

(b) Orthogonal Transformation of Vectors.

If $\mathbf{x}$ is expressed in terms of coordinates $\mathbf{e}_j$, and $\bar{\mathbf{x}}$ is the value of the vector expressed in terms of coordinates $\bar{\mathbf{e}}_i$, then:

$$\bar{\mathbf{x}} = \mathbf{S}\mathbf{x}, \qquad \bar{x}_i = S_{ij} x_j \qquad 4.29$$

and

$$\mathbf{x} = \mathbf{S}'\bar{\mathbf{x}} \qquad 4.30$$

(c) Transformation from Cartesian to Cylindrical Coordinates, Fig. 4-1.

$$\mathbf{e} = (\mathbf{e}_x, \mathbf{e}_y, \mathbf{e}_z)$$

$$\bar{\mathbf{e}} = (\mathbf{e}_r, \mathbf{e}_\theta, \mathbf{e}_z)$$

$$\mathbf{S} = \begin{bmatrix} \cos\theta & \sin\theta & 0 \\ -\sin\theta & \cos\theta & 0 \\ 0 & 0 & 1 \end{bmatrix} \qquad 4.31$$

(d) Transformation from Cartesian to Spherical Coordinates, Fig. 4-2.

$$\mathbf{e} = (\mathbf{e}_x, \mathbf{e}_y, \mathbf{e}_z)$$

$$\bar{\mathbf{e}} = (\mathbf{e}_r, \mathbf{e}_\theta, \mathbf{e}_\phi)$$

$$\mathbf{S} = \begin{bmatrix} \sin\theta\cos\phi & \sin\theta\sin\phi & \cos\theta \\ \cos\theta\cos\phi & \cos\theta\sin\phi & -\sin\theta \\ -\sin\phi & \cos\phi & 0 \end{bmatrix} \qquad \mathbf{4.32}$$

4.3 EULERIAN ANGLES

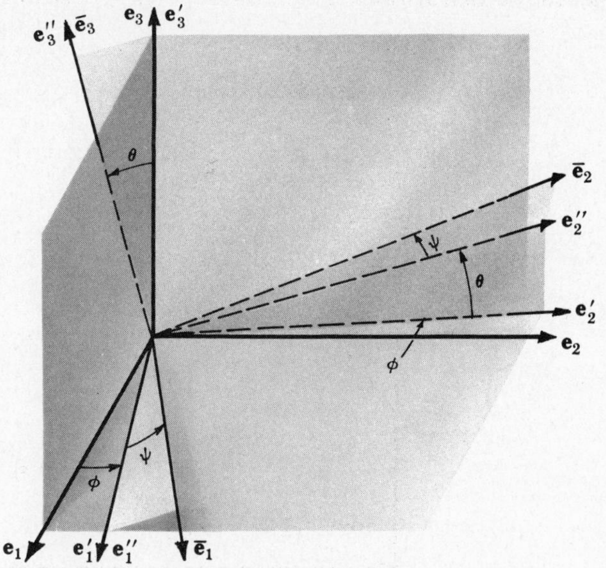

Fig. 4-5. The Eulerian Angles.

Referring to Fig. 4-5, the Eulerian angles define an orthogonal coordinate system $\bar{\mathbf{e}}_1, \bar{\mathbf{e}}_2, \bar{\mathbf{e}}_3$ that results from three successive rotations from a fixed coordinate system, $\mathbf{e}_1, \mathbf{e}_2, \mathbf{e}_3$. The three successive rotations are defined as follows:

1. Rotation ϕ about the $\mathbf{e}_3$ axis giving $\mathbf{e}_1', \mathbf{e}_2', \mathbf{e}_3'$.
2. Rotation θ about the $\mathbf{e}_1'$ axis giving $\mathbf{e}_1'', \mathbf{e}_2'', \mathbf{e}_3''$.
3. Rotation ψ about the $\mathbf{e}_3''$ axis giving $\bar{\mathbf{e}}_1, \bar{\mathbf{e}}_2, \bar{\mathbf{e}}_3$.

The transformation matrix $\bar{\mathbf{x}} = \mathbf{S}\mathbf{x}$ is:

$$\mathbf{S} = \begin{bmatrix} \begin{pmatrix} \cos\psi\cos\phi \\ -\sin\psi\cos\theta\sin\phi \end{pmatrix} & \begin{pmatrix} \cos\psi\sin\phi \\ +\sin\psi\cos\theta\cos\phi \end{pmatrix} & (\sin\psi\sin\theta) \\ \begin{pmatrix} -\sin\psi\cos\phi \\ -\cos\psi\cos\theta\sin\phi \end{pmatrix} & \begin{pmatrix} -\sin\psi\sin\phi \\ +\cos\psi\cos\theta\cos\phi \end{pmatrix} & (\cos\psi\sin\theta) \\ (\sin\theta\sin\phi) & (-\sin\theta\cos\phi) & \cos\theta \end{bmatrix} \qquad \mathbf{4.33}$$

4.4 MOVING FRAMES OF REFERENCE

Methods are given for expressing velocity, acceleration, angular momentum and kinetic energy referred to a fixed (or Newtonian) frame of reference in terms of vectors referred to moving coordinate systems.

(a) Velocity and Acceleration.

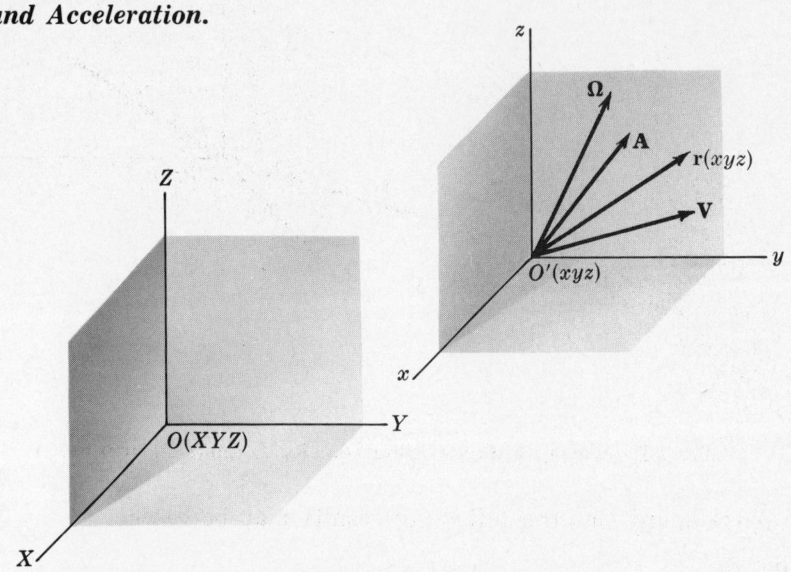

Fig. 4-6. Moving Frames of Reference for Velocity and Acceleration.

Referring to Fig. 4-6, let $O(XYZ)$ be a Newtonian frame of reference, and $O'(xyz)$ be a moving frame of reference. Let $\mathbf{r}(xyz)$ be the position vector relative to $O'(xyz)$, $\mathbf{V}$ = velocity of the moving origin O', $\mathbf{A}$ = acceleration of the origin O', $\boldsymbol{\Omega}$ = angular velocity of $O'(xyz)$. The subscript (xyz) means relative to the $O'(xyz)$ frame. (xyz) denotes the derivative referred to $O'(xyz)$, and (XYZ) denotes operation with respect to the Newtonian frame $O(XYZ)$.

Velocity:

$$\mathbf{v}_{(XYZ)} = \mathbf{V} + \mathbf{v}_{(xyz)} + \boldsymbol{\Omega} \times \mathbf{r}_{(xyz)} \qquad \textbf{4.34}$$

Acceleration:

$$\mathbf{a}_{(XYZ)} = \mathbf{A} + \left(\frac{d\boldsymbol{\Omega}}{dt}\right)_{(xyz)} \times \mathbf{r}_{(xyz)} + 2\boldsymbol{\Omega} \times \mathbf{v}_{(xyz)} + \boldsymbol{\Omega} \times (\boldsymbol{\Omega} \times \mathbf{r}_{(xyz)}) + \left(\frac{d^2\mathbf{r}}{dt^2}\right)_{(xyz)} \qquad \textbf{4.35}$$

and the following vector identity is useful:

$$\boldsymbol{\Omega} \times (\boldsymbol{\Omega} \times \mathbf{r}_{(xyz)}) = \boldsymbol{\Omega}(\boldsymbol{\Omega} \cdot \mathbf{r}_{(xyz)}) - \mathbf{r}_{(xyz)}|\boldsymbol{\Omega}|^2 \qquad \textbf{4.36}$$

It should be remembered that $\left(\frac{d\boldsymbol{\Omega}}{dt}\right)_{(XYZ)} = \left(\frac{d\boldsymbol{\Omega}}{dt}\right)_{(xyz)}$ since $\boldsymbol{\Omega} \times \boldsymbol{\Omega} = 0$.

(b) Angular Momentum Referred to a Frame of Reference Moving in Translation.

Referring to Fig. 4-7 below, we define:

$\mathbf{h}_{(xyz)}$ = angular momentum relative to system $O'(xyz)$ moving in translation

$\mathbf{h}_{(XYZ)}$ = angular momentum relative to a fixed origin $O(XYZ)$

$\mathbf{R}$ = position vector of the moving origin O'

$\mathbf{r}_c$ = position vector of the mass center of the system relative to $O'(xyz)$

M = total mass of the system.

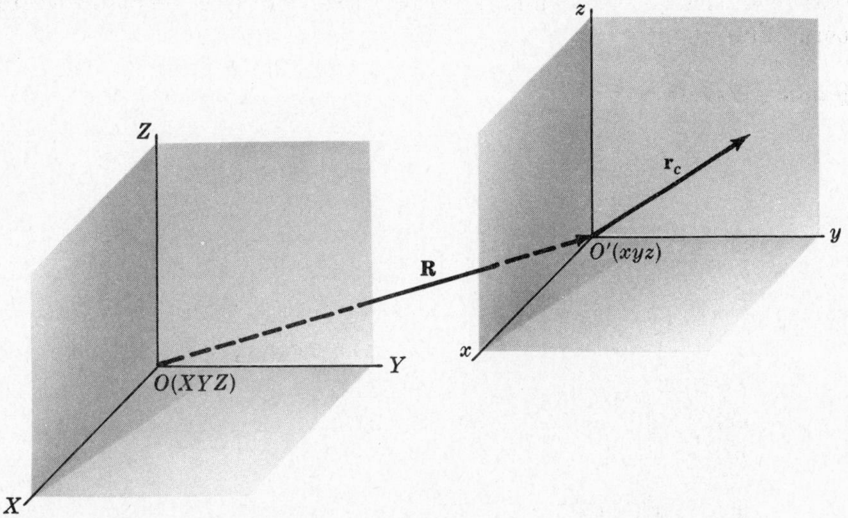

Fig. 4-7. Moving Frame of Reference for Angular Momentum.

With the above definitions the following results may be listed:

1. In general,

$$\mathbf{h}_{(XYZ)} = \mathbf{h}_{(xyz)} + \mathbf{R} \times M\dot{\mathbf{R}} + \mathbf{R} \times M\dot{\mathbf{r}}_c + \mathbf{r}_c \times M\dot{\mathbf{R}} \qquad \textbf{4.37}$$

$$\dot{\mathbf{h}}_{(XYZ)} = \dot{\mathbf{h}}_{(xyz)} + \mathbf{R} \times M\ddot{\mathbf{R}} + \mathbf{R} \times M\ddot{\mathbf{r}}_c + \mathbf{r}_c \times M\ddot{\mathbf{R}} \qquad \textbf{4.38}$$

2. Moving origin O' coincides instantaneously with fixed origin O. Then $\mathbf{R} = 0$, and O' is called the instant center.

$$\mathbf{h}_{(XYZ)} = \mathbf{h}_{(xyz)} + \mathbf{r}_c \times M\dot{\mathbf{R}} \qquad \textbf{4.39}$$

$$\dot{\mathbf{h}}_{(XYZ)} = \dot{\mathbf{h}}_{(xyz)} + \mathbf{r}_c \times M\ddot{\mathbf{R}} \qquad \textbf{4.40}$$

Note that $\dot{\mathbf{h}}_{(XYZ)} = \dot{\mathbf{h}}_{(xyz)}$ when $\mathbf{r}_c$, the position vector of the mass center, is in the same direction as the acceleration vector of the accelerating origin, $\ddot{\mathbf{R}}$.

3. If the moving origin O' is the mass center, $\mathbf{r}_c = 0$ and $\mathbf{R} = \mathbf{R}_c$.

$$\mathbf{h}_{(XYZ)} = \mathbf{h}_c + \mathbf{R}_c \times M\dot{\mathbf{R}}_c \qquad \textbf{4.41}$$

$$\dot{\mathbf{h}}_{(XYZ)} = \dot{\mathbf{h}}_c + \mathbf{R}_c \times M\ddot{\mathbf{R}}_c \qquad \textbf{4.42}$$

4. In general the following useful observation may be made:

   The angular momentum of a system about the origin $O(XYZ)$ equals the angular momentum of the system relative to the mass center plus the angular momentum, relative to $O(XYZ)$, of the mass of the system concentrated at the mass center.

5. If both frames of reference have their origin at the mass center, $\mathbf{R} = O$ and $\mathbf{r}_c = O$. Then,

$$\mathbf{h}_{(XYZ)} = \mathbf{h}_{(xyz)}, \qquad \dot{\mathbf{h}}_{(XYZ)} = \dot{\mathbf{h}}_{(xyz)} \qquad \textbf{4.43}$$

6. It may be concluded from the above statement that the angular momentum about the mass center is the same for all frames of reference.

(c) Acceleration of Instant Centers.

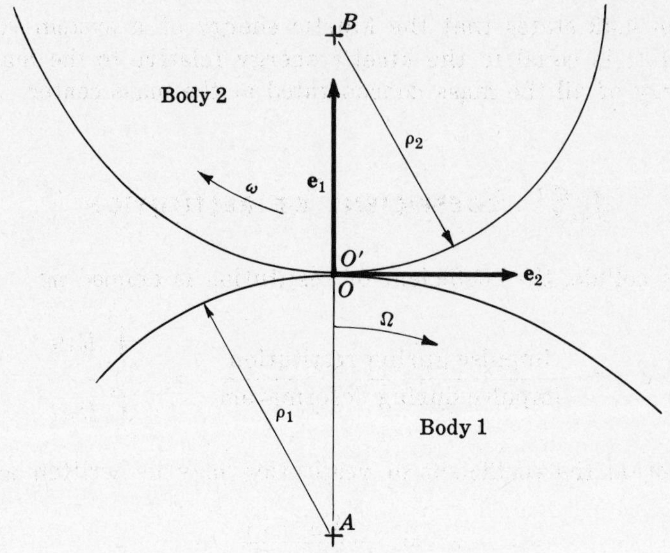

Fig. 4-8. Instant Center formed by Body 2 rolling on Body 1.

Fig. 4-8 shows an instant center O' in body 2 which is making rolling contact with point O in stationary body 1. ρ_1 is the radius of curvature of the contact surface in body 1 and ρ_2 is the radius of curvature in body 2. Ω is the angular velocity of line OA and ω is the angular velocity of body 2 and line $O'B$. The acceleration of the instant center O' is the value of $\ddot{\mathbf{R}}$ which may be substituted in equation 4.38 to determine $\dot{\mathbf{h}}_{(XYZ)}$.

1. In general,

$$\mathbf{a}_{O'} = \frac{\rho_1 \rho_2}{\rho_1 + \rho_2}\,\omega^2 \mathbf{e}_1 \qquad \textbf{4.44}$$

Substituting $\omega = \dfrac{\rho_1 + \rho_2}{\rho_2}\Omega$ gives

$$\mathbf{a}_{O'} = \frac{\rho_1}{\rho_2}(\rho_1 + \rho_2)\Omega^2 \mathbf{e}_1 \qquad \textbf{4.45}$$

2. Special case of body 2 rolling on a plane body 1, $\rho_1 = \infty$.

$$\mathbf{a}_{O'} = \rho_2 \omega^2 \mathbf{e}_1 \qquad \textbf{4.46}$$

3. Special case of body 2, a plane surface, rolling on body 1, $\rho_2 = \infty$.

$$\mathbf{a}_{O'} = \rho_1 \omega^2 \mathbf{e}_1 \qquad \textbf{4.47}$$

(d) Kinetic Energy Referred to a Frame of Reference Moving in Translation.

Define T as the kinetic energy of a system, defining all other symbols according to Fig. 4-7.

1. In general,

$$T_{(XYZ)} = T_{(xyz)} + \tfrac{1}{2}M[\dot{\mathbf{R}} \cdot \dot{\mathbf{R}} + \dot{\mathbf{R}} \cdot \dot{\mathbf{r}}_c] \qquad \textbf{4.48}$$

2. Moving origin at the mass center, (Theorem of König):

$$T_{(XYZ)} = T_{(xyz)} + \tfrac{1}{2}M\dot{\mathbf{R}}_c \cdot \dot{\mathbf{R}}_c \qquad 4.49$$

Equation 4.49 states that the kinetic energy of a system referred to a fixed origin $O(XYZ)$ is equal to the kinetic energy relative to the mass center plus the kinetic energy of all the mass concentrated at the mass center.

4.5 COEFFICIENT OF RESTITUTION

When two bodies collide, the coefficient of restitution is defined as

$$\epsilon = \frac{\text{impulse during restitution}}{\text{impulse during deformation}} = \frac{\int R\,dt}{\int D\,dt} \qquad 4.50$$

In rectilinear motion the coefficient of restitution may be written as

$$\epsilon = -\frac{V_{2f} - V_{1f}}{V_{2i} - V_{1i}} \qquad 4.51$$

where the subscript i refers to the initial velocities and f to final velocities. The velocities are measured at the point of impact. The coefficient of restitution may be written in terms of energy as

$$\epsilon^2 = \frac{\text{restoration energy}}{\text{deformation energy}} \qquad 4.52$$

Fig. 4-9. Collision of Two Bodies in Rectilinear Motion.

4.6 THE INERTIA TENSOR

(a) Definitions.

The inertia tensor **I** is defined as

$$\mathbf{I} = \begin{bmatrix} I_{xx} & -I_{xy} & -I_{yz} \\ -I_{xy} & I_{yy} & -I_{yz} \\ -I_{xz} & -I_{yz} & I_{zz} \end{bmatrix} \qquad 4.53$$

where for a discrete system:

$$\begin{aligned} I_{xx} &= \sum m_i(z_i^2 + y_i^2), & I_{xy} &= \sum m_i x_i y_i \qquad 4.54 \\ I_{yy} &= \sum m_i(x_i^2 + z_i^2), & I_{xz} &= \sum m_i x_i z_i \\ I_{zz} &= \sum m_i(x_i^2 + y_i^2), & I_{yz} &= \sum m_i y_i z_i \end{aligned}$$

and for a continuous system (where ρ is the mass density):

$$I_{xx} = \iiint \rho(z^2 + y^2)\,dx\,dy\,dz \qquad \textbf{4.55}$$

$$I_{yy} = \iiint \rho(x^2 + z^2)\,dx\,dy\,dz$$

$$I_{zz} = \iiint \rho(x^2 + y^2)\,dx\,dy\,dz$$

$$I_{xy} = \iiint \rho xy\,dx\,dy\,dz$$

$$I_{xz} = \iiint \rho xz\,dx\,dy\,dz$$

$$I_{yz} = \iiint \rho yz\,dx\,dy\,dz$$

In order to find the moment of inertia about a line k-k, let (l, m, n) be the direction cosines of the line k-k, and $\mathbf{e}_k(l, m, n)$ be a unit vector along k-k. The moment of inertia about k-k is

$$I_{kk} = \sum m_i(\mathbf{r}_i \times \mathbf{e}_k) \cdot (\mathbf{r}_i \times \mathbf{e}_k) \qquad \textbf{4.56}$$

$$I_{kk} = l^2 I_{xx} + m^2 I_{yy} + n^2 I_{zz} - 2lmI_{xy} - 2lnI_{xz} - 2mnI_{yz}$$

The product of inertia in a plane is defined by two perpendicular lines k-k and q-q, with unit vectors and direction cosines $\mathbf{e}_k(l, m, n)$ and $\mathbf{e}_q(l', m', n')$ respectively:

$$I_{qk} = \sum m_i(\mathbf{r}_i \times \mathbf{e}_k) \cdot (\mathbf{r}_i \times \mathbf{e}_q) \qquad \textbf{4.57}$$

$$I_{qk} = -ll'I_{xx} - mm'I_{yy} - nn'I_{zz} + (lm' + ml')I_{xy} + (ln' + nl')I_{xz} + (mn' + nm')I_{yz}$$

(b) *Transformation of Coordinates for Moments of Inertia and Products of Inertia in Tensor Form.*

Let a_{ki} and a_{qi} be the respective direction cosines for axis k-k and q-q, and define the moments of inertia to be

$$I_{11} = \sum m_i(x_2^2 + x_3^2) \qquad \textbf{4.58}$$

$$I_{12} = -\sum m_i(x_1 x_2)$$

Then the expressions for the transformed moments and products of inertia are

$$I_{kk} = \sum_j \sum_i a_{ki}\,a_{kj}\,I_{ij} \qquad \textbf{4.59}$$

and

$$I_{kq} = \sum_j \sum_i a_{ki}\,a_{qj}\,I_{ij} \qquad \textbf{4.60}$$

where a_{kj} and a_{qj} are the direction cosines.

(c) *The Momental Ellipsoid.*

Definition: The momental ellipsoid of a rigid body about an origin is the locus of points in space whose distance from the origin is $r = 1/\sqrt{I_{kk}}$ where I_{kk} is the moment of inertia about a line passing through the point and the origin.

The equation for the momental ellipsoid is

$$I_{xx}x^2 + I_{yy}y^2 + I_{zz}z^2 - 2I_{xy}xy - 2I_{xz}xz - 2I_{yz}yz = 1 \qquad 4.61$$

For axes of principal moments of inertia, the equation for the momental ellipsoid is

$$I'_{x'x'}x'^2 + I'_{y'y'}y'^2 + I'_{z'z'}z'^2 = 1 \qquad 4.62$$

where x', y', and z' are the principal axes.

(d) *Diagonalization of the Inertia Tensor* **I**, *Principal Moments of Inertia.*

The inertia tensor **I** is a real symmetric operator, and the principal axes are the axes which transform the inertia tensor into a diagonalized matrix **I′** whose elements are the principal moments of inertia. It follows that:

1. The trace is invariant, i.e. trace **I** = trace **I′**, or

$$I_{xx} + I_{yy} + I_{zz} = I'_{x'x'} + I'_{y'y'} + I'_{z'z'} \qquad 4.63$$

2. The determinant is invariant

$$\text{Det. } \mathbf{I} = \text{Det. } \mathbf{I}' = I'_{x'x'}I'_{y'y'}I'_{z'z'} \qquad 4.64$$

3. The elements of **I′**, the principal moments of inertia, are the eigenvalues of **I**, that is,

$$\begin{bmatrix} (I_{xx}-I') & -I_{xy} & -I_{xz} \\ -I_{xy} & (I_{yy}-I') & -I_{yz} \\ -I_{xz} & -I_{yz} & (I_{zz}-I') \end{bmatrix} \begin{bmatrix} x_1^k \\ x_2^k \\ x_3^k \end{bmatrix} = 0 \qquad 4.65$$

where the normalized values of the eigenvectors, $\mathbf{x}^k$, are the rows of the transformation matrix **S**, where $\mathbf{I}' = \mathbf{SIS}'$; that is,

$$x_i^k = S_{ki}, \qquad S_{11} = x_1^1, \qquad S_{12} = x_2^1, \qquad \text{etc.} \qquad 4.66$$

4. The principal moments of inertia are the roots of the determinantal equation

$$\begin{vmatrix} (I_{xx}-I') & -I_{xy} & -I_{xz} \\ -I_{xy} & (I_{yy}-I') & -I_{yz} \\ -I_{xz} & -I_{yz} & (I_{zz}-I') \end{vmatrix} = 0 \qquad 4.67$$

4.7 DYNAMICS OF RIGID BODIES

(a) *Angular Momentum.*

Let angular velocity $\boldsymbol{\omega} = \omega_1\mathbf{i} + \omega_2\mathbf{j} + \omega_3\mathbf{k}$ = the column vector $\begin{bmatrix} \omega_1 \\ \omega_2 \\ \omega_3 \end{bmatrix}$.

Let angular momentum $\mathbf{h} = h_1\mathbf{i} + h_2\mathbf{j} + h_3\mathbf{k}$ = the column vector $\begin{bmatrix} h_1 \\ h_2 \\ h_3 \end{bmatrix}$.

The angular momentum in matrix form is

$$\begin{bmatrix} h_1 \\ h_2 \\ h_3 \end{bmatrix} = \begin{bmatrix} I_{xx} & -I_{xy} & -I_{xz} \\ -I_{xy} & I_{yy} & -I_{yz} \\ -I_{xz} & -I_{yz} & I_{zz} \end{bmatrix} \begin{bmatrix} \omega_1 \\ \omega_2 \\ \omega_3 \end{bmatrix}, \qquad \mathbf{h} = \mathbf{I}\boldsymbol{\omega} \tag{4.68}$$

or written out,

$$\begin{aligned} h_1 &= I_{xx}\omega_1 - I_{xy}\omega_2 - I_{xz}\omega_3 \\ h_2 &= -I_{xy}\omega_1 + I_{yy}\omega_2 - I_{yz}\omega_3 \\ h_3 &= -I_{xz}\omega_1 - I_{yz}\omega_2 + I_{zz}\omega_3 \end{aligned} \tag{4.69}$$

For principal axes:

$$\begin{bmatrix} h_1 \\ h_2 \\ h_3 \end{bmatrix} = \begin{bmatrix} I_{xx} & 0 & 0 \\ 0 & I_{yy} & 0 \\ 0 & 0 & I_{zz} \end{bmatrix} \begin{bmatrix} \omega_1 \\ \omega_2 \\ \omega_3 \end{bmatrix} \tag{4.70}$$

and in vector form,

$$\mathbf{h} = I_{xx}\omega_1\mathbf{i} + I_{yy}\omega_2\mathbf{j} + I_{zz}\omega_3\mathbf{k} \tag{4.71}$$

(b) *Kinetic Energy Associated with the Angular Momentum of a Rigid Body.*

The kinetic energy is $T = \frac{1}{2}\boldsymbol{\omega} \cdot \mathbf{h}$. In matrix form:

$$T = \tfrac{1}{2}[\omega_1 \ \omega_2 \ \omega_3] \begin{bmatrix} I_{xx} & -I_{xy} & -I_{xz} \\ -I_{xy} & I_{yy} & -I_{yz} \\ -I_{xz} & -I_{yz} & I_{zz} \end{bmatrix} \begin{bmatrix} \omega_1 \\ \omega_2 \\ \omega_3 \end{bmatrix} = \tfrac{1}{2}\boldsymbol{\omega}' \cdot \mathbf{I}\boldsymbol{\omega} \tag{4.72}$$

In terms of any general axes,

$$T = \tfrac{1}{2}(I_{xx}\omega_1^2 + I_{yy}\omega_2^2 + I_{zz}\omega_3^2 - 2I_{xy}\omega_1\omega_2 - 2I_{yz}\omega_2\omega_3 - 2I_{xz}\omega_1\omega_3) \tag{4.73}$$

and for the principal axes,

$$T = \tfrac{1}{2}(I_{xx}\omega_1^2 + I_{yy}\omega_2^2 + I_{zz}\omega_3^2) \tag{4.74}$$

(c) *General Equations of Motion for a Rigid Body about a Fixed Point or Mass Center.*

Let the coordinates (XYZ) be a fixed nonrotating system, and the coordinates (xyz) be a rotating system in the body, but not necessarily rotating at the same angular velocity as the body. The following terms are defined:

$\boldsymbol{\Omega}$ = angular velocity of the moving axes (xyz).

$\boldsymbol{\omega}$ = angular velocity of the body.

Note that $\mathbf{\Omega}$ is not necessarily equal to $\boldsymbol{\omega}$. The sum of the external torques acting on the body is denoted as **G**. The general equations of motion are then

$$\mathbf{G} = \left(\frac{d\mathbf{h}}{dt}\right)_{XYZ} = \left(\frac{d\mathbf{h}}{dt}\right)_{xyz} + \mathbf{\Omega}\times\mathbf{h} \qquad 4.75$$

which can be written out as

$$\mathbf{G} = \left.\frac{d\mathbf{I}}{dt}\right|_{xyz}\cdot\boldsymbol{\omega} + \mathbf{I}\cdot\left.\frac{d\boldsymbol{\omega}}{dt}\right|_{xyz} + \mathbf{\Omega}\times\mathbf{h} \qquad 4.76$$

It should be noted that the angular momentum **h** should be taken in its general form as indicated in equation 4.68. If the angular velocities $\mathbf{\Omega}$ and $\boldsymbol{\omega}$ are different, i.e. the rotating axes (xyz) move with respect to the body, the moments and products of inertia change with time.

If the moving axes system (xyz) is permanently fixed in the body so that $\mathbf{\Omega} = \boldsymbol{\omega}$, and the origin is fixed at the mass center or a fixed point, the moments and products of inertia are constant. Then the derivative of $\boldsymbol{\omega}$ is the same referred to either the (XYZ) or (xyz) coordinate system:

$$\left(\frac{d\boldsymbol{\omega}}{dt}\right)_{XYZ} = \left(\frac{d\boldsymbol{\omega}}{dt}\right)_{xyz} + \boldsymbol{\omega}\times\boldsymbol{\omega} = \left(\frac{d\boldsymbol{\omega}}{dt}\right)_{xyz} = \dot{\boldsymbol{\omega}} \qquad 4.77$$

The equations of motion take the following form then for $\mathbf{\Omega} = \boldsymbol{\omega}$:

$$G_1 = I_{xx}\dot{\omega}_1 + \omega_2\omega_3(I_{zz} - I_{yy}) + I_{xy}(\omega_3\omega_1 - \dot{\omega}_2) - I_{xz}(\dot{\omega}_3 + \omega_2\omega_1) - I_{yz}(\omega_2^2 - \omega_3^2) \qquad 4.78$$

$$G_2 = I_{yy}\dot{\omega}_2 + \omega_3\omega_1(I_{xx} - I_{zz}) + I_{yz}(\omega_1\omega_2 - \dot{\omega}_3) - I_{xy}(\dot{\omega}_1 + \omega_3\omega_2) - I_{zx}(\omega_3^2 - \omega_1^2)$$

$$G_3 = I_{zz}\dot{\omega}_3 + \omega_1\omega_2(I_{yy} - I_{xx}) + I_{xz}(\omega_2\omega_3 - \dot{\omega}_1) - I_{yz}(\dot{\omega}_2 + \omega_1\omega_3) - I_{xy}(\omega_1^2 - \omega_2^2)$$

(d) *Euler's Equations.*

If the axes system (xyz) is fixed in the body and taken as the principal axes, the products of inertia are zero and the resulting equations are known as Euler's equations:

$$G_1 = I_{xx}\dot{\omega}_1 - (I_{yy} - I_{zz})\omega_2\omega_3 \qquad 4.79$$

$$G_2 = I_{yy}\dot{\omega}_2 - (I_{zz} - I_{xx})\omega_1\omega_3$$

$$G_3 = I_{zz}\dot{\omega}_3 - (I_{xx} - I_{yy})\omega_2\omega_1$$

(e) *Components of Angular Velocity and its Derivatives in Terms of Eulerian Angles* (see Fig. 4-5).

$$\omega_1 = \cos\psi\,\dot{\theta} + \sin\theta\sin\psi\,\dot{\phi} \qquad 4.80$$

$$\omega_2 = -\sin\psi\,\dot{\theta} + \sin\theta\cos\psi\,\dot{\phi}$$

$$\omega_3 = \dot{\psi} + \cos\theta\,\dot{\phi}$$

$$\dot{\omega}_1 = \cos\psi\,\ddot{\theta} - \sin\psi\,\dot{\psi}\,\dot{\theta} + \sin\theta\sin\psi\,\ddot{\phi} + \sin\theta\cos\psi\,\dot{\psi}\,\dot{\phi} + \cos\theta\sin\psi\,\dot{\theta}\,\dot{\phi} \quad \textbf{4.81}$$

$$\dot{\omega}_2 = -\sin\psi\,\ddot{\theta} - \cos\psi\,\dot{\psi}\,\dot{\theta} + \sin\theta\cos\psi\,\ddot{\phi} - \sin\theta\sin\psi\,\dot{\psi}\,\dot{\phi} + \cos\theta\cos\psi\,\dot{\theta}\,\dot{\phi}$$

$$\dot{\omega}_3 = \ddot{\psi} + \cos\theta\,\ddot{\phi} - \sin\theta\,\dot{\theta}\,\dot{\phi}$$

The expressions for $\omega_1, \omega_2, \omega_3$ and $\dot{\omega}_1, \dot{\omega}_2, \dot{\omega}_3$ may be simplified by choosing space axes such that one or more of the Eulerian angles have values of zero or multiples of 90 degrees, making some of the sine or cosine terms assume values of zero or one. However, the simplified expressions for the derivatives, $\dot{\omega}_1, \dot{\omega}_2, \dot{\omega}_3$, must be determined from equations 4.81, and not from the simplified form of 4.80.

(f) Torque-Free Motion.

Let $\mathbf{h} = \mathbf{h}_0 = h_0\mathbf{K}$ by selecting the $\mathbf{K}$ axis to coincide with the direction of $\mathbf{h}$, the angular momentum. The angular momentum may be written: $\mathbf{h}_0 = I_{xx}\omega_1\mathbf{i} + I_{yy}\omega_2\mathbf{j} + I_{zz}\omega_3\mathbf{k}$. The components of angular velocity in terms of h_0 and the Eulerian angles are

$$\omega_1 = \frac{h_0 \sin\theta\sin\psi}{I_{xx}} \quad \textbf{4.82}$$

$$\omega_2 = \frac{h_0 \sin\theta\cos\psi}{I_{yy}}$$

$$\omega_3 = \frac{h_0 \cos\theta}{I_{zz}}$$

Euler's equations for torque-free motion are

$$I_{xx}\frac{d}{dt}\left[\frac{h_0\sin\theta\sin\psi}{I_{xx}}\right] + \frac{I_{zz}-I_{yy}}{I_{zz}I_{yy}}\,h_0^2\sin\theta\cos\theta\cos\psi = 0 \quad \textbf{4.83}$$

$$I_{yy}\frac{d}{dt}\left[\frac{h_0\sin\theta\cos\psi}{I_{yy}}\right] + \frac{I_{xx}-I_{zz}}{I_{xx}I_{zz}}\,h_0^2\sin\theta\cos\theta\sin\psi = 0$$

$$I_{zz}\frac{d}{dt}\left[\frac{h_0\cos\theta}{I_{zz}}\right] + \frac{I_{yy}-I_{xx}}{I_{yy}I_{xx}}\,h_0^2\sin^2\theta\sin\psi\cos\psi = 0$$

(g) Torque-free Motion of a Body of Revolution, the Gyroscope.

For a body of revolution, $I_{xx} = I_{yy} = I$, giving

$$\frac{h_0\cos\theta}{I_{zz}} = \text{a constant} \quad \textbf{4.84}$$

$$\theta = \theta_0 = \text{Nutation angle} \quad \textbf{4.85}$$

$$\dot{\phi} = \frac{h_0}{I} = \text{Precession velocity} \quad \textbf{4.86}$$

$$\dot{\psi} = \frac{I - I_{zz}}{I\,I_{zz}}\,h_0\cos\theta_0 \quad \textbf{4.87}$$

(h) Motion of a Body of Revolution or a Gyroscope about a Torque-free Axis.

Let the $\mathbf{k}$ axis be torque-free and $I_{xx} = I_{yy} = I$. Arbitrarily define $\psi = 0$. Then,

$$G_1 = I\dot{\omega}_1 + \omega_2\omega_3(I_{zz} - I) \quad \textbf{4.88}$$
$$G_2 = I\dot{\omega}_2 + \omega_1\omega_3(I - I_{zz})$$
$$G_3 = 0 = I_{zz}\dot{\omega}_3$$

or in terms of Eulerian angles,

$$G_1 = I(\ddot{\theta} - \dot{\phi}^2 \sin\theta\cos\theta) + I_{zz}\dot{\phi}\sin\theta\,(\dot{\psi} + \dot{\phi}\cos\theta) \quad \textbf{4.89}$$
$$G_2 = I(\ddot{\phi}\sin\theta + 2\dot{\phi}\dot{\theta}\cos\theta) - I_{zz}\dot{\theta}(\dot{\psi} + \dot{\phi}\cos\theta)$$
$$G_3 = I_{zz}\frac{d}{dt}(\dot{\psi} + \dot{\phi}\cos\theta) = 0$$

From $G_3 = 0$, $(\dot{\psi} + \dot{\phi}\cos\theta) = S$, a constant. The constant S is defined as the spin. The symmetry of the body about the **k** axis allows the choice of an (**i**-**j**) axis system that makes $\psi = 0$ at any instant, even though the body axes (xyz) rotates with the body.

In terms of the spin, the equations of motion are

$$G_1 = I(\ddot{\theta} - \dot{\phi}^2 \sin\theta\cos\theta + I_{zz}S\dot{\phi}\sin\theta) \quad \textbf{4.90}$$
$$G_2 = I(\ddot{\phi}\sin\theta + 2\dot{\phi}\dot{\theta}\cos\theta) - I_{zz}S\dot{\theta}$$

The angular momentum is

$$\mathbf{h} = I\dot{\theta}\mathbf{i} + I\dot{\phi}\sin\theta\,\mathbf{j} + I_{zz}S\mathbf{k} \quad \textbf{4.91}$$

and the kinetic energy is

$$T = \tfrac{1}{2}(I\dot{\theta}^2 + I\dot{\phi}^2\sin^2\theta + I_{zz}S^2) \quad \textbf{4.92}$$

(i) *Motion of a Top.*

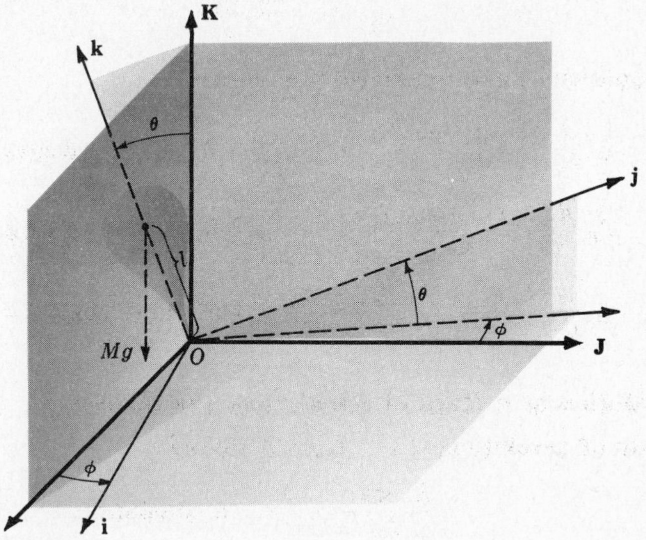

Fig. 4-10. The Spinning Top.

The origin of the body axes (**i**, **j**, **k**) of the spinning top is at its fixed base as shown in Fig. 4-10 above. The body axis **k** and the space axis **K** are both torque-free. The applied torque G_1 acts about the body axis **i** and $G_2 = G_3 = 0$. For the gravity top,

$$G_1 = Mgl\sin\theta \quad \textbf{4.93}$$

where M = the mass of the top, l = distance from the origin to the center of gravity, and g is the acceleration of gravity.

The top is symmetrical, $I_{xx} = I_{yy} = I$, and the body axes can be defined so that $\psi = 0$. The equations of motion are equations 4.90 and the angular momentum $\mathbf{h}$ is given by 4.91. With the torque about axis $\mathbf{K}$ equal to zero, its component of angular momentum is constant, giving

$$\mathbf{K} \cdot \mathbf{h} \quad = \quad I\dot{\phi}\sin^2\theta + I_{zz}S\cos\theta \quad = \quad h_k \qquad \textbf{4.94}$$

The total energy is also constant:

$$E \quad = \quad Mgl\cos\theta + \tfrac{1}{2}(I\dot{\theta}^2 + I\dot{\phi}^2\sin^2\theta + I_{zz}S^2) \qquad \textbf{4.95}$$

where S is the spin, $(\dot{\psi} + \dot{\phi}\cos\theta)$.

4.8 LAGRANGE'S EQUATIONS

(a) General Case.

$$\frac{d}{dt}\left(\frac{\partial L}{\partial \dot{q}^j}\right) - \frac{\partial L}{\partial q^j} \quad = \quad Q_j \qquad \textbf{4.96}$$

where $L = T - V$, the Lagrangian

T = kinetic energy

V = potential energy

Q_j = forces not arising from a potential.

The generalized force Q_j is defined by

$$\sum \mathbf{F}_i \cdot \delta\mathbf{r}_i \quad = \quad \sum Q_j \delta q^j \qquad \textbf{4.97}$$

where $\mathbf{F}_i$ is a dissipative force and $\delta\mathbf{r}_i$ is a virtual displacement.

(b) The Rayleigh Dissipation Function.

When frictional forces are proportional to the velocities of the particles of the system, $F_{fx} = -k_x v_x$, and similarly for the y and z components. The Rayleigh dissipation function $\mathcal{F}$ is defined as

$$\mathcal{F} \quad = \quad \frac{1}{2}\sum_i (k_x v_{ix}^2 + k_y v_{iy}^2 + k_z v_{iz}^2) \qquad \textbf{4.98}$$

where the summation is taken over the i particles of the system. Hence the frictional force may be written as

$$\mathbf{F}_f \quad = \quad \mathbf{i}\frac{\partial \mathcal{F}}{\partial v_x} + \mathbf{j}\frac{\partial \mathcal{F}}{\partial v_y} + \mathbf{k}\frac{\partial \mathcal{F}}{\partial v_z} \qquad \textbf{4.99}$$

The rate of energy dissipation due to friction is then $2\mathcal{F}$. From energy considerations,

$$Q_{fj} \quad = \quad -\frac{\partial \mathcal{F}}{\partial \dot{q}^j} \qquad \textbf{4.100}$$

where Q_{fj} is the generalized dissipation force due to friction, so that Lagrange's equations become

$$\frac{d}{dt}\left(\frac{\partial L}{\partial \dot{q}^j}\right) - \frac{\partial L}{\partial q^j} + \frac{\partial \mathcal{F}}{\partial \dot{q}^j} \quad = \quad 0 \qquad \textbf{4.101}$$

(c) Lagrange Multipliers.

Given a system having n generalized coordinates and m constraints of the type

$$\phi^s(q^1, \ldots, q^n, t) = 0 \qquad \textbf{4.102}$$

Lagrange's equations may be written as

$$\frac{d}{dt}\left(\frac{\partial L}{\partial \dot{q}^k}\right) - \frac{\partial L}{\partial q^k} = \sum_s \lambda_s(t) \frac{\partial \phi^s}{\partial q^k} \qquad \textbf{4.103}$$

where the m values of the λ_s are the undetermined Lagrange multipliers. Equations 4.102 and 4.103 constitute $(m+n)$ equations in $(m+n)$ unknowns, the q^k and λ_s.

4.9 HAMILTON'S EQUATIONS

The generalized momenta of a system is defined as

$$p_j = \frac{\partial L}{\partial \dot{q}^j} \qquad \textbf{4.104}$$

where $L(q^j, \dot{q}^j, t)$ is the Lagrangian of the system. From Lagrange's equations,

$$\dot{p}_j = \frac{\partial L}{\partial q^j} \qquad \textbf{4.105}$$

The Hamiltonian H is defined by

$$H(q^j, p_j, t) = p_j \dot{q}^j - L \qquad \textbf{4.106}$$

where the summation is taken over j, i.e. $p_j \dot{q}^j = \sum_j p_j \dot{q}^j$.

The Hamilton canonical equations are

$$\dot{q}^j = \frac{\partial H}{\partial p_j} \qquad \textbf{4.107}$$

$$\dot{p}_j = -\frac{\partial H}{\partial q^j}, \quad \frac{\partial H}{\partial t} = -\frac{\partial L}{\partial t}$$

4.10 HAMILTON'S PRINCIPLE

For a conservative system the motion of a system from time t_1 to time t_2 is such that the line integral

$$I = \int_{t_1}^{t_2} L\,dt \qquad \textbf{4.108}$$

is an extremum for the path of the motion. Here $L = T - V$, the Lagrangian. Lagrange's equations may be derived from Hamilton's principle by performing the variation of the action integral I. The integral of 4.108 is known as the action integral and I as the action. Hamilton's principle is consequently known as the principle of Least Action.

4.11 LIST OF SYMBOLS USED IN CHAPTER 4

$\mathbf{A}$	=	Acceleration of a moving origin
$\mathbf{a}$	=	Acceleration
D	=	Impulsive force during deformation
E	=	Total energy
$\mathbf{F}$	=	Force
$\mathcal{F}$	=	Rayleigh dissipation function
$\mathbf{h}$	=	Angular momentum
h_0	=	Angular momentum about a torque-free axis
$\mathbf{I}$	=	Inertia tensor
I_{kk}	=	Moment of inertia about line k-k
I_{qk}	=	Product of inertia in the plane qk
L	=	Lagrangian
M	=	Mass
m_i	=	Mass of ith particle
p_j	=	Generalized momentum
q^m	=	Generalized coordinate
$\mathbf{R}$	=	Position vector of a moving origin
$\mathbf{R}_c$	=	Position vector of the mass center as a moving origin
$\mathbf{r}_c$	=	Position vector of the mass center relative to a moving origin
S	=	Spin
$\mathbf{S}$	=	Orthogonal transformation matrix
$\mathbf{S}'$	=	Transpose of matrix $\mathbf{S}$
$\mathbf{S}^{-1}$	=	Inverse of matrix $\mathbf{S}$
T	=	Kinetic energy
V	=	Potential energy
$\mathbf{v}$	=	Velocity
$(\mathbf{I}, \mathbf{J}, \mathbf{K};\ \mathbf{i}, \mathbf{j}, \mathbf{k};\ \mathbf{e}_1, \mathbf{e}_2, \mathbf{e}_3;\ \mathbf{e}_r, \mathbf{e}_\theta, \mathbf{e}_z;\ \mathbf{e}_r, \mathbf{e}_\theta, \mathbf{e}_\phi;\ \hat{x}, \hat{y}, \hat{z})$	=	Various sets of unit vectors forming an orthogonal triad
λ^n	=	Contravariant component of a vector
λ_n	=	Covariant component of a vector
(l, m, n)	=	Direction cosines
ρ	=	Radius of curvature; mass density
ϵ	=	Coefficient of restitution
$\boldsymbol{\omega}$	=	Angular velocity of a rigid body
$\boldsymbol{\Omega}$	=	Angular velocity of a moving axes system
ϕ, θ, ψ	=	Eulerian angles

4.12 REFERENCES

1. Corben, H. C., and Stehle, P., *Classical Mechanics,* Wiley, 1950
2. Goldstein, H., *Classical Mechanics,* Addison-Wesley, 1950
3. Shames, I., *Engineering Mechanics,* Prentice Hall, 1958
4. Synge, J. L., and Griffith, B. A., *Principles of Mechanics,* McGraw Hill, 1959
5. Whittaker, E. T., *Analytical Dynamics,* Cambridge University Press, 1937, or Dover, 1944

Appendix

Mathematical Relationships

A.1 VECTOR IDENTITIES

A is a vector defined as

$$\mathbf{A} = \mathbf{e}_1 A_1 + \mathbf{e}_2 A_2 + \mathbf{e}_3 A_3$$

where $\mathbf{e}_1, \mathbf{e}_2$, and $\mathbf{e}_3$ are unit vectors in the coordinate directions and A_1, A_2, and A_3 are the components of the vector. A scalar is denoted as Φ. ∇ is the operator "del".

$$\mathbf{A}\cdot\mathbf{B} = A_1B_1 + A_2B_2 + A_3B_3 \qquad \textbf{A.1}$$

$$\mathbf{A}\cdot\mathbf{B} = \mathbf{B}\cdot\mathbf{A} \qquad \textbf{A.2}$$

$$\mathbf{A}\cdot(\mathbf{B}+\mathbf{C}) = \mathbf{A}\cdot\mathbf{B} + \mathbf{A}\cdot\mathbf{C} \qquad \textbf{A.3}$$

$$\mathbf{A}\times\mathbf{B} = -\mathbf{B}\times\mathbf{A} = \begin{vmatrix} \mathbf{e}_1 & \mathbf{e}_2 & \mathbf{e}_3 \\ A_1 & A_2 & A_3 \\ B_1 & B_2 & B_3 \end{vmatrix} \qquad \textbf{A.4}$$

$$(\mathbf{A}+\mathbf{B})\times\mathbf{C} = (\mathbf{A}\times\mathbf{C}) + (\mathbf{B}\times\mathbf{C}) \qquad \textbf{A.5}$$

$$\mathbf{A}\times(\mathbf{B}+\mathbf{C}) = (\mathbf{A}\times\mathbf{B}) + (\mathbf{A}\times\mathbf{C}) \qquad \textbf{A.6}$$

$$\mathbf{A}\times(\mathbf{B}\times\mathbf{C}) = \mathbf{B}(\mathbf{A}\cdot\mathbf{C}) - \mathbf{C}(\mathbf{A}\cdot\mathbf{B}) \qquad \textbf{A.7}$$

$$\mathbf{A}\cdot(\mathbf{B}\times\mathbf{C}) = (\mathbf{A}\times\mathbf{B})\cdot\mathbf{C} = \mathbf{B}\cdot(\mathbf{C}\times\mathbf{A}) = \begin{vmatrix} A_1 & A_2 & A_3 \\ B_1 & B_2 & B_3 \\ C_1 & C_2 & C_3 \end{vmatrix} \qquad \textbf{A.8}$$

$$(\mathbf{A}\times\mathbf{B})\cdot(\mathbf{C}\times\mathbf{D}) = (\mathbf{A}\cdot\mathbf{C})(\mathbf{B}\cdot\mathbf{D}) - (\mathbf{A}\cdot\mathbf{D})(\mathbf{B}\cdot\mathbf{C}) \qquad \textbf{A.9}$$

$$\begin{aligned}(\mathbf{A}\times\mathbf{B})\times(\mathbf{C}\times\mathbf{D}) &= \mathbf{B}[\mathbf{A}\cdot(\mathbf{C}\times\mathbf{D})] - \mathbf{A}[\mathbf{B}\cdot(\mathbf{C}\times\mathbf{D})] \\ &= \mathbf{C}[\mathbf{A}\cdot(\mathbf{B}\times\mathbf{D})] - \mathbf{D}[\mathbf{A}\cdot(\mathbf{B}\times\mathbf{C})]\end{aligned} \qquad \textbf{A.10}$$

$$\nabla^2\Phi = \nabla\cdot\nabla\Phi \qquad \textbf{A.11}$$

$$\nabla^2\mathbf{A} = (\nabla\cdot\nabla)\mathbf{A} \qquad \textbf{A.12}$$

$$\nabla\cdot\nabla\times\mathbf{A} = 0 \qquad \textbf{A.13}$$

$$\nabla \times \nabla\Phi = 0 \qquad \text{A.14}$$

$$\nabla \times (\nabla \times \mathbf{A}) = \nabla(\nabla \cdot \mathbf{A}) - \nabla^2\mathbf{A} \qquad \text{A.15}$$

$$(\mathbf{A} \cdot \nabla)\mathbf{A} = \nabla\left(\frac{|\mathbf{A}|^2}{2}\right) - \mathbf{A} \times (\nabla \times \mathbf{A}) \qquad \text{A.16}$$

$$\nabla \times (\mathbf{A} \times \mathbf{B}) = (\mathbf{B} \cdot \nabla)\mathbf{A} - \mathbf{B}(\nabla \cdot \mathbf{A}) - (\mathbf{A} \cdot \nabla)\mathbf{B} + \mathbf{A}(\nabla \cdot \mathbf{B}) \qquad \text{A.17a}$$

$$\nabla \cdot (\mathbf{A} \times \mathbf{B}) = \mathbf{B} \cdot \nabla \times \mathbf{A} - \mathbf{A} \cdot \nabla \times \mathbf{B} \qquad \text{A.17b}$$

$$\nabla(\mathbf{A} \cdot \mathbf{B}) = (\mathbf{B} \cdot \nabla)\mathbf{A} + (\mathbf{A} \cdot \nabla)\mathbf{B} + \mathbf{B} \times (\nabla \times \mathbf{A}) + \mathbf{A} \times (\nabla \times \mathbf{B}) \qquad \text{A.18}$$

A.2 VECTOR INTEGRALS

Listed below are the more common vector integral theorems.

(a) Stokes' Theorem.

$$\oint_C \mathbf{A} \cdot d\mathbf{l} = \int_S (\nabla \times \mathbf{A}) \cdot d\mathbf{S} \qquad \text{A.19}$$

where the curve C defines the surface S. Fig. A-1 below illustrates the surface. The sense of the line integral is counterclockwise with respect to the vector $d\mathbf{S}$.

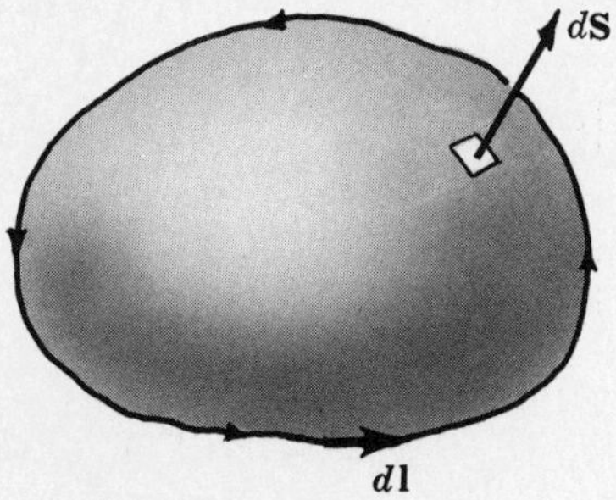

Fig. A-1

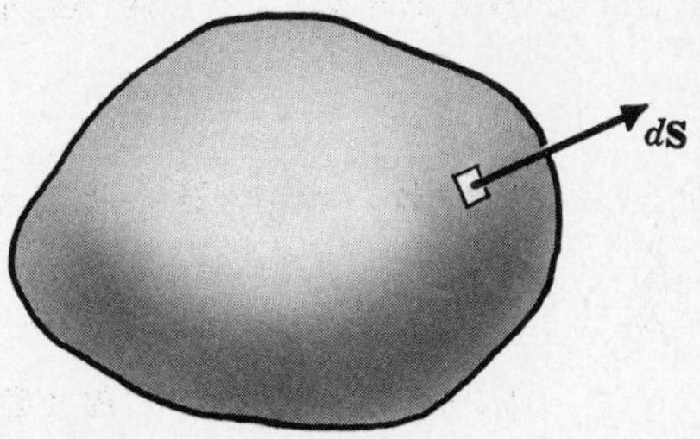

Fig. A-2

(b) Gauss' Theorem or Divergence Theorem.

$$\int_V \nabla \cdot \mathbf{A}\, dV = \int_S \mathbf{A} \cdot d\mathbf{S} \qquad \text{A.20}$$

where the surface S defines the volume V. Fig. A-2 above shows this surface and volume.

(c) Green's Theorems.

If a vector $\mathbf{A}$ is derived from a potential Φ as

$$\mathbf{A} = \nabla\Phi$$

then the line integral of the vector $\mathbf{A}$ can be expressed as

$$\int_A^B \mathbf{A} \cdot d\mathbf{l} = \int_A^B d\Phi \qquad \text{A.21}$$

Under the above condition the following theorem may be stated:

$$\int_V \nabla\Phi \cdot \nabla\psi \, dV = \int_S \Phi\nabla\psi \cdot d\mathbf{S} - \int_V \Phi\nabla^2\psi \, dV \qquad \textbf{A.22}$$

$$= \int_S \psi\nabla\Phi \cdot d\mathbf{S} - \int_V \psi\nabla^2\Phi \, dV$$

A.3 VECTOR OPERATIONS IN VARIOUS COORDINATE SYSTEMS

Referring to Fig. A-3 below, which shows the various coordinate systems, the basic vector operations can be written.

(a) Gradient.

Cartesian:

$$(\nabla\Phi)_x = \frac{\partial\Phi}{\partial x} \qquad \textbf{A.23}$$

$$(\nabla\Phi)_y = \frac{\partial\Phi}{\partial y}$$

$$(\nabla\Phi)_z = \frac{\partial\Phi}{\partial z}$$

Cylindrical:

$$(\nabla\Phi)_r = \frac{\partial\Phi}{\partial r} \qquad \textbf{A.24}$$

$$(\nabla\Phi)_\theta = \frac{1}{r}\frac{\partial\Phi}{\partial\theta}$$

$$(\nabla\Phi)_z = \frac{\partial\Phi}{\partial z}$$

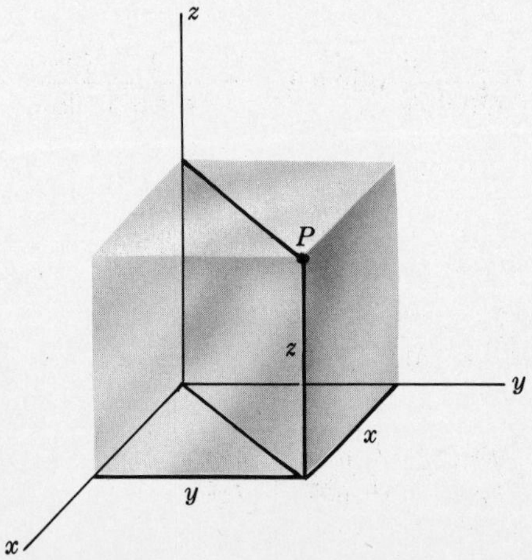

Cartesian Coordinates

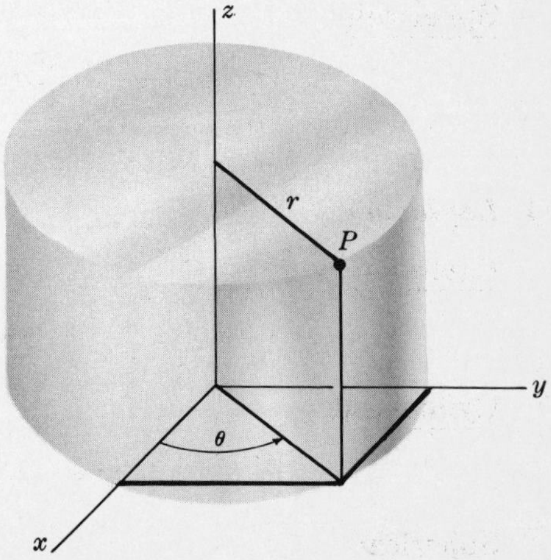

Cylindrical Coordinates

Fig. A-3. The Basic Coordinate Systems.

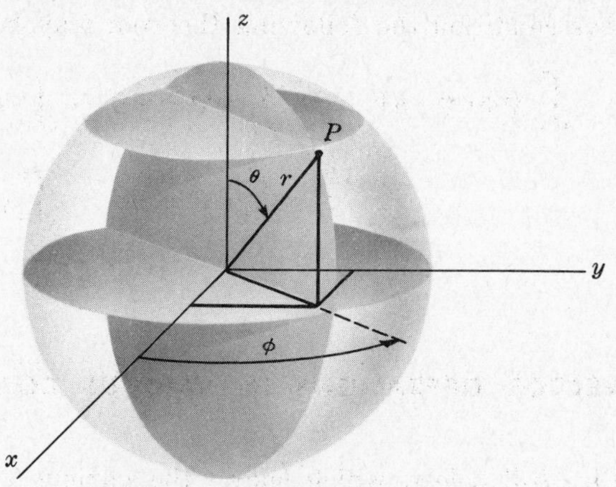

Spherical Coordinates

Fig. A-3. The Basic Coordinate Systems (cont.).

Spherical:

$$(\nabla\Phi)_r = \frac{\partial\Phi}{\partial r} \tag{A.25}$$

$$(\nabla\Phi)_\theta = \frac{1}{r}\frac{\partial\Phi}{\partial\theta}$$

$$(\nabla\Phi)_\phi = \frac{1}{r\sin\theta}\frac{\partial\Phi}{\partial\phi}$$

(b) Divergence.

Cartesian:

$$\nabla\cdot\mathbf{A} = \frac{\partial A_x}{\partial x} + \frac{\partial A_y}{\partial y} + \frac{\partial A_z}{\partial z} \tag{A.26}$$

Cylindrical:

$$\nabla\cdot\mathbf{A} = \frac{1}{r}\frac{\partial}{\partial r}(rA_r) + \frac{1}{r}\frac{\partial A_\theta}{\partial\theta} + \frac{\partial A_z}{\partial z} \tag{A.27}$$

Spherical:

$$\nabla\cdot\mathbf{A} = \frac{1}{r^2}\frac{\partial}{\partial r}(r^2A_r) + \frac{1}{r\sin\theta}\frac{\partial}{\partial\theta}(\sin\theta A_\theta) + \frac{1}{r\sin\theta}\frac{\partial A_\phi}{\partial\phi} \tag{A.28}$$

(c) Laplacian.

Cartesian:

$$\nabla^2\Phi = \frac{\partial^2\Phi}{\partial x^2} + \frac{\partial^2\Phi}{\partial y^2} + \frac{\partial^2\Phi}{\partial z^2} \tag{A.29}$$

Cylindrical:

$$\nabla^2\Phi = \frac{1}{r}\frac{\partial}{\partial r}\left(r\frac{\partial\Phi}{\partial r}\right) + \frac{1}{r^2}\frac{\partial^2\Phi}{\partial\theta^2} + \frac{\partial^2\Phi}{\partial z^2} \tag{A.30}$$

Spherical:

$$\nabla^2\Phi = \frac{1}{r^2}\frac{\partial}{\partial r}\left(r^2\frac{\partial\Phi}{\partial r}\right) + \frac{1}{r^2\sin\theta}\frac{\partial}{\partial\theta}\left(\sin\theta\frac{\partial\Phi}{\partial\theta}\right) + \frac{1}{r^2\sin^2\theta}\frac{\partial^2\Phi}{\partial\phi^2} \tag{A.31}$$

(d) Curl.

Cartesian:

$$(\nabla \times \mathbf{A})_x = \left(\frac{\partial A_z}{\partial y} - \frac{\partial A_y}{\partial z}\right) \qquad \textbf{A.32}$$

$$(\nabla \times \mathbf{A})_y = \left(\frac{\partial A_x}{\partial z} - \frac{\partial A_z}{\partial x}\right)$$

$$(\nabla \times \mathbf{A})_z = \left(\frac{\partial A_y}{\partial x} - \frac{\partial A_x}{\partial y}\right)$$

Cylindrical:

$$(\nabla \times \mathbf{A})_r = \left(\frac{1}{r}\frac{\partial A_z}{\partial \theta} - \frac{\partial A_\theta}{\partial z}\right) \qquad \textbf{A.33}$$

$$(\nabla \times \mathbf{A})_\theta = \left(\frac{\partial A_r}{\partial z} - \frac{\partial A_z}{\partial r}\right)$$

$$(\nabla \times \mathbf{A})_z = \frac{1}{r}\left[\frac{\partial}{\partial r}(rA_\theta) - \frac{\partial A_r}{\partial \theta}\right]$$

Spherical:

$$(\nabla \times \mathbf{A})_r = \frac{1}{r \sin\theta}\left[\frac{\partial}{\partial \theta}(\sin\theta A_\phi) - \frac{\partial A_\theta}{\partial \phi}\right] \qquad \textbf{A.34}$$

$$(\nabla \times \mathbf{A})_\theta = \frac{1}{r \sin\theta}\frac{\partial A_r}{\partial \phi} - \frac{1}{r}\frac{\partial}{\partial r}(rA_\phi)$$

$$(\nabla \times \mathbf{A})_\phi = \frac{1}{r}\left[\frac{\partial}{\partial r}(rA_\theta) - \frac{\partial A_r}{\partial \theta}\right]$$

(e) Scalar Product.

Cartesian:

$$\mathbf{A} \cdot \mathbf{B} = A_x B_x + A_y B_y + A_z B_z \qquad \textbf{A.35}$$

Cylindrical:

$$\mathbf{A} \cdot \mathbf{B} = A_r B_r + A_\theta B_\theta + A_z B_z \qquad \textbf{A.36}$$

Spherical:

$$\mathbf{A} \cdot \mathbf{B} = A_r B_r + A_\theta B_\theta + A_\phi B_\phi \qquad \textbf{A.37}$$

(f) Vector Product.

Cartesian:

$$(\mathbf{A} \times \mathbf{B})_x = A_y B_z - A_z B_y \qquad \textbf{A.38}$$

$$(\mathbf{A} \times \mathbf{B})_y = A_z B_x - A_x B_z$$

$$(\mathbf{A} \times \mathbf{B})_z = A_x B_y - A_y B_x$$

Cylindrical:

$$(\mathbf{A} \times \mathbf{B})_r = A_\theta B_z - A_z B_\theta \qquad \textbf{A.39}$$

$$(\mathbf{A} \times \mathbf{B})_\theta = A_z B_r - A_r B_z$$

$$(\mathbf{A} \times \mathbf{B})_z = A_r B_\theta - A_\theta B_r$$

Spherical:

$$(\mathbf{A}\times\mathbf{B})_r = A_\theta B_\phi - A_\phi B_\theta \qquad \text{A.40}$$

$$(\mathbf{A}\times\mathbf{B})_\theta = A_\phi B_r - A_r B_\phi$$

$$(\mathbf{A}\times\mathbf{B})_\phi = A_r B_\theta - A_\theta B_r$$

(g) Material Derivative.

The material derivative is also known as the substantial or Stokes' derivative. The operation is different depending on whether it operates on a vector or scalar component. The equations listed below are for operation on a scalar. The general operation on a vector has been indicated in the derivation and discussion of the fluid dynamical acceleration and will not be repeated here. The reader is referred to Section 1.5 of Chapter 1.

Cartesian:

$$\frac{D}{Dt} = \frac{\partial}{\partial t} + u\frac{\partial}{\partial x} + v\frac{\partial}{\partial y} + w\frac{\partial}{\partial z} \qquad \text{A.41}$$

Cylindrical:

$$\frac{D}{Dt} = \frac{\partial}{\partial t} + v_r\frac{\partial}{\partial r} + \frac{v_\theta}{r}\frac{\partial}{\partial \theta} + v_z\frac{\partial}{\partial z} \qquad \text{A.42}$$

Spherical:

$$\frac{D}{Dt} = \frac{\partial}{\partial t} + v_r\frac{\partial}{\partial r} + \frac{v_\theta}{r}\frac{\partial}{\partial \theta} + \frac{v_\phi}{r\sin\theta}\frac{\partial}{\partial \phi} \qquad \text{A.43}$$

(h) The Biharmonic Operator, ∇^4.

Cartesian:

$$\nabla^4 = \frac{\partial^4}{\partial x^4} + \frac{\partial^4}{\partial y^4} + \frac{\partial^4}{\partial z^4} + 2\frac{\partial^4}{\partial x^2\,\partial y^2} + 2\frac{\partial^4}{\partial x^2\,\partial z^2} + 2\frac{\partial^4}{\partial y^2\,\partial z^2} \qquad \text{A.44}$$

Cylindrical:

$$\nabla^4 = \left[\frac{1}{r}\frac{\partial}{\partial r}\left(r\frac{\partial}{\partial r}\right) + \frac{1}{r^2}\frac{\partial^2}{\partial \theta^2} + \frac{\partial^2}{\partial z^2}\right]\cdot\left[\frac{1}{r}\frac{\partial}{\partial r}\left(r\frac{\partial}{\partial r}\right) + \frac{1}{r^2}\frac{\partial^2}{\partial \theta^2} + \frac{\partial^2}{\partial z^2}\right] \qquad \text{A.45}$$

Spherical:

$$\nabla^4 = \left[\frac{1}{r^2}\frac{\partial}{\partial r}\left(r^2\frac{\partial}{\partial r}\right) + \frac{1}{r^2\sin\theta}\frac{\partial}{\partial\theta}\left(\sin\theta\frac{\partial}{\partial\theta}\right) + \frac{1}{r^2\sin^2\theta}\frac{\partial^2}{\partial\phi^2}\right] \qquad \text{A.46}$$

$$\cdot\left[\frac{1}{r^2}\frac{\partial}{\partial r}\left(r^2\frac{\partial}{\partial r}\right) + \frac{1}{r^2\sin\theta}\frac{\partial}{\partial\theta}\left(\sin\theta\frac{\partial}{\partial\theta}\right) + \frac{1}{r^2\sin^2\theta}\frac{\partial^2}{\partial\phi^2}\right]$$

A.4 ORTHOGONAL CURVILINEAR COORDINATES

The orthogonal coordinates are denoted as x_1, x_2, and x_3. The line element of length is given by

$$ds^2 = h_1^2\,dx_1^2 + h_2^2\,dx_2^2 + h_3^2\,dx_3^2 \qquad \text{A.47}$$

and the element of volume as

$$dV = h_1h_2h_3\,dx_1\,dx_2\,dx_3 \qquad \text{A.48}$$

The table below lists various orthogonal coordinate systems and the values of the metric coefficients h_1, h_2, and h_3, together with the relationships between the coordinates and the Cartesian coordinates x, y, and z. For a more complete discussion of the general theory of orthogonal transformation theory and the matrix formulation, the reader is referred to the chapter on dynamics (Chapter 4).

Listed below, then, is an outline of the coordinate systems. For a more complete discussion of the physical significance of the coordinate systems the reader is referred to the references at the end of this appendix. In particular, the reference to Margenau and Murphy is useful.

Tables of Orthogonal Coordinate Systems

	Cartesian	Cylindrical $x = r\cos\theta$ $y = r\sin\theta$ $z = z$	Spherical $x = r\sin\theta\cos\phi$ $y = r\sin\theta\sin\phi$ $z = r\cos\theta$	Confocal Ellipsoidal (a, b and c are constants) $x^2 = \frac{(a^2-\lambda)(a^2-\mu)(a^2-\nu)}{(b^2-a^2)(c^2-a^2)}$ $y^2 = \frac{(b^2-\lambda)(b^2-\mu)(b^2-\nu)}{(a^2-b^2)(c^2-b^2)}$ $z^2 = \frac{(c^2-\lambda)(c^2-\mu)(c^2-\nu)}{(a^2-c^2)(b^2-c^2)}$
x_1	x	r	r	λ
h_1^2	1	1	1	$\frac{1}{4}\left\{\frac{(\mu-\lambda)(\nu-\lambda)}{(a^2-\lambda)(b^2-\lambda)(c^2-\lambda)}\right\}$
x_2	y	θ	ϕ	μ
h_2^2	1	r^2	$r^2\sin^2\theta$	$\frac{1}{4}\left\{\frac{(\nu-\mu)(\lambda-\mu)}{(a^2-\mu)(b^2-\mu)(c^2-\mu)}\right\}$
x_3	z	z	θ	ν
h_3^2	1	1	r^2	$\frac{1}{4}\left\{\frac{(\lambda-\nu)(\mu-\nu)}{(a^2-\nu)(b^2-\nu)(c^2-\nu)}\right\}$

	Prolate Spheroidal $x = a\sinh u\sin v\cos\phi$ $y = a\sinh u\sin v\sin\phi$ $z = a\cosh u\cos v$	Oblate Spheroidal $x = a\cosh u\sin v\cos\phi$ $y = a\cosh u\sin v\sin\phi$ $z = a\sinh u\cos v$	Elliptic Cylindrical $x = a\cosh u\cos v$ $y = a\sinh u\sin v$ $z = z$
x_1	u	u	u
h_1^2	$a^2(\sinh^2 u + \sin^2 v)$	$a^2(\sinh^2 u + \cos^2 v)$	$a^2(\sinh^2 u + \sin^2 v)$
x_2	v	v	v
h_2^2	$a^2(\sinh^2 u + \sin^2 v)$	$a^2(\sinh^2 u + \cos^2 v)$	$a^2(\sinh^2 u + \sin^2 v)$
x_3	ϕ	ϕ	z
h_3^2	$a^2(\sinh^2 u\sin^2 v)$	$a^2\cosh^2 u\sin^2 v$	1

Tables of Orthogonal Coordinate Systems (cont.)

	Conical coordinates	Confocal Paraboloidal	Parabolic coordinates
	$x^2 = \dfrac{u^2v^2w^2}{b^2c^2}$ $y^2 = \dfrac{u^2(v^2-b^2)(w^2-b^2)}{b^2(b^2-c^2)}$ $z^2 = \dfrac{u^2(v^2-c^2)(w^2-c^2)}{c^2(c^2-b^2)}$	$x^2 = \dfrac{(a^2-\lambda)(a^2-\mu)(a^2-\nu)}{(b^2-a^2)}$ $y^2 = \dfrac{(b^2-\lambda)(b^2-\mu)(b^2-\nu)}{(a^2-b^2)}$ $z = \frac{1}{2}(a^2+b^2-\lambda-\mu-\nu)$	$x = \xi\eta\cos\phi$ $y = \xi\eta\sin\phi$ $z = (\eta^2-\xi^2)/2$
x_1	u	λ	ξ
h_1^2	1	$\dfrac{1}{4}\dfrac{(\mu-\lambda)(\nu-\lambda)}{(a^2-\lambda)(b^2-\lambda)}$	$(\xi^2+\eta^2)$
x_2	v	μ	η
h_2^2	$\dfrac{u^2(v^2-w^2)}{(v^2-b^2)(c^2-v^2)}$	$\dfrac{1}{4}\dfrac{(\nu-\mu)(\lambda-\mu)}{(a^2-\mu)(b^2-\mu)}$	$(\xi^2+\eta^2)$
x_3	w	ν	ϕ
h_3^2	$\dfrac{u^2(v^2-w^2)}{(w^2-b^2)(w^2-c^2)}$	$\dfrac{1}{4}\dfrac{(\lambda-\nu)(\mu-\nu)}{(a^2-\nu)(b^2-\nu)}$	$\xi^2\eta^2$

	Parabolic Cylindrical	Bipolar coordinates	Toroidal coordinates
	$x = \xi\eta$ $y = (\eta^2-\xi^2)/2$ $z = z$	$x = \dfrac{a\sinh\eta}{\cosh\eta-\cos\xi}$ $y = \dfrac{a\sin\xi}{\cosh\eta-\cos\xi}$ $z = z$	$x = r\cos\psi$ $y = r\sin\psi$ $r = \dfrac{a\sinh\eta}{\cosh\eta-\cos\xi}$ $z = \dfrac{a\sin\xi}{\cosh\eta-\cos\xi}$
x_1	ξ	ξ	ξ
h_1^2	$(\xi^2+\eta^2)$	$\dfrac{a^2}{(\cosh\eta-\cos\xi)^2}$	$\dfrac{a^2}{(\cosh\eta-\cos\xi)^2}$
x_2	η	η	η
h_2^2	$(\xi^2+\eta^2)$	$\dfrac{a^2}{(\cosh\eta-\cos\xi)^2}$	$\dfrac{a^2}{(\cosh\eta-\cos\xi)^2}$
x_3	z	z	ψ
h_3^2	1	1	$\dfrac{a^2\sinh^2\eta}{(\cosh\eta-\cos\xi)^2}$

Vector Operations in Orthogonal Curvilinear Coordinates.

Gradient:

$$(\nabla\Phi)_1 = \frac{1}{h_1}\frac{\partial\Phi}{\partial x_1} \qquad \text{A.49}$$

$$(\nabla\Phi)_2 = \frac{1}{h_2}\frac{\partial\Phi}{\partial x_2}$$

$$(\nabla\Phi)_3 = \frac{1}{h_3}\frac{\partial\Phi}{\partial x_3}$$

Divergence:

$$\nabla\cdot\mathbf{A} = \frac{1}{h_1h_2h_3}\left[\frac{\partial}{\partial x_1}(h_2h_3A_1) + \frac{\partial}{\partial x_2}(h_3h_1A_2) + \frac{\partial}{\partial x_3}(h_1h_2A_3)\right] \qquad \text{A.50}$$

Curl:

$$(\nabla\times\mathbf{A})_1 = \frac{1}{h_2h_3}\left[\frac{\partial}{\partial x_2}(h_3A_3) - \frac{\partial}{\partial x_3}(h_2A_2)\right] \qquad \text{A.51}$$

$$(\nabla\times\mathbf{A})_2 = \frac{1}{h_1h_3}\left[\frac{\partial}{\partial x_3}(h_1A_1) - \frac{\partial}{\partial x_1}(h_3A_3)\right]$$

$$(\nabla\times\mathbf{A})_3 = \frac{1}{h_1h_2}\left[\frac{\partial}{\partial x_1}(h_2A_2) - \frac{\partial}{\partial x_2}(h_1A_1)\right]$$

Laplacian:

$$\nabla^2\Phi = \frac{1}{h_1h_2h_3}\left[\frac{\partial}{\partial x_1}\left(\frac{h_2h_3}{h_1}\frac{\partial\Phi}{\partial x_1}\right) + \frac{\partial}{\partial x_2}\left(\frac{h_3h_1}{h_2}\frac{\partial\Phi}{\partial x_2}\right) + \frac{\partial}{\partial x_3}\left(\frac{h_1h_2}{h_3}\frac{\partial\Phi}{\partial x_3}\right)\right] \qquad \text{A.52}$$

Material Derivative:

$$\frac{D}{Dt} = \frac{\partial}{\partial t} + \frac{w_1}{h_1}\frac{\partial}{\partial x_1} + \frac{w_2}{h_2}\frac{\partial}{\partial x_2} + \frac{w_3}{h_3}\frac{\partial}{\partial x_3} \qquad \text{A.53}$$

where w_1, w_2, and w_3 are the velocities in the coordinate directions.

A.5 TRIGONOMETRIC RELATIONSHIPS

(a) Trigonometric Identities.

$$\sin^2\theta + \cos^2\theta = 1 \qquad \text{A.54}$$

$$1 + \tan^2\theta = \sec^2\theta \qquad \text{A.55}$$

$$1 + \text{ctn}^2\theta = \csc^2\theta \qquad \text{A.56}$$

$$\sin 2\theta = 2\sin\theta\cos\theta \qquad \text{A.57}$$

$$\cos 2\theta = 2\cos^2\theta - 1 = \cos^2\theta - \sin^2\theta \qquad \text{A.58}$$

$$\tan 2\theta = \frac{2\tan\theta}{1-\tan^2\theta} \qquad \text{A.59}$$

$$\sin\frac{\theta}{2} = \pm\sqrt{\frac{1-\cos\theta}{2}} \qquad \textbf{A.60}$$

$$\cos\frac{\theta}{2} = \pm\sqrt{\frac{1+\cos\theta}{2}} \qquad \textbf{A.61}$$

$$\tan\frac{\theta}{2} = \frac{1-\cos\theta}{\sin\theta} = \frac{\sin\theta}{1+\cos\theta} = \pm\sqrt{\frac{1-\cos\theta}{1+\cos\theta}} \qquad \textbf{A.62}$$

$$\sin(\theta\pm\phi) = \sin\theta\cos\phi \pm \cos\theta\sin\phi \qquad \textbf{A.63}$$

$$\cos(\theta\pm\phi) = \cos\theta\cos\phi \mp \sin\theta\sin\phi \qquad \textbf{A.64}$$

$$\tan(\theta\pm\phi) = \frac{\tan\theta\pm\tan\phi}{1\mp\tan\theta\tan\phi} \qquad \textbf{A.65}$$

$$\sin\theta + \sin\phi = 2\sin\tfrac{1}{2}(\theta+\phi)\cos\tfrac{1}{2}(\theta-\phi) \qquad \textbf{A.66}$$

$$\sin\theta - \sin\phi = 2\cos\tfrac{1}{2}(\theta+\phi)\sin\tfrac{1}{2}(\theta-\phi) \qquad \textbf{A.67}$$

$$\cos\theta + \cos\phi = 2\cos\tfrac{1}{2}(\theta+\phi)\cos\tfrac{1}{2}(\theta-\phi) \qquad \textbf{A.68}$$

$$\cos\theta - \cos\phi = -2\sin\tfrac{1}{2}(\theta+\phi)\sin\tfrac{1}{2}(\theta-\phi) \qquad \textbf{A.69}$$

$$\sin 3\theta = 3\sin\theta - 4\sin^3\theta \qquad \textbf{A.70}$$

$$\cos 3\theta = 4\cos^3\theta - 3\cos\theta \qquad \textbf{A.71}$$

$$\sin n\theta = 2\sin(n-1)\theta\cos\theta - \sin(n-2)\theta \qquad \textbf{A.72}$$

$$\cos n\theta = 2\cos(n-1)\theta\cos\theta - \cos(n-2)\theta \qquad \textbf{A.73}$$

$$\sin^2\theta = \tfrac{1}{2}(1-\cos 2\theta) \qquad \textbf{A.74}$$

$$\cos^2\theta = \tfrac{1}{2}(1+\cos 2\theta) \qquad \textbf{A.75}$$

$$\sin\theta\cos\phi = \tfrac{1}{2}\sin(\theta+\phi) + \tfrac{1}{2}\sin(\theta-\phi) \qquad \textbf{A.76}$$

$$\sin\theta\sin\phi = \tfrac{1}{2}\cos(\theta-\phi) - \tfrac{1}{2}\cos(\theta+\phi) \qquad \textbf{A.77}$$

$$\cos\theta\cos\phi = \tfrac{1}{2}\cos(\theta-\phi) + \tfrac{1}{2}\cos(\theta+\phi) \qquad \textbf{A.78}$$

$$\sin^3\theta = \tfrac{1}{4}(3\sin\theta - \sin 3\theta) \qquad \textbf{A.79}$$

$$\cos^3\theta = \tfrac{1}{4}(\cos 3\theta + 3\cos\theta) \qquad \textbf{A.80}$$

(b) Oblique Triangles.

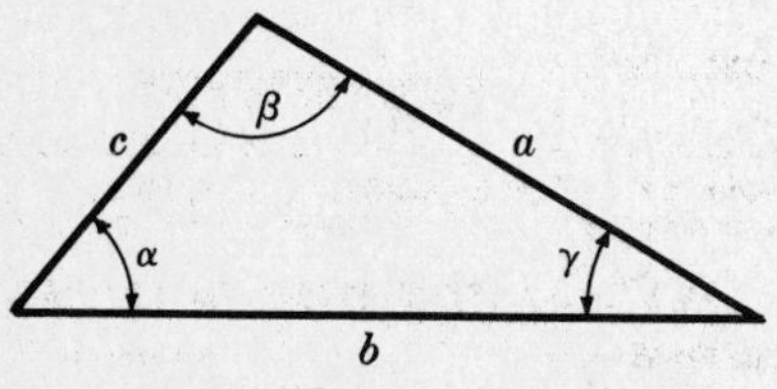

Fig. A-4. The Oblique Triangle

Referring to Fig. A-4, we can write:

$$\frac{a}{\sin\alpha} = \frac{b}{\sin\beta} = \frac{c}{\sin\gamma} \qquad \textbf{A.81}$$

$$a^2 = b^2 + c^2 - 2bc\cos\alpha \qquad \textbf{A.82}$$

$$\frac{a+b}{a-b} = \frac{\tan\frac{1}{2}(\alpha+\beta)}{\tan\frac{1}{2}(\alpha-\beta)} \qquad \textbf{A.83}$$

A.6 HYPERBOLIC FUNCTIONS

(a) Relationships Involving Hyperbolic Functions.

$$\sinh x = \tfrac{1}{2}(e^{x} - e^{-x}) \qquad \text{A.84}$$

$$\cosh x = \tfrac{1}{2}(e^{x} + e^{-x}) \qquad \text{A.85}$$

$$\tanh x = \frac{e^{x} - e^{-x}}{e^{x} + e^{-x}} \qquad \text{A.86}$$

$$\operatorname{csch} x = \frac{1}{\sinh x} \qquad \text{A.87}$$

$$\operatorname{sech} x = \frac{1}{\cosh x} \qquad \text{A.88}$$

$$\coth x = \frac{1}{\tanh x} \qquad \text{A.89}$$

$$\sinh(-x) = -\sinh x \qquad \text{A.90}$$

$$\cosh(-x) = \cosh x \qquad \text{A.91}$$

$$\tanh(-x) = -\tanh x \qquad \text{A.92}$$

$$\cosh^2 x - \sinh^2 x = 1 \qquad \text{A.93}$$

$$\operatorname{sech}^2 x + \tanh^2 x = 1 \qquad \text{A.94}$$

$$\operatorname{csch}^2 x - \coth^2 x = -1 \qquad \text{A.95}$$

$$\tanh x = \frac{\sinh x}{\cosh x} \qquad \text{A.96}$$

$$\sinh(x \pm y) = \sinh x \cosh y \pm \cosh x \sinh y \qquad \text{A.97}$$

$$\cosh(x \pm y) = \cosh x \cosh y \pm \sinh x \sinh y \qquad \text{A.98}$$

$$\sinh 2x = 2 \sinh x \cosh x \qquad \text{A.99}$$

$$\cosh 2x = \cosh^2 x + \sinh^2 x \qquad \text{A.100}$$

(b) Hyperbolic Functions of Complex Arguments.

$$\sin x = -\tfrac{1}{2}i(e^{ix} - e^{-ix}) = -i \sinh ix \qquad \text{A.101}$$

$$\cos x = \cosh ix \qquad \text{A.102}$$

$$\sinh ix = i \sin x \qquad \text{A.103}$$

$$\cosh ix = \cos x \qquad \text{A.104}$$

$$\tanh ix = i \tan x \qquad \text{A.105}$$

$$\sinh(x \pm iy) = \sinh x \cos y \pm i \cosh x \sin y$$ **A.106**

$$\cosh(x \pm iy) = \cosh x \cos y \pm i \sinh x \sin y$$ **A.107**

$$\sin ix = i \sinh x$$ **A.108**

$$\cos ix = \cosh x$$ **A.109**

A.7 SERIES EXPANSIONS

(a) Expansions of Common Functions.

$$e = 1 + \frac{1}{1!} + \frac{1}{2!} + \frac{1}{3!} + \cdots$$ **A.110**

$$e^x = 1 + x + \frac{x^2}{2!} + \frac{x^3}{3!} + \cdots$$ **A.111**

$$a^x = 1 + x \ln a + \frac{(x \ln a)^2}{2!} + \frac{(x \ln a)^3}{3!} + \cdots$$ **A.112**

$$e^{-x^2} = 1 - x^2 + \frac{x^4}{2!} - \frac{x^6}{3!} + \frac{x^8}{4!} - \cdots$$ **A.113**

$$\ln x = (x-1) - \tfrac{1}{2}(x-1)^2 + \tfrac{1}{3}(x-1)^3 - \cdots, \qquad 0 < x \leq 2$$ **A.114**

$$\ln x = \frac{x-1}{x} + \frac{1}{2}\left(\frac{x-1}{x}\right)^2 + \frac{1}{3}\left(\frac{x-1}{x}\right)^3 + \cdots, \qquad x > \tfrac{1}{2}$$ **A.115**

$$\ln x = 2\left[\frac{x-1}{x+1} + \frac{1}{3}\left(\frac{x-1}{x+1}\right)^3 + \frac{1}{5}\left(\frac{x-1}{x+1}\right)^5 + \cdots\right], \qquad x > 0$$ **A.116**

$$\ln(1+x) = x - \frac{x^2}{2} + \frac{x^3}{3} - \frac{x^4}{4} + \cdots, \qquad |x| \leq 1$$ **A.117**

$$\ln(a+x) = \ln a + 2\left[\frac{x}{2a+x} + \frac{1}{3}\left(\frac{x}{2a+x}\right)^3 + \frac{1}{5}\left(\frac{x}{2a+x}\right)^5 + \cdots\right],$$
$$a > 0, \; -a < x < +\infty$$ **A.118**

$$\ln\left(\frac{1+x}{1-x}\right) = 2\left(x + \frac{x^3}{3} + \frac{x^5}{5} + \frac{x^7}{7} + \cdots\right), \qquad x^2 < 1$$ **A.119**

$$\ln\left(\frac{x+1}{x-1}\right) = 2\left[\frac{1}{x} + \frac{1}{3}\left(\frac{1}{x}\right)^3 + \frac{1}{5}\left(\frac{1}{x}\right)^5 + \frac{1}{7}\left(\frac{1}{x}\right)^7 + \cdots\right], \qquad x^2 > 1$$ **A.120**

$$\ln\left(\frac{1+x}{x}\right) = 2\left[\frac{1}{2x+1} + \frac{1}{3(2x+1)^3} + \frac{1}{5(2x+1)^5} + \cdots\right], \qquad x > 0$$ **A.121**

$$\sin x = x - \frac{x^3}{3!} + \frac{x^5}{5!} - \frac{x^7}{7!} + \cdots \qquad \textbf{A.122}$$

$$\cos x = 1 - \frac{x^2}{2!} + \frac{x^4}{4!} - \frac{x^6}{6!} + \cdots \qquad \textbf{A.123}$$

$$\tan x = x + \frac{x^3}{3} + \frac{2x^5}{15} + \frac{17x^7}{315} + \frac{62x^9}{2835} + \cdots, \qquad x^2 < \frac{\pi^2}{4} \qquad \textbf{A.124}$$

$$\sin^{-1} x = x + \frac{x^3}{6} + \frac{1}{2}\cdot\frac{3}{4}\cdot\frac{x^5}{5} + \frac{1}{2}\cdot\frac{3}{4}\cdot\frac{5}{6}\cdot\frac{x^7}{7} + \cdots, \qquad x^2 < 1 \qquad \textbf{A.125}$$

$$\tan^{-1} x = x - \tfrac{1}{3}x^3 + \tfrac{1}{5}x^5 - \tfrac{1}{7}x^7 + \cdots, \qquad x^2 < 1 \qquad \textbf{A.126}$$

$$\tan^{-1} x = \frac{\pi}{2} - \frac{1}{x} + \frac{1}{3x^3} - \frac{1}{5x^5} + \cdots, \qquad x^2 > 1 \qquad \textbf{A.127}$$

$$\sinh x = x + \frac{x^3}{3!} + \frac{x^5}{5!} + \frac{x^7}{7!} + \cdots \qquad \textbf{A.128}$$

$$\cosh x = 1 + \frac{x^2}{2!} + \frac{x^4}{4!} + \frac{x^6}{6!} + \cdots \qquad \textbf{A.129}$$

$$\tanh x = x - \frac{x^3}{3} + \frac{2x^5}{15} - \frac{17x^7}{315} + \cdots \qquad \textbf{A.130}$$

$$\sinh^{-1} x = x - \frac{1}{2}\cdot\frac{x^3}{3} + \frac{1\cdot 3}{2\cdot 4}\cdot\frac{x^5}{5} - \frac{1\cdot 3\cdot 5}{2\cdot 4\cdot 6}\cdot\frac{x^7}{7} + \cdots, \qquad x^2 < 1 \qquad \textbf{A.131}$$

$$\sinh^{-1} x = \ln 2x + \frac{1}{2}\cdot\frac{1}{2x^2} - \frac{1\cdot 3}{2\cdot 4}\cdot\frac{1}{4x^4} + \frac{1\cdot 3\cdot 5}{2\cdot 4\cdot 6}\cdot\frac{1}{6x^6} - \cdots, \qquad x > 1 \qquad \textbf{A.132}$$

$$\cosh^{-1} x = \ln 2x - \frac{1}{2}\cdot\frac{1}{2x^2} - \frac{1\cdot 3}{2\cdot 4}\cdot\frac{1}{4x^4} - \frac{1\cdot 3\cdot 5}{2\cdot 4\cdot 6}\cdot\frac{1}{6x^6} - \cdots \qquad \textbf{A.133}$$

$$\tanh^{-1} x = x + \frac{x^3}{3} + \frac{x^5}{5} + \frac{x^7}{7} + \cdots, \qquad x^2 < 1 \qquad \textbf{A.134}$$

(b) Binomial Theorem.

$$(a+x)^n = a^n + na^{n-1}x + \frac{n(n-1)}{2!}a^{n-2}x^2 + \frac{n(n-1)(n-2)}{3!}a^{n-3}x^3 + \cdots, \qquad x^2 < a^2 \qquad \textbf{A.135}$$

(c) Taylor Series Expansion.

A function $f(x)$ may be expanded about $x = a$ if the function is continuous, and its derivatives exist and are finite at $x = a$.

$$f(x) = f(a) + f'(a)\frac{(x-a)}{1!} + f''(a)\frac{(x-a)^2}{2!} + f'''(a)\frac{(x-a)^3}{3!} + \cdots + f^{n-1}(a)\frac{(x-a)^{n-1}}{(n-1)!} + R_n \qquad \textbf{A.136}$$

(d) Maclaurin Series Expansion.

The Maclaurin series expansion is a special case of the Taylor series expansion for $a = 0$.

$$f(x) = f(0) + f'(0)\frac{x}{1!} + f''(0)\frac{x^2}{2!} + f'''(0)\frac{x^3}{3!} + \cdots \qquad \textbf{A.137}$$

$$+ f^{(n-1)}(0)\frac{x^{n-1}}{(n-1)!} + R_n$$

(e) Arithmetic Progression.

The sum to n terms of the arithmetic progression

$$S = a + (a+d) + (a+2d) + \cdots + [a+(n-1)d] \qquad \textbf{A.138}$$

is (in terms of the last number l)

$$S = \frac{n}{2}(a+l) \qquad \textbf{A.139}$$

where $l = a + (n-1)d$.

(f) Geometric Progression.

The sum of the geometric progression to n terms is

$$S = a + ar + ar^2 + \cdots + ar^{n-1} = a\left(\frac{1-r^n}{1-r}\right) \qquad \textbf{A.140}$$

(g) Sterling's Formula for Factorials.

$$n! \approx \sqrt{2\pi}\, n^{n+1/2}\, e^{-n} \qquad \textbf{A.141}$$

A.8 LIST OF REFERENCES

1. Aris, R., *Vectors, Tensors, and the Basic Equations of Fluid Mechanics,* Prentice Hall, 1962

2. Borg, S. F., *Matrix-Tensor Methods in Continuum Mechanics,* Van Nostrand, 1963

3. Margenau, H., and Murphy, G. M., *The Mathematics of Physics and Chemistry,* Van Nostrand, 1943

4. Morse, P. M., and Feshbach, H., *Methods of Theoretical Physics, Vols. I and II,* McGraw Hill, 1953

5. Spiegel, M., *Vector Analysis,* Schaum Publishing Co., 1959

6. Synge, J. L., and Schild, A., *Tensor Calculus,* University of Toronto Press, 1949

INDEX